NEGOTIATE TO WIN

NEGOTIATE TO WIN

Gaining

The Psychological Edge

ALAN N. SCHOONMAKER

Schoonmaker and Associates

PRENTICE HALL
Englewood Cliffs, New Jersey 07632

Library of Congress Cataloging-in-Publication Data

Schoonmaker, Alan N.
    Negotiate to win : gaining the psychological edge / Alan N. Schoonmaker
    p.   cm.
    Bibliography: p.
    Includes index.
    ISBN 0-13-611385-0
    1. Negotiation in business. 2. Persuasion (Psychology)
    I. Title.
HD58.6.S36   1989
658—dc19   88-38417
                                                  CIP

Editorial/production supervision
    and interior design: Gertrude Szyferblatt
Cover design: George Cornell
Manufacturing Buyer: Mary Ann Gloriande

© 1989 by Prentice-Hall, Inc.
A Division of Simon & Schuster
Englewood Cliffs, New Jersey 07632

The publisher offers discounts on this book when ordered
in bulk quantities. For more information, write:
        Special Sales/College Marketing
        College Technical and Reference Division
        Prentice Hall
        Englewood Cliffs, New Jersey 07632

10 9 8 7 6 5 4 3 2 1

ISBN   0-13-611385-0

PRENTICE-HALL INTERNATIONAL (UK) LIMITED, *London*
PRENTICE-HALL OF AUSTRALIA PTY. LIMITED, *Sydney*
PRENTICE-HALL CANADA INC., *Toronto*
PRENTICE-HALL HISPANOAMERICANA, S.A., *Mexico*
PRENTICE-HALL OF INDIA PRIVATE LIMITED, *New Delhi*
PRENTICE-HALL OF JAPAN, INC., *Tokyo*
SIMON & SCHUSTER ASIA PTE. LTD., *Singapore*
EDITORA PRENTICE-HALL DO BRASIL, LTDA, *Rio de Janerio*

Contents

Appendices:

Preface

When you think of negotiations, you probably think of high level ones—international treaties, athletes' salaries, union management negotiations. You may also think that the only people in business who have to negotiate are buyers and sellers. But virtually everyone in business has to negotiate from time to time. In fact, you negotiate more often than you think you do. You may never sit down at a formal negotiating session, but every time you try to reach an agreement on a budget, or who will be assigned to a project, or how your job will be defined, you probably have to negotiate.

Your ability to negotiate can greatly affect your career. If you improve it, you can probably control more resources, look better to your boss, and earn more money. In fact, some of the world's most powerful and highly paid people are primarily negotiators. For example, some "hired guns" who negotiate for athletes, singers, and actors earn millions of dollars a year. Top investment bankers earn even more. And Carl Icahn made tens of millions of dollars by getting Pennzoil and Texaco to settle their dispute after years of nastiness and enormous legal fees. Why are skilled negotiators rewarded so highly? Because so few people can negotiate well.

Since negotiations are so common and so important, I have devoted more than twenty years to teaching people how to negotiate. My doctoral dissertation at Berkeley in 1966 was based on collective bargaining negotiations. Since then my associates of and I have taught it to organizations in more than twenty countries on all six continents. This book comes from these experiences.

My major conclusion after all these years is that not many people negotiate well. I certainly don't negotiate as well as I would like, even though I am allegedly an expert. Several factors combine to make negotiating a rare skill. Perhaps the most important one is that the demands are so contradictory: you have to be tough but sensitive, analytic but flexible. You need to know when to push and when to back off.

Another factor, and a major theme of this book, is that there is no such thing as an ideal negotiating style, nor can anyone negotiate effectively in every situation. The same personal qualities that help you to succeed in one kind of situation can cause a disaster in other situations. For example, a cooperative approach will work very well with many people, but be perceived by others as a sign of weakness. A highly competitive, "let's take every last dollar on the table" approach, might get you a bargain on a used car lot, but alienate your co-workers or boss.

In addition, the process is so complex that it creates many conflicting demands during the same negotiation. While competing on one issue, you may cooperate on others. You may also have to work together with the other side to convince your managements to accept your deal. Satisfying these conflicting demands requires characteristics that do not normally go together. A first-class negotiator combines a tough-minded competitive attitude, the ability to compromise, intellectual mastery of complex issues, and sensitivity to other people. Very few people have all these qualities.

Our own inhibitions also create problems. In fact, most people (including me) dislike negotiations, especially highly adversarial ones. For example, many people will not take unreasonable positions, even when the other side has done so. Nearly all of us fear that hard bargaining will lead to rejection, and shrewd negotiators take advantage of our inhibitions by acting insulted, hurt, or angry.

We can be so uncomfortable with conflict that we react to our discomfort rather than to the objective, situational demands. These reactions tend toward two extremes —fight and flight. We may avoid negotiating, settle too easily, stonewall, or make personal attacks. All of these reactions interfere with the negotiating process.

These inhibitions are particularly strong in North America and Northern Europe because negotiating conflicts with our values and customs. We have been trained since birth to be fair, reasonable, unemotional, and objective, and we rarely haggle about anything; in fact, most of us would not even consider bargaining in a supermarket or department store. People from many other cultures feel quite differently, and bargaining is a natural part of most transactions—food, taxi rides, even the payment for weddings.

Our culture not only inhibits negotiations; it actively discourages them. Negotiating is often perceived as cheap, devious, or dishonest. For example, most tourists feel uncomfortable when bargaining for a taxi in Cairo or Bangkok. They simply cannot accept that, in these cultures, bargaining is legitimate and normal.

People from our culture also dislike and avoid many essential negotiating rituals. For example, the mutual concession ritual seems unreasonable and a waste of time. We do not want to offer less than we expect to pay, then trade a series of small concessions. We would rather decide on a fair price, then offer it. However, since people's perceptions of "fair" are often quite different, the mutual concession ritual is often essential. Ignoring it can cause a poor deal or a deadlock.

Since negotiating skill is both rare and important, one would expect help from the educational system. Alas, it has not provided it, perhaps because of educators' inhibitions. Very few business or law schools offer courses. A few books have been published, but they generally focus on non-business topics. They may help you when you buy a car or real estate, but they do not provide useful guidance for business negotiations.

This book has three objectives: *(1) to reduce your inhibitions and discomfort; (2) develop your skills and sensitivity; and (3) increase your flexibility.*

The essential first step is to make you more comfortable when negotiating. Otherwise your discomfort can cause you to avoid negotiating, settle too quickly, miss the other side's signals, or stonewall. As you understand the negotiating process and your reactions to it, you will slowly become more comfortable and effective.

The second objective is to increase your understanding of negotiating principles and your ability to apply them. For example, this book will show you how to analyze situations, set your own objectives, make appropriate first offers, and understand the other side's signals.

You need sensitivity to the other side, your own style, and the negotiating process. Sensitivity is so important that we will spend more time on it than on any other subject.

First, and most important, you must understand the other side. Most people do not seriously try to do so; they focus their attention on themselves, thereby missing much of the information coming from the other side. You will learn how to understand their offers, words, and actions. In fact, developing this understanding is our major theme. *The key to successful negotiations is understanding the other side.*

You also need to understand your own negotiating style, its impact on people, and the kinds of situations that fit or conflict with it. Finally, since each negotiation makes different demands, you need sensitivity to the situation. Then you can choose between competition, cooperation, or a mixture of both.

The net result of this sensitivity should be a greater ability to adjust your strategy. There is no such thing as a good, all-purpose negotiating strategy. Different situations require different strategies. As you learn more about them, yourself, and the negotiation process, you will become more flexible.

I sincerely believe that this book is unique in several ways. First, it presents a clear, conceptual structure, while most (but not all) other books are a grab bag of tips and tactics—do this, do that, do something else. One best selling book has no organization at all; it is a number of chapters arranged alphabetically! The tips may be good, but they do not hang together, and it is hard to know when to do what. This book provides a structured model and relates every principle to it. You can therefore understand what is happening, so you can plan and execute coherent strategies.

Second, it does not teach just one negotiating approach. Many books present *the* system, such as "win-win" or "winning through intimidation." But one approach cannot work everywhere. This book describes a variety of approaches, shows where and when each is appropriate, thereby developing skill at analyzing and adjusting to situations.

Third, it emphasizes understanding the other side. Most people really need help there. They are so concerned with their own positions—their needs, their logic, their strengths, their weaknesses—that they overlook the other side's signals. We will teach you how to determine what the other side wants, and move toward a deal that satisfies *both* sides, while letting you get most of the "money on the table."

Fourth, it integrates negotiations with personality theory. Nearly everyone recognizes that you must adjust to both parties' personalities, but they offer little more than vague generalizations: "read the other person," "adjust to their signals." We present a clear, well-validated personality theory, and show you how to understand and adjust to your own and other people's personalities.

Fifth, it also shows you how to adjust to the effects of team factors. Negotiating as a team offers substantial benefits, but creates some serious problems. We will therefore analyze these costs and benefits, then show you how to organize and control a team.

Finally, it discusses a subject that becomes more important every day—cultural factors affecting international negotiations. The coauthor of this chapter is former Ambassador Stephen Rhinesmith, a distinguished authority. His doctoral dissertation was *Managing the Human Side of Multinational Organizations,* and he has studied the effects of cultural factors affecting management for two decades in literally dozens of countries. As our trade deficit and foreign policy problems clearly indicate, Americans have not understood or adjusted to these cultural factors.

A little story might help you to understand how this book can help you. Years ago, a major New York bank asked me to train their junior officers. Since the bank was changing its corporate strategy and needed more creative young bankers, they asked me to meet with senior managers to learn about their corporate culture and the objectives of their training program.

In addition to the obvious questions about the bank's culture and strategy, I asked every manager two questions: How have you changed since you were a junior officer? What should I teach your junior officers?

The details of their answers varied, but there were two consistent themes that seem to be universally expressed in the corporate world.

Be tougher. They expressed it in a variety of ways. "I have more confidence in my authority and positions." "I don't give things away the way I used to." "I'm more confident and assertive." "I don't make one-way concessions any more. I trade concessions."

Understand and satisfy the customer. This theme was expressed quite forcefully by every single manager and executive. They clearly regarded it as more important than anything else. The banker's job was to understand their customers' objectives and priorities, and satisfy them in a way that was also profitable to the bank.

At first, these themes may seem inconsistent; toughness, understanding, and flexibility do not seem to go together. But a senior vice-president showed me that they really support each other. I spent the most educational morning of my life watching him negotiate over a speakerphone and chatting with him when he had a free moment. I was awed by his combination of toughness and sensitivity. He never took the easy way out, never accepted a waffling answer, always probed for more information, especially information that customers did not want to give him. One of our brief conversations summarized his negotiating approach.

> Alan, you may think that toughness and understanding and satisfying the customer are incompatible, but, in fact, you can't understand and satisfy the customer unless you are tough. The art of the dealmaker is to be able to put together a deal in three, four, maybe even six ways and to keep probing until you put it together in the *right* way. I'm an experienced banker. If I talk to a customer and study the situation, I can put together a satisfactory deal. It will be acceptable to the customer and the bank. But, if I don't take that first deal, if I ask some more questions, I can put together a better deal for both of us. And, if I really work at it, reject the so-so deals, ask those hard questions that the customer really does not want to answer, keep trying out different combinations, a little more of this, a little less of that, I'll make the *right* deal, the one that really satisfies the customer. If I do that, if I give the customers what they really need, they do not care if the bank makes a bigger profit. It just does not matter to them.

I cannot think of any better way to summarize my beliefs about negotiations. If you can resist that temptation to accept just any deal; if you can ask those embarrassing questions and refuse to accept waffling answers; if you can keep cutting and fitting the deal as if you were a master carpenter building a cabinet, you can often end up with the *right* deal, the one that gives *both* sides what they really need.

I believe this book can help you achieve that objective.

Acknowledgments

The author would like to thank the people who helped to write this book. My sister and president of our company, Sue Ann Schoonmaker, read every word several times, proofreading, improving the grammar, correcting unclear writing. Carole Johnstone, director of our Minneapolis office, spent countless hours on the same tasks. Gertrude Schoonmaker, our researcher, identified many of the historical examples of good and bad negotiations.

Phyllis Rosen of Bankers Trust made an extraordinary number of suggestions, nearly all of which have been implemented.

Kathy Terwilliger and Suzanne DeLaPointe had a huge impact on this book (and on all of our training materials). While working together on our videos, they clarified many negotiations principles and suggested numerous examples of good and bad negotiations tactics. Kathy then read the entire manuscript, making countless, invaluable recommendations; she is certainly the best editor I have ever had.

I especially appreciate the patience and tolerance of Jeff Krames, the acquisitions editor at Prentice Hall. He stuck by me when I got way behind schedule.

Gertrude Szyferblatt, production editor at Prentice Hall also showed great patience and professionalism. Very few editors would tolerate extensive last minute changes made while cruising down the Nile River.

Michael Carroll and Peter Davidson made many useful suggestions.

Phil Johnson and Doug Lind have provided numerous comments over more than ten years. Bruce Wilson, Mervyn Collins, and Raymond Dubois have done the same for shorter periods.

Jay Meagher provided numerous suggestions about structuring this material, including the basic form of the Three-Phase Model, the very foundation of our work.

We owe special thanks to the thousands of students, from all over the world, who have taken our workshops, commented on our earlier works on negotiations, and clarified the principles with their questions and comments.

Fran Zagorski and Joan Wolkenberg helped enormously in preparing earlier drafts and the final manuscript.

1

The Negotiating Process

Many people regard negotiations as some sort of mystical art, a gift with which one is born or can never possess. We disagree. It is more an art than a science, but even arts such as music and painting have rules, and you can improve your skill by learning how to apply the rules. Exactly the same principle applies to negotiations: Some people are born with natural negotiating skill, but all of us can become more effective by understanding and applying the rules.

This chapter will help you to understand those rules. It contains six major sections:

I. A Sample Negotiation
II. Definitions
III. Pure Bargaining versus Joint Problem Solving
IV. The Negotiations Model
V. Overview of the Rest of the Book
VI. Summary

A SAMPLE NEGOTIATION

Before discussing the theory, let's look at a sample business negotiation. Because a complex negotiation can take years, we shall describe only one of the last meetings in a long series of negotiating sessions.

This particular negotiation is between two parties, but some negotiations can have three, four, five, or more parties: the more parties there are, the harder it is to work out a mutually acceptable solution.

Management Enterprises is a small consulting company owned and operated by Mike, Sharon, and Jack. They provide advice and training related to installing new systems, especially computer systems.

Today's negotiation is with George, a fairly senior manager of the Tadmar Corporation, and a long term client. Jack knows that George is a tough negotiator. He is friendly and likes to start with a little warm-up period, but when it comes to money, he is really tough. He even brags about how much he saved on his office furniture.

Management Enterprises has completed several projects for George, and he has always been satisfied by their work. Today's negotiation concerns a contract for about $150,000. Jack knows that George has ordered nearly two million dollars worth of computer and related equipment. The equipment will be delivered in two months, but it cannot be used effectively without considerable help from Management Enterprises or some other consultants. Jack feels confident that George has not requested bids from another consulting company.

There have been numerous meetings, and they have agreed on almost all the issues. Jack believes that today's meeting is to settle the final details on price and payment terms. Management Enterprises has already submitted a written proposal covering these issues. Although it appears that only the financial issues must be negotiated, Jack's partners have warned him that other issues often come up during the final negotiations.

Jack calls at George's office. After a very brief delay, he is invited to go in.

As he enters, George walks toward him, smiles, and says, "Thanks for coming, Jack. How are you today?"

"Fine, George. Did you get a chance to read our proposal?"

George frowns slightly at Jack's abruptness, then says: "Yes, and it seems to satisfy most of our needs."

Jack misses the significance of the word "most" and continues, "I'm sure that you will find that it is an excellent proposal."

"Jack, I have a lot of confidence in your firm. You have always done good work for us."

"Thank you, George."

"But I am concerned about the training."

Jack is a bit surprised. "Oh?"

"You said that one of your people will do it."

"That's right."

"Well, we have a qualified person who could handle it. Her name is Joan McIntyre. Here is her resume." George hands Jack the resume and sits back, waiting for him to read it.

Jack does not even look at it because he has already dismissed the idea of using Joan. "Well, George, we've found that our staff does a much better job than internal people."

George starts to object, "Perhaps, but..."

Jack interrupts, "Using one of our trained consultants would provide much better quality control."

George is obviously annoyed. "Before you jump to conclusions, let me tell you a little about Joan. She is fairly new to Tadmar, but she has an excellent background in computer systems. She has also conducted numerous seminars."

Jack ignores George's point and blunders on. "I don't doubt her qualifications, George, but the only way we can guarantee the good results you want is to do the training ourselves."

George, becoming more annoyed, flatly states, "I really want Joan to do it."

"Be reasonable, George. Your equipment arrives in two months. If we had to train Joan, and then wait for her to train your people, we'd never finish on time."

"If necessary, we could delay the equipment's delivery."

Jack is astonished. "What? I thought the schedule was your key priority."

"No, it's important, but not as important as having Joan on the project."

Jack is now quite exasperated. "George, this just doesn't make sense. Why delay such an important project when we are totally qualified to do the training within your original schedule?"

"There are a couple of reasons. First, I want to develop her for some other things, and she needs this visibility. Second, it will save us some money."

Jack ignores the first point and says, "Oh, you wouldn't save that much."

"How much?"

Since he is unprepared for the question, Jack stalls, jots down some numbers, then replies, "Well, let's see.... Our original proposal was for $150,000.... About $10,000 of that was for training."

"So we would save $10,000 if she did the training?"

"No,... we would still have to train and supervise Joan."

"How much would that cost?"

"I couldn't say. We have never even considered that possibility."

Frowning, George says, "I see."

"George, this just doesn't make sense. The money you saved on our fee would be less than you would spend for Joan's time."

"Jack," George pauses for emphasis and speaks very firmly, "Joan can't be cut out of this process. It's as simple as that."

By now Jack is so frustrated that he does not know what to do. "George, could we just set this whole issue of training aside and talk about the price and everything else?"

George pushes back from his desk and abruptly says, "I'm not ready to talk price yet... You figure out how much you can reduce your bid by using Joan, then get back to me." He then stands up and walks around his desk, dismissing Jack.

Jack looks stunned as he rises from his chair and shakes George's hand. "Okay.... I'll put some figures together and get back to you tomorrow. How does that sound?"

"Fine, thanks for your time."

Jack leaves.

If we had a cash register, we would ring up "No sale." The session was a disaster. Before analyzing why it went so poorly, let's make some general points.

First, even though George expected to negotiate price, the key issue for this session was staffing, not money. That point has two implications: (1) Unexpected issues come up all the time; you expect to negotiate a certain issue, but spend most of your time discussing a different one. (2) Many people believe that negotiations usually concern money, but they deal far more frequently with staffing, schedules, responsibilities, policies, and other non-monetary issues.

Second, this session was part of a much longer series of sessions about this contract, and that series was part of an even longer term relationship. That pattern is true for most business negotiations. Relatively few business negotiations can be settled in one session, and most of them are part of an ongoing relationship. Therefore, both parties must consider both the deal they reach today and the effects of this negotiation on their overall relationship.

Third, even though this session was a disaster, the deal is far from dead. If Jack carefully analyzes what has happened and learns from his mistakes, he can still save the contract. This pattern is quite common. Most business negotiations are not like a tennis tournament—lose once and you are finished. You usually have a chance to think things over, then try again.

Fourth, this session was unsuccessful because Jack made several mistakes. We will discuss the specific errors in a minute, but the critical point is that he was working *against* George, not with him. His specific errors were obvious, perhaps too obvious, but most of us make similar mistakes all the time. Let's see what we can learn from Jack's mistakes.

His first mistake was a lack of preparation. He walked in expecting to discuss price and payment terms, then found that George had a different agenda. It happens to all of us because new issues arise, priorities change, and so forth.

His biggest mistake was not adjusting to the new situation. When George raised the training issue, Jack should have realized that his own plans had been based upon incorrect assumptions and then shifted to understanding what George really wanted. Instead he tried to sell George on his original proposal.

He abruptly started to talk business while George was still socializing. Since he knew that George liked a little warm-up period, he should have slowed down and made small talk for a few moments.

Jack stated his position on a take it or leave it basis, not as a starting point to a mutually acceptable compromise. George essentially did the same. That communication pattern virtually guaranteed a win-lose conflict. Only one of them could win. Joan was on the project or off it. They should have discussed what they wanted to accomplish; they could then search for a solution that would satisfy both of them.

Jack also disrespectfully dismissed George's position by not reading Joan's resume, arguing, and even saying, "Be reasonable" and "This just does not make sense." In fact, he never even learned why George wanted Joan on the project. George said that he wanted to save money, develop Joan, and give her some visibility, but Jack never learned his reasons for developing her.

The combination of abruptness, the way both parties expressed their positions, and Jack's disrespect and lack of interest in understanding George created the wrong kind of atmosphere. It started friendly, but quickly deteriorated. This combination also prevented them from creating any momentum toward a deal. The negotiation essentially never got started.

We have used an unsuccessful negotiation as our example because it helps us to illustrate many important principles. We will refer to this sample negotiation again and again. We will also return to their next negotiating session in chapter 4.

DEFINITIONS

A first step toward understanding is defining a few basic terms.

Negotiations

Negotiations are a method for reaching agreement with both cooperative and competitive elements. *Method* means that there is a series of steps that should be followed in certain ways in a certain order. The flow-chart model discussed later in this chapter illustrates this method. Failing to take a step or performing it badly has predictable and undesirable consequences. Learning and applying this method will improve your results.

The *cooperative element* derives from both parties' desire to reach a mutually acceptable agreement. Without that desire, you would not negotiate; you would sue each other, fight, appeal to authority, or use some other kind of force.

The *competitive element* comes from both parties' desire to get the best results for themselves. There are a certain number of dollars or other things on the table, and both parties usually want to get most of them. If there were no competitive elements, if your interests did not at least partially conflict, there would be no need to negotiate.

The tension between cooperation and competition is absolutely central to negotiations, and we shall encounter it again and again. Overemphasizing either can lead to a disaster. Overemphasizing competition can cause deadlocks, lost orders, strikes, or even wars. Overemphasizing cooperation can cause such bad deals that your company loses money or even goes bankrupt. In fact, one of your most difficult and important tasks is to find the right balance between cooperation and conflict for *this* negotiation (because each one is different).

Conditions Requiring Negotiations

Negotiations are appropriate *only* if all three of the following conditions are present. First, there must be a conflict of interests. If there is no conflict, there is no need to negotiate. You may be the best of friends, but on this issue your interests at least partially conflict. You want a higher price; they want a lower one. You want an earlier deadline; they want to delay it. You want Bob on the project; they want Jane.

Second, there must be some ambiguity about the right solution. If the solution is clear, there is no reason to negotiate. For example, if you and your boss know that a report must be submitted on Friday afternoon, you should not even try to negotiate the deadline. You can, however, negotiate other issues such as time off next week, secretarial or other assistance, perhaps even a bonus.

Third, there must be an opportunity to compromise, to reach a deal that satisfies both parties. Neither of you may get exactly what you want, but you can both live with the deal. If compromise is impossible, for example, if the highest price that you will pay is much less than the lowest price that a vendor will accept, do not bother to negotiate. Of course, you may be unable to tell that a compromise is impossible until after you have negotiated, but at other times the initial positions are so far apart that it is fairly obvious that no deal is possible.

A Good Negotiation

A good negotiation produces two types of desirable results: objective and psychological. Think of it as a puzzle—a good deal fits the pieces together just right. The difference between a puzzle and a negotiation is that a puzzle's pieces are made in advance, while negotiations force you to cut and fit the pieces until you put together a deal that produces both types of results.

Good objective results means that the deal makes sense; it fits everyone's priorities. Both parties get what they really need and make acceptable sacrifices. For example, if the buyer's critical priority is time, and the seller's is price, a good deal would include a premium price and speedy delivery.

Conversely, a bad deal would be a discounted price and slow delivery. That sort of deal could easily occur. The buyer might conceal the time pressures and negotiate hard on price. After agreeing to a discount, the seller might not be able, or willing, to deliver promptly. Therefore, the buyer's hard bargaining actually costs *both* parties. They would both be better off with a higher price and quicker delivery.

Banking provides a more dramatic example. Let's imagine that you, the owner of a small business, are in a desperate cash bind; unless you raise $100,000 by next Wednesday, you will fail to meet an important deadline, and your entire business will collapse. Your creditors will start demanding payment, your suppliers will not deliver, and so on. To complicate matters, your loan is borderline—it is not one that the banker can easily approve.

A good deal would be one that will give you the necessary cash quickly, although you will pay a high price for it. A bad deal would be a loan offer for $75,000 ($25,000 less than you desperately need), with a delay of three weeks, and a savings on the fee and interest.

You don't care about the price. Your entire business is at stake. What you care about is money and time. The creative, flexible banker will satisfy you *and* get a good profit.

Therefore, some critical tasks are to decide upon your own priorities, learn their priorities, and then move toward a deal that satisfies everyone's top priorities.

Good psychological results mean that everyone feels good about both the deal and the process by which it was reached. Everyone is a winner, and nobody has lost face. Of course, no one likes a bad deal, but even a good deal can create bad feelings if it has been reached in the wrong way. For example, how would you feel about an objectively good deal that a domineering person jammed down your throat? He dominated the process, cross-examined you, ignored your questions, and then told you: "Take it or leave it."

Giving in too easily can create a different kind of dissatisfaction. Let's say that a used car is for sale for $12,000. You like it and think it is worth about $11,200. To give yourself bargaining room you say, "I'll offer you $10,500." The dealer gives you a big smile and says, "You've got it."

At first you may be delighted, but you could soon get an attack of buyer's remorse. You may wonder if you offered too much, or even suspect that something is wrong with the car. If the dealer had bargained a little, the price would have been higher, and you would have felt better.

The Foundation of Negotiations

This example illustrates a critically important principle, one that we call "The Foundation of Negotiations": *Nothing has an objective value.* Absolutely everything is worth whatever the seller will accept and the buyer will pay. The market, production costs, customs, and other objective factors will influence what people will accept and pay, but each pair of buyers and sellers may reach a different agreement. This seller is a little less hungry; that buyer is a little shrewder.

Let's relate that principle to the stock market. On Black Monday, October 19, 1988, about one trillion dollars was lost on the world's stock exchanges. How much change had occurred in the assets, profits, sales, and other objective values of the listed companies since the preceding Friday?

Exactly none. Companies do not report or even compute their profits and assets daily; they do so every quarter or six months. The only thing that had changed was the psychology. People suddenly changed their minds about what stocks were worth.

The same principle applies to much smaller transactions. For example, many antique dealers tell this sort of story: "I tried to sell that chest for $500 and could not move it. I put it up for auction and sold it for $650. And the person who bought it had seen it several times in my shop!"

This principle has important implications for most negotiations. Of course you have to conduct research, study the markets, and perform other analyses because objective factors will usually determine the general range within which you will negotiate. But then, when you are actually negotiating, you have to set those objective analyses a little to the side and focus on the other people. What do *they* think this item is worth?

PURE BARGAINING VERSUS JOINT PROBLEM SOLVING

Now that we have defined our terms and indicated when you should negotiate, let's discuss *how* you should negotiate. There are two diametrically opposed approaches: pure bargaining (PB) and joint problem solving (JPS). PB is a way to cut up a pie;

who gets what? The more you get, the less I get. JPS is a method for making the pie bigger so we both get more. JPS seems clearly superior so concentrating on it should benefit everyone.

That superiority has clearly been demonstrated by the wealth of western societies. One reason, for our wealth is that we tend to be problem solvers with all the related values, such as objective analysis of information, relatively open communications, and emphasis upon trust.

Societies that emphasize bargaining, such as most Third World countries, are much less successful. They spend so much time and energy dividing up the pie that they do not make enough of it. Class, tribe, and other conflicts take most of their time and energy; trust is minimal; objectivity and openness are rare, even despised.

However, there is another side to the story. The problem-solving approach benefits both parties *only* if they both use it. If one side is problem solving, while the other is bargaining, the problem solver will usually be exploited. This obvious fact has been ignored again and again. Some people are so uncomfortable with conflict that they try to wish it away.

But conflict is a fact of life, and ignoring it will just make you vulnerable to those who can manage it. You must therefore base your strategic choice, not on your discomfort, but on an objective analysis of the situation.

Most people respond emotionally to conflict. They either fight excessively or run away. This fight-flight pattern is a sure sign that the reactions are based, not on an objective analysis, but on personal emotions. You must be more rational. In fact, one of your critical tasks is to balance competition and cooperation, to select the appropriate point on the bargaining- problem-solving continuum (and it varies from one negotiation to the next).

There are three critical issues. First, how much do your interests conflict? The more they conflict, the more appropriate bargaining becomes. Second, how important is the long-term relationship? The more important it is, the more you should usually emphasize problem solving. Third, what approach is the other party using? If they are bargaining, while you are problem solving, you are probably going to lose, at least in the short term. However, you may also become so angry or distrustful that you refuse to make necessary concessions or even to deal with them at all. It is generally best to have both parties use similar approaches so that neither side has an advantage, and neither feels exploited.

Selecting the right approach is obviously difficult since you must balance the demands of the degree of conflict, the importance of the relationship, and your perception of the other's approach. Your task is complicated by the fact that bargaining and problem solving are incompatible: Most actions that support one detract from the other. Ultimately bargaining is based on power, while problem solving is based on trust and information, and *almost everything that builds power reduces trust and the flow of information and vice versa.* For example, filing a lawsuit may strengthen your bargaining position, but it certainly inhibits problem solving. We shall therefore contrast the two approaches, and provide guidelines for choosing between them.

Contrasting the Approaches

The following diagram illustrates several points, First, there are not just two approaches; there is a whole range of approaches. Pure bargaining is near one end of the range; joint problem solving is near the other end. Usually you are working someplace in the middle, the vague central area in which trading predominates. You give something in return for something else; they do the same.

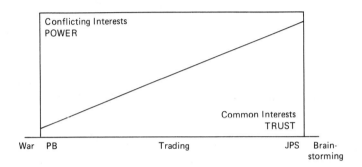

Second, note that neither pure bargaining nor joint problem solving is at the extreme end of the continuum. All negotiating approaches involve both conflicting and common interests, both trust and power, while the extreme actions (war and brain storming) involve only one of them. You may want the best possible deal, but you prefer a negotiated settlement to no deal at all.

Third, all approaches require some power and some trust. Pure bargaining is based on power, but it cannot succeed without some trust. At a minimum, both sides must believe that the other will implement the agreement. Without a minimum of trust people will simply wage war or its more civilized alternatives, such as strikes or lawsuits. JPS is based on trust, but without some conflicting interests people have no need to negotiate, and unless both sides have some power they probably cannot resolve their conflicts. The party with all the power could simply force the other to capitulate.

Trading is in the middle of the continuum because it is a mixed approach containing elements of both. A good trade increases the overall value because each party gets more value than it gives, but both parties will normally try for trades that favor themselves.

The rest of this section will focus on the extremes by contrasting bargaining and problems solving on several dimensions.

PB is win-lose; JPS is win-win

Game theorists call win-lose games *zero-sum.* The gain for one side equals the loss for the other. For example, if you sell your car for $500 more, the buyer has $500 less. Their loss exactly equals your gain. The net for both parties is zero.

Win-win games are *variable-sum*. Some agreements are better for both parties collectively. For example, if you are selling your car to someone who lives 100 miles away, agreeing to exchange it when you are both in the same place for other purposes saves you both the expense, time, and trouble of making a special trip.

Price negotiations are almost always pure bargaining because each dollar that one side gains, the other side loses. However, a good solution to a common problem, such as equipment maintenance or scheduling, benefits both sides.

Some people, including a few alleged authorities, claim that one should always strive for a win-win approach. Such exhortations are naive, childish, and cowardly. The people making them simply lack the courage to face the reality that there are genuine conflicts of interest, that wars, strikes, and lawsuits are facts of life. Alas, some of these naive people have reached extremely high positions, including the American presidency.

Jimmy Carter's legacy in Afghanistan, Panama, and many other places clearly illustrates the effects of wishing away conflict and being too trusting. A preferable principle is the one that Reagan and Gorbachev have repeatedly stated: "trust, but verify."

PB involves conflicting interests; JPS involves common interests

Price is not the only PB issue. Negotiations to end a war could divide a particular piece of territory, but the negotiators might also try to agree on common interests such as the humane treatment of prisoners.

PB is a competitive process; JPS is a cooperative one

Since your interests conflict, PB is essentially a competitive process: Both sides try to get the best deal for themselves. But, when you have common interests, you should work together to develop the best joint solution.

PB is based on power; JPS is based on trust and information

Because your interests directly conflict, PB is ultimately based upon power. You probably cannot convince them to lose for your gain, but you may be able to force them to do so. Your power may come from any source, such as an offer from another vendor, a good lawyer and legal position, your relationship with top management, or even your possession of embarrassing information.

The "Godfather" in Puzo's novel presents a superb example of power bargaining. With a gun in his hand, he said, "I'm going to make you an offer you can't refuse. Either your signature or your brains will be on that contract."

Trust and information are the foundation of problem solving, and trust is the critical element. Without trust, neither party will communicate openly, nor will they take actions that might give away an advantage.

The central problem has already been identified: Actions that build power usually reduce trust and information flow and vice versa. You may therefore be forced to make an unequivocal choice between the approaches. For example, you cannot use the Godfather approach and then say, "Trust me."

Irrationality and emotions often help PB, but they interfere with JPS

Irrationality and anger can greatly increase a pure bargainer's power. The other side may make concessions because they fear a walkout, strike, or other punishment. In diplomacy they call it the Madman's Advantage. For example, Hitler, Gadhafi, and The Ayatollah got away with outrageous actions because they were clearly irrational; democratic leaders are constrained by their rationality. Angry, abusive customers often get better service than polite ones — the squeaky wheel gets the grease.

Other emotions can also help PB. Some negotiators act hurt in order to make people feel guilty or sorry for them. This ploy can make some people yield to assuage their guilt.

However, emotions and irrationality usually interfere with JPS by reducing communications and trust.

Distorted communications can further pure bargaining, but inhibit joint problem solving

In PB it often pays to withhold or distort information by bluffing or perhaps even lying. You cannot, for example, tell the other party your bottom line or weaknesses. However, distorting communications reduces both trust and information, the essential ingredients of JPS.

The communications pattern is often the most visible indication of whether one is bargaining or problem solving. Because you cannot see people's intentions, you may not know whether they are playing win-win or win-lose. In fact, some highly skilled bargainers deliberately conceal their intentions; they pretend to be problem solving, while they are really out to get every penny on the table (plus whatever they can steal from your pockets). But you can usually see how they communicate. In addition, the communications pattern frequently has quite dramatic effects.

For example, let's say that I am trying to sell you my services as a consultant on a firm, fixed-price basis. I quote you a price of $25,000 plus travel expenses for the project, and you suspect that my price has some padding built into it. We therefore have a bargaining issue: You want to drive the price down, while I want to keep it up.

We might also have a joint problem-solving issue, scheduling. Neither of us wants me to fly to your city, and spend your money on hotels, air fares, and meals for meetings that disrupt your operations or conflict with your other demands.

A few simple sentences can affect both issues. If I am very naive, I might, for example, say: "I'm glad we are negotiating this contract now because I just had two large contracts cancelled. Since I have only four days' work over the next three months, we can get together whenever you like." My openness certainly helps us to arrange a good schedule, but what does it do to my bargaining position on price?

The communications pattern can also have extreme effects on your relationship. Many people regard lying or even withholding information as morally repugnant.

Lying to them—even during pure bargaining—can ruin your entire relationship. Conversely, many other people feel that all's fair in love and war, and negotiations are a form of warfare. They regard honesty as a sign of weakness and take advantage of it. Therefore, until you know the other people's styles and values, it is best to be cautious and avoid either extreme of open or distorted communication.

Selecting the Right Approach

Since bargaining and problem solving require fundamentally incompatible tactics, you must determine what the situation requires and select the right approach. Some people approach all negotiations competitively or cooperatively. They may rationalize that it produces better results, but it probably just makes them more comfortable. Effective negotiators select the right approach, even when it makes them uncomfortable.

Sometimes you should use only one approach for an entire negotiation. However, many negotiations require a bargaining approach on some issues, problem solving on others. Of course, it is not necessarily either/or. You will rarely move all the way to either extreme. In some negotiations or on some issues, emphasize JPS; on others bargain as hard as you can.

Your choice should be influenced by the other side's approach. Of course, you should try to create an atmosphere that will encourage the other side to use the approach that favors you, but you may be unsuccessful. If you cannot influence them, adjust to them (i.e., if you can't beat them, join them). Use their approach because mismatches are usually bad for both parties if there is a long-term relationship. If there is no long-term relationship, or if that relationship is relatively unimportant, the pure bargainer has a distinct advantage.

Emphasizing bargaining

Emphasize bargaining when:

- Your interests clearly conflict
- You are much more powerful
- You do not need or want a long-term harmonious relationship
- You do not trust the other party
- The agreement is easy to implement
- The other party is pure bargaining

PB's competitive elements may be obscured by elaborate rituals, such as expressions of friendship, golf games, gourmet meals, or formal agendas. Both parties may be polite and strive to create an air of objective analysis, but the essential nature rarely changes: You both want to win to get the best deal you can. That emphasis upon winning can be as clear in multibillion dollar contract negotiations as it is in brief negotiations to sell a used car. Let's use the car negotiations because they illustrate the principles more clearly.

If you are selling a car to a stranger, do not need to sell it quickly, and have two other interested prospects, you can bargain hard. If you do not make this deal, or if you irritate this buyer, so what?

On the other hand, if you were selling the same car to your brother-in-law, had no other prospects, were short of cash, and were leaving on vacation the next morning, you should obviously be much more accommodating. Driving too hard a bargain can cost you a sale you really need, or worse yet, create family problems that last for years.

Even when they should be problem solving, many people emphasize bargaining. For example, some people bargain on nearly all issues, even ones on which they clearly have common interests. They emphasize bargaining because power is more tangible and less fragile than trust. Using power creates a feeling of security, while trusting almost always involves some risks. The other party can easily take advantage of you.

Disarmament negotiations are an excellent example. The United States and the Soviet Union have numerous and extremely important common interests: An accidental nuclear war could destroy us all. The arms race is extremely expensive to us, and even more expensive to them. Whenever another country gets nuclear weapons the dangers increase. Yet nearly thirty years of disarmament negotiations have accomplished very little. Despite the 1987 agreement, both sides have far more missiles than they had when the negotiations began, and many other countries have joined or can soon join the "nuclear club." The negotiations have essentially failed because we cannot trust each other; we both know that the other side could take advantage of any weakness.

This example illustrates another reason for the emphasis on bargaining: internal politics. Even if the negotiators wanted to work together, the hard-liners in both governments would not let them. When two groups are competing, people who want to cooperate are seen as traitors. Those who fight are heroes, even if their fighting damages their own side's interests.

Emphasizing JPS

Emphasize JPS when:

- You have common interests
- You are weaker or power is approximately equal
- You need or want a continuing, harmonious relationship
- You trust the other party
- Implementing the agreement may be difficult
- The other party is problem solving

Solving joint problems during a negotiation is often quite difficult. The adversarial nature of most negotiations can cause both parties to emphasize pure bargaining, even when they should be working together. Therefore, if you want to cooperate, take the following steps.

Move slowly

This is the most important and most frequently violated principle. Many people feel that large concessions and extreme openness will improve the atmosphere and encourage the other side to reciprocate. Unfortunately, the other side may regard these actions as signs of weakness. They may then raise their expectations, anticipating additional concessions. In fact, they may get so greedy that a deal becomes impossible.

These actions may also create distrust. The other side may wonder: "What is their little game?" For example, how would you react if someone trying to sell you a house lowered the price by 10% before you made your first offer? You might start worrying about termites or other problems. The same principle can apply to information; excessive openness can actually build distrust. For example, if you were a union leader, negotiating with management, what would you think of an offer to let you see their books? You might wonder whether they have two sets of books.

Build trust without giving away too much

Trust can only be built gradually, and you should usually guard against excessive risks. Some trust building actions create no risks at all. You can, for instance, often build it by creating a friendly atmosphere, listening to the other side's position, and addressing their concerns.

Giving away either information or substantive concessions almost inevitably creates some risks, and you should usually limit your vulnerability. Give them a little information or a small concession, but insist they reciprocate. If you share some information, they must share some. If you make a small concession, they must make one. This gradual process slowly builds trust without making either side too vulnerable or creating unrealistic expectations or cynicism.

Identify issues with clearly cooperative elements

Without cooperative elements, there is no opportunity for problem solving. If you have no common interests, you should just go out there and bargain. Fortunately, there are more common interests than you may suspect, but you may have to work hard to find them. They fall into three broad classes: third parties, efficiencies, and profitable trades. We will discuss trades elsewhere. Now we will just look at the first two.

Third parties can add value directly or indirectly, and in America the biggest and most benevolent third party is the U.S. government. Each year hundreds of thousands of deals are structured in ways that save taxes or maximize government subsidies. For example, tax free municipal bonds are often issued to build factories that would normally be financed through corporate bonds. The borrower gets a lower interest rate; the lenders (bond holders) get tax free income; the city gets jobs and other benefits, and the federal government essentially subsidizes everyone.

Efficiencies are the second source of added value, and they can affect almost any kind of negotiation. For example, if a computer company can show a customer how to process its information more efficiently, they both gain. The customer gets better value for money, and the computer company probably gets additional business.

General Motors and The United Automobile Workers jointly found the importance of efficiency. GM discovered that Blue Cross and other health insurance companies were among its biggest suppliers. Health insurance premiums amounted to literally hundreds of dollars for every car! Since every dollar spent on insurance cannot be spent on something else, such as wages, the company and the union had a common interest in cutting medical costs. They have worked together to save tens of millions of dollars a year through purchasing generic drugs, requiring second opinions for some surgery, and negotiating discounts with hospitals and other health care organizations.

You may not be able to work together cooperatively unless you clearly identify the issues on which your interests at least partially overlap. While preparing, classify issues into three types: competitive, cooperative, and mixed. For example, in a union-management negotiation, wages would probably be competitive; developing a common lobbying position on imports would be cooperative; and revising the grievance procedure could be mixed.

Confirm your definition of the issues

If you are problem solving because you have defined an issue as primarily cooperative, while the other side is bargaining because they believe that your interests conflict, you will probably get the worst of the deal.

Conversely, if you are bargaining while they are problem solving, you may damage, perhaps even destroy, your relationship. They may see you as cheating or devious, perhaps even dishonest. You should therefore try to have both sides define the issues the same way.

If possible, separate cooperative issues from the competitive negotiations

Because bargaining is so power oriented, both parties may be reluctant to use problem-solving techniques in the central negotiations. If possible, have technical experts work separately on the cooperative issues. For example, engineers from both sides might agree on the best way to build a piece of equipment; the chief negotiators would then bargain over the price and terms.

Start with the primarily cooperative issues

Create trust and momentum by starting with these issues, keeping the following suggestions in mind:

1. *Talk in terms of problems, not solutions.* Let them know what you want and why you want it, but focus on what you must accomplish, not the exact means for accomplishing it. Stating your proposal can look as if you are telling them what to do, and their natural reaction is to make a counter proposal, thereby creating a bargaining atmosphere. You both may then argue that your own proposal is the best, or trade one part of your proposal for a different part of theirs. "We will accept your proposal for staffing the design team, if you will agree with our engineering specifications."

The negotiation between Jack and George illustrated the effects of talking in terms of solutions. In effect, George said, "I want Joan on the project." Jack said, "You can't have her." George said, "I insist," and Jack told him he was being unreasonable. Since only one of them could win they got nowhere.

This kind of approach creates a bargaining atmosphere, narrows both parties' focus, and prevents people from considering other ideas that could be better than *either* side's original proposal. The results would probably be better, and people would almost certainly feel better if the problem is raised as one for everyone to discuss. More ideas would be considered, and more people would be involved in the solution. The best solutions to problems occur when people focus, not on "my idea versus your idea," but on the problem itself.

For example, if the issue is a reorganization, state what you want from the new organization, but do not draw a new organization chart. Doing so encourages the other side to draw its organization chart, then bargain with you about which chart to use. It is better to agree first on what the new organization should accomplish, then draw the chart together.

2. *Encourage the other side to do the same.* Show that you are interested in hearing their ideas, and listen carefully. In addition to learning something, listening helps to build that essential trust, openness, and flexibility.

3. *Clarify and discuss differences in priorities.* These differences will usually suggest opportunities for value-added trades, the ones that allow both parties to get back more than they give. You concede on one of their higher priority issues in return for a concession on one of your important issues. That way you both gain.

4. *Propose many alternatives, and discuss each one as just a possibility, not the final solution.* The more alternatives both sides consider, the better the deal is likely to be. In fact, a very visible difference between bargaining and problem solving is the number of alternatives considered. In PB it is usually the same as the number of parties (e.g., two parties, two alternatives, yours and ours), while many more alternatives may be considered while problem solving. Obviously, the more alternatives you consider, the better chance you have of achieving the best solution.

5. *Select the alternative that balances objective quality and mutual acceptability.* Sometimes both sides will like the same alternative, but compromises are often needed. Alternative A might be a little cheaper, faster, or easier, but they really like alternative B. Alternative C might not be as attractive to either of you as your first preference, but it is both parties' second choice. If neither of you can convince the other, perhaps you should take C.

Ignore the source of each suggestion and evaluate each one on its merits. Acceptability may depend as much on the problem-solving process as on the quality of the decision. If the other party feels you have dominated the process or ignored their suggestions, they may reject a solution which is objectively better for them. "I don't care if it is better; no way am I going along with his proposal!"

6. *Listen respectfully.* It is the best way to create trust and open-mindedness. It also increases your power because knowledge is power. In fact, the ability to listen well is probably the most important quality for both bargaining and problem solving.

Balancing PB and JPS

Balancing is both important and difficult, and requires constant attention to the situation. Sometimes you must lean toward bargaining, sometimes the other way, but do not go too far, or you may fall on your face. Balance trust and caution—again, trust, but verify. Temper your desire for the best possible deal by your need for a good relationship.

Despite the need for balance, this book will generally emphasize the bargaining side of the continuum. We will certainly not overemphasize bargaining. We will always be looking for ways to move toward a mutually satisfactory deal, but we will put somewhat more stress on bargaining strategies and tactics.

There are several reasons for this emphasis. First, we must emphasize bargaining to counteract our culture's extreme emphasis upon problem solving. Americans and Europeans are natural problem solvers. Our culture values and encourages qualities such as openness, objectivity, fairness, cooperation, reason, and mutual trust.

Second, because of our culture, you are probably much better at problem solving, but need help when bargaining. When there is little or no conflict, you can usually get good results by acting naturally. But, when interests conflict, or the other side uses bargaining tactics, you must act in unnatural, perhaps even distasteful ways. Since this is the kind of help you need, it will be our emphasis.

Third, bargaining is where the money is. Too many companies have inadequate profit levels; too many billions of dollars in bad loans will have to be written off, too many bad deals have been made.

One reason for these bad deals is that Americans and Europeans tend to be naive. We are trusting and objective even when we should be tougher and more skeptical. In fact, the Russians, Arabs, Japanese, and members of other non-western cultures regard us as naive fools for problem solving when they are bargaining, for trusting them when they are unquestionably lying. The best negotiations are between two sincere problem solvers, and it would be extremely foolish to shift toward bargaining when the other side is being open, honest, and cooperative. But it is suicidal to be open, honest, and trusting when the other side is obviously lying and exploitative. Yet that is exactly what we have done, again, and again, and again.

Jimmy Carter repeatedly ignored the Russians' intransigence and violations of countless agreements; then, when they invaded Afghanistan, he lamented that he did not understand what they were really like. OPEC expropriated billions of dollars worth of oil wells that had been developed by western capital and talent, and raised the price of oil by a factor of twelve. In an earlier era the threat to nationalize would have been met by the threat of military action.

Rice in Japan costs six times the world market price, and hundreds of Japanese products are cheaper in New York, Toronto, or Frankfurt than they are in Tokyo. The Japanese even insist that, because their bodies are different, they cannot buy our beef, fruit, or medical instruments. Anyone who challenges such obvious nonsense is called prejudiced or a "Japan basher." By manipulating the media, the Japanese have gotten many people to accept the obvious lie that their markets are as open as ours! We could open their markets with ridiculous ease: All we have to do is tell them we will be exactly as protectionist as they are.

A fourth reason for emphasizing pure bargaining is that you cannot get much of the help you need. There are numerous books and courses on joint problem solving, but hardly any that seriously discuss pure bargaining. In fact, many popular books on negotiations essentially ignore conflict. They pander to people's discomfort with conflict by pretending it does not exist and lead one to believe that *all* negotiations can be win-win. Tell that to a trade negotiator who is trying to ensure that an American car costs as much in Seoul as a Korean one costs in New York.

Although we will show you ways to soften conflict, to build and preserve relationships while rationally seeking to advance your own interests, we will never forget that conflict is a fact of life, and that ignoring it is dangerous. Nor will we overlook the obvious fact that people do lie while negotiating and that excessive trust can lead to disaster.

John Maynard Keynes, the great economist, made this point brilliantly in his analysis of the Versailles negotiations that ended World War II. He definitely sympathized with Woodrow Wilson's ideals, but regarded him as a naive fool, a preacher playing poker with card sharks. The cynical French and British prime ministers manipulated Wilson into agreements that protected their short-term interests, but, as Keynes predicted, had disastrous long-term effects on everyone—including the French and British—Germany's ruinous inflation, the Great Depression, and World War II.

You cannot afford to be as naive as Presidents Wilson and Carter. Your naivity will not have such disastrous consequences for other people, but it could destroy your own career. Corporations do not forgive naive, costly errors.

THE NEGOTIATIONS MODEL

Our entire theory is built on a flow-chart model of the negotiations process. It presents a clear, structured series of steps that should be taken in a definite order.

It also shows that negotiations are not just the face-to-face meetings, the back-and-forth wheeling and dealing that most people regard as the essence of negotiations. The process is actually much broader. It includes positioning actions that can be taken long before a negotiating session, the preparation just before the meetings, the actual discussions, and the reviews afterward.

The model is divided into three phases: preparing, negotiating, and reviewing. Positioning yourself (getting ready for actions before you take them) is not represented in the model because it is a more general concept, and positioning actions can occur at any time. Virtually everything you do affects your bargaining position, reputation, and people's attitudes toward you.

The next sections briefly describe the major parts and purpose of each step and explain why they are in this order and how they affect each other. Later chapters will discuss each step in considerable detail. Positioning yourself will be analyzed in chapter 5.

THE THREE-PHASE MODEL

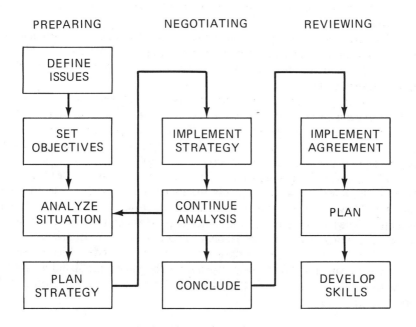

Preparing

The four major preparation steps are:

1. Defining issues
2. Setting objectives
3. Analyzing the situation (from their perspective)
4. Planning your strategy

Defining issues

What are you negotiating about? What are the key issues? Set aside (at least temporarily) the issues that have already been decided, and focus only on the ones that either party might want to discuss.

Then ask where and how your interests conflict or coincide. The answer to that question will have a major impact on your strategy. In fact, a major preparation task is often to determine how much your interests conflict.

Setting objectives

In negotiations, as in most other activities, you need to set clear objectives. You must know what you want to accomplish or you almost certainly will not accomplish it. You will drift or take actions that conflict with each other, and your strategy will have no sense of direction.

Objectives are normally divided into two classes: essential and desirable. You *must* reach your essential objectives, and you would like to reach the desirable ones. However, if necessary, you will make sacrifices and forego a desirable objective to reach an essential one.

At this stage, an absolutely critical task is to decide what you *must* get: *your minimum/maximum settlement point (MSP)*. The MSP is not your goal; it *is your bottom line, the worst deal you can accept.* If you cannot get at least that much, you do not want a deal at all. You will try, of course, for more, but will not take less (unless you learn that your MSP is incorrect).

We must point out that senior managers *love* the MSP concept, the idea that you should walk away rather than accept less, the attitude that no deal is better than a bad deal. When they hear us say that, many senior managers have said: "That's it! That's what our people have to learn. . . . .I'm so sick of people coming in and telling me that we have to cut margins or even lose money to get a certain piece of business."

A few years ago the name of the game was grow, grow, grow—get the business even if you lose money at first. Today, the name of the game is profitability—get only the business that makes a satisfactory profit. If a deal is not profitable, forget it. We could not agree more.

Analyzing the situation (from their perspective)

Despite your limited information, make a preliminary analysis of the situation from their point of view. First, estimate their objectives. You will revise this estimate as you get more information, but you need a starting point to plan your initial strategy.

Second, analyze the power balance. Carefully examine both sides' alternatives. The important question is: Who needs the deal more? The more one side needs the deal, the weaker they are. Since your information is incomplete, plan to probe about this subject.

Third, analyze their personality, political situation, and probable strategy. What kind of people are they? What political pressures do they face? How will they probably negotiate?

Planning your strategy

Since you have so little information, your plans, although tentative, should focus on the start of the negotiations. Do not ignore the later stages, but emphasize the early tasks: creating the right atmosphere, communicating your initial position, and learning their position.

First and foremost, decide whether you will emphasize bargaining or problem solving. This decision comes first because it affects every other strategic decision. For example, if you want to emphasize problem solving, you cannot make an attacking first offer.

Decide whether you will make the first offer. If so, how much will it be? What atmosphere will you create? On which issues will you make your first concessions? On which issues will you hold firm? What questions will you ask? Should you negotiate by yourself or with a team? If you are negotiating as a team, which role will each member take? These questions are not easy, but you should make preliminary answers. Later, when you have more information, you will modify those answers.

Negotiating

There are three major steps during the negotiations phase:

1. Implementing your original strategy
2. Continuing your analysis and revising your plans (using the Feedback Loop)
3. Concluding the negotiations

Implementing your original strategy

You should obviously implement your strategy well, but many people's actions conflict with their plans. For example, they say that they intend to be indifferent, then sell very hard. Or they plan to be cooperative, but act aggressively.

Make sure your signals fit your strategy, and remember that the adversarial nature of negotiations makes most people quite skeptical. You may therefore believe that you are reasonable and accommodating, while they feel that you are unyielding or even hostile.

Continuing your analysis

The ongoing analysis is critically important, and many people disregard or minimize it. Again and again, we have seen people persist with an ineffective strategy because they ignore signals that their initial analysis was incorrect. They are so intent on their own plans that they ignore contradictory information.

Observe that the model has a line from "continue analysis" to "analyze situation." In flow-chart terms that line plus the one to "plan (revise) strategy" and "implement strategy" is called a *Feedback Loop*. This term comes from computers and other control devices. For example, a thermostat is a feedback loop. As the temperature gets higher, it turns off the heat. When the temperature drops, it turns on the heat.

This Feedback Loop is the single most important part of our model and the one that is most often neglected. Far too many people simply do not adjust their negotiating strategy to fit the situation. They may not ask enough questions, or misinterpret the answers, or ignore the implications of the new information, but, in one way or another, they continue a strategy long after it has shown that it will not work. For example, we saw that Jack ignored George's signals and tried to sell an unacceptable proposal. He should have learned why using Joan was so important, then worked with George to develop a mutually satisfactory arrangement.

In fact, *we believe that the most important difference between effective and ineffective negotiators is their ability to use the Feedback Loop.* Good negotiators adjust their strategy to fit the situation; poor ones continue ineffective strategies.

Concluding the negotiations

Eventually the negotiations must end, and there are really only two possible outcomes: a deal or a deadlock. You reach an agreement or you decide you cannot reach one. Closing the deal is an art that many people never master. Concluding a negotiation that ends without a deal is an even more difficult art; you should end it in a way that preserves your relationship and allows both parties to reopen the negotiations or work on another deal without losing face.

The beginning, middle, and end games

The negotiating phase can also be broken down another way, into the Beginning, Middle, and End Games. The Beginning Game sets the stage for the entire negotiation. The three critical tasks are: (1) create the right atmosphere; (2) communicate your position; and (3) learn their position. Our sample negotiation showed that these tasks are interdependent. Jack's dogmatic way of presenting his position and his failure to understand George's position changed a pleasant atmosphere into an adversarial one. If it is done properly, the Beginning Game essentially establishes the gap between both sides' positions; they understand each other's positions and know how far they have to go to close the gap between them.

The Middle Game is concerned with closing that gap. First, you must create momentum by having both sides start moving toward a deal. Your ability to do so depends upon how well you have performed the Beginning Game's tasks. For example, because the atmosphere was so negative and Jack did not understand George's position, he could not create any momentum.

Once you have created momentum, you must maintain it. You have to keep moving by avoiding the obstacles to momentum such as the belief that "we are moving faster than they are." But, you must also control that momentum to make sure that you move in a slow, deliberate way toward the *right* deal. Any fool can put together a deal, but it takes hard work and discipline to put together the right one.

The End Game is the final, often stressful period when both sides frequently make the painful concessions that they strenuously resisted earlier. You have four critical tasks. First, you should test their limits to learn how far they can be pushed. Second, you must communicate finality; let them know that you cannot be pushed too far.

Third, use that deadline pressure; make it work for you. Fourth, you should let them save face; make them feel good about both the deal and the way it was reached.

Because each game makes different demands, you must modify your approach as the negotiations progress. For example, the way you communicate your positions must change. In the Beginning Game you must communicate a readiness to negotiate, but not be so soft that they do not take your opening position seriously. In the Middle Game you must move, but only in a slow, deliberate, controlled way. In the End Game you must make them believe that you have run out of bargaining room, and that you cannot go another inch. The need to change your actions as the negotiations progress can cause serious psychological and strategic problems. The personal qualities that help you at one stage in the process can hurt you in another. The actions that fit the Beginning Game may clash with the End Game's demands. Expert negotiators understand how the game changes, and they adjust their approaches to fit the changing demands.

Reviewing

Regardless of how the negotiations end, you should immediately review them. Doing so can provide three benefits:

1. Fewer implementation problems
2. Better strategies for future negotiations with these people
3. Development of your own skills

Implementing the agreement

Implementation problems often occur because the parties have different ideas of their agreement. These misunderstandings increase dramatically when people other than the negotiators must implement all or part of the agreement. In fact, negotiations to clarify an agreement are often much longer and more difficult than those that produced the original agreement.

Reviewing can reduce, but not eliminate these problems. A quick review before breaking can save many frustrating phone calls and letters. A memo of understanding can further reduce these problems, and it is particularly valuable if other people will become involved in the implementation process. Without that memo, they can easily misinterpret your agreement.

Planning future negotiations with these people

Nearly all of your negotiations are part of a continuing relationship. Whether you like it or not, you will probably have to negotiate with the same people again, and the ideal time to make your general plans is right now. Your memory is fresh; you now know more about how they negotiate and the way to get the best results than you will know if you wait until your next negotiation.

Carefully review everything that happened, then decide how you can get better results the next time. Do not worry about details; look at the overall strategy. Write a memo to yourself or to the file listing things you want to remember. Should you be more friendly, factual, or power oriented? Should your first offer be more or less reasonable? What signals should you look for? What kinds of probing will produce the most information? A few minutes spent on your general strategy can greatly improve the results of the next negotiation.

Developing skills

Do not just consider ways to negotiate more effectively with these people; try to improve your overall skills. Reviewing your negotiations will reveal patterns, such as making overly generous first offers, failing to probe enough, or being too aggressive.

If you look at many different negotiations, you will probably see that you have repeatedly shown the same strengths and weaknesses. You can then decide how to develop your skills. By building on your strengths and overcoming your weaknesses, you will become a much better negotiator.

OVERVIEW OF THE REST OF THE BOOK

The next seven chapters follow the organization of the Flow Chart Model. They give detailed instructions on how to take each step. The negotiating phase is so complex that it is divided into three separate chapters: the Beginning Game, the Middle Game, and the End Game.

The final three chapters discuss the effects of three additional factors. They will show you how to adjust for the effects of personal styles, negotiating as a team, and cultural factors during international negotiations.

The first four appendices are questionnaires or tools to help you prepare for negotiations, keep track of offers while negotiating, use the Feedback Loop, or analyze your own negotiating style. Appendix 5 is a list of recommended readings.

Throughout this book we illustrate negotiating principles with stories. Some are based on personal experience; many have been told to us by friends, associates, and seminar participants; and lots of them are straight from the newspapers and history books. Some business people feel uncomfortable with stories about Jimmy Carter, Woodrow Wilson, or other historical figures because they do not get involved in the same kinds of negotiations.

True, but the principles are the same. Presidents, prime ministers, and diplomats make the same kinds of good and bad moves as business people. We use them as examples for two reasons. First, many people know the people involved, the general issues, and the context, while a manufacturing manager computer analyst, sales rep, and insurance adjuster may know hardly anything about each other's worlds.

Second, some politicians and diplomats have made such spectacularly stupid mistakes that they are wonderful negative examples. Their egos and political constraints have caused them to act in ineffective ways, often with tragic consequences. What significant business executive would ever waste billions of dollars and thousands of lives trying to win an argument over the shape of a negotiating table?

Yet Henry Kissinger and the North Vietnamese foreign minister did it, and they won the Nobel Peace Prize!

SUMMARY

This chapter has described the basic elements of the negotiating process. We began by defining negotiations as a method for reaching agreement, with both cooperative and competitive elements. Negotiating is not a mystical art; you can become a more skilled and effective negotiator by taking the right steps in the right order. You must also balance cooperation and competition. Overemphasizing cooperation can encourage other people to exploit you, while overemphasizing competition will alienate people and result in deadlocks.

You should negotiate only when three conditions exist: a conflict of interests, ambiguity about the result, and an opportunity to compromise.

A good negotiation will produce good objective and good psychological results. The deal will make sense, and everyone will feel good about it. These feelings depend upon both the deal and the process by which it was reached.

Selecting your basic strategic emphasis affects everything else. There is a range of strategies, with pure bargaining and joint problem solving near the opposite ends of a strategic continuum. However, neither is at the exact end of that continuum because both require both trust and power, while the extreme positions (war or brainstorming) involve only one of them.

Pure bargaining is a win-lose, zero-sum, competitive game, involving conflicting interests. It is based upon power that can be enhanced by irrationality, emotions, and distorted communications. Joint problem solving is a win-win, variable-sum, cooperative game involving common interests. It is based on trust and information that are reduced by emotions, irrationality, and distorted communications. Therefore, nearly every action that increases power reduces trust and the flow of information and vice versa.

Most people select the strategy that makes them most comfortable, but *good* negotiators select the one that fits the situation.

Pure bargaining should be emphasized when interests clearly conflict; you are much more powerful; you do not care about the long-term relationship; you do not trust the other party; the ageement is easy to implement; or they are pure bargaining.

Joint problem solving should be emphasized when you have common interests; you are weaker or equal in power; you want a long-term relationship; you trust them; the agreement is hard to implement; or they are joint problem solving.

Because negotiations are essentially adversarial, pure bargaining normally dominates the negotiating process, even when it is inappropriate. To overcome this tendency, you must work hard to create a JPS atmosphere. The text describes several helpful actions such as moving slowly, building trust without making large concessions, and starting with cooperative issues.

The negotiations model showed that the process is clearly structured, and it includes much more than the wheeling and dealing that most people regard as the essence of negotiations. There is a series of rationally ordered steps that are divided into three distinct phases: *preparation, negotiation, and review.*.

In addition, there is a Feedback Loop. You cannot just implement the strategy you planned during the preparation phase; you must also acquire information, interpret it, use it to revise your strategy, and then implement that revised strategy. Many people, perhaps most of them, do not use the Feedback Loop effectively. One of our major themes is that you must work harder on the Feedback Loop. Keep trying to understand the other side and continuously adjust your strategy. Work toward a deal that satisfies *both* parties, but gives you most of the money on the table.

2

Getting Ready to Negotiate

Good preparation can mean the difference between success and failure, but many people do not prepare carefully. They enter negotiations without clearly understanding the issues, their own objectives, or the other side's, and their strategy is little more than a vague hope. A few hours spent preparing can mean the difference between a successful negotiation and a failure. *The more thoroughly you prepare, the better deal you will get.*

You should prepare both economically and psychologically, but even the people who prepare their economics carefully often ignore or minimize psychological factors. They may carefully analyze the costs and benefits of various kinds of deals, but pay little attention to the way other parties see the situation, the kinds of atmosphere they should create, the strategy that the other side will follow, or the likely reactions to their own strategy. The net result can be a deadlock or a relatively poor deal.

Your decisions while preparing will usually be more rational than those made during the negotiations. You have more time to think, can break to get information or advice, and are not under the psychological pressure of having to respond immediately.

Our flow chart model divided preparation into four distinct steps, and this chapter will devote a section to each step.

   I. Define the Issues
  II. Set Your Objectives
 III. Analyze the Situation (from Their Perspective)
  IV. Plan Your Strategy

DEFINE THE ISSUES

The way you define the issues can affect every other step. You should therefore take three simple steps: list all the issues, group them, and relate the issues to the overall relationship.

List All the Issues

First, just list all the issues that either party might raise. You can usually omit issues that have already been settled. However, even if you have already agreed on, perhaps, the staffing of a project, one side or the other might want to renegotiate it because of disagreements over other issues.

If you are unsure of whether to include or exclude an issue, include it. It is far better to prepare for an issue that never arises than to be surprised during the negotiation. We saw, for example, in the first chapter, that Jack became flustered and ineffective when George wanted to change the training plans.

A union-management negotiation might include the following issues:

General wage increase
Wage differentials between skilled and unskilled jobs
Wage differentials for night and weekend work
Increase in the number of paid holidays
Increase in vacation time for long-term employees
Maternity/paternity leave
Sick leave
Pension contributions and benefits
Changes in the grievance procedure
Many different ways to increase productivity
Cost of living allowances
Rules for changing from lower- to higher-paid jobs
Seniority and bumping
Layoffs
Use of subcontractors
Rules for allocating overtime
Administering the health insurance plan

Group the Issues

The above list is quite formidable; many negotiations cover even more issues! The longer the list, the greater the need to divide them into logical categories. Trying to deal with them individually virtually guarantees confusion.

You might find it useful to use more than one grouping system so that you can look at them in a variety of ways. The first grouping should usually be based on priorities: high, medium, and low. If you prioritize issues for both parties, you may find that some of your high priorities are not particularly important to the other side and vice versa. *Every difference in priorities can create an opportunity for a profitable trade*, one in which both sides give up something to gain a more important concession.

For example, let's say that increasing productivity is extremely important to management, while maternity/paternity leave is a low priority. The union might be under pressure from its members to get maternity/paternity leave, but be relatively indifferent to some work rule changes that would increase productivity. A profitable trade would be a change in the work rules for maternity/paternity leave.

Another possible grouping could be based on the degree of conflict. High conflict issues such as wages and the use of subcontractors would be approached competitively. Management wants lower costs and the flexibility to use subcontractors frequently; the union wants to increase wages and protect its members' jobs. Low conflict issues such as changing the grievance procedure and administering the health insurance plan would be approached cooperatively. Both sides often want a more efficient grievance procedure and more value for money from their health insurance plan. Mixed issues, such as some ways to increase productivity, would require a balanced negotiating approach.

Both parties would normally bargain hard on the high conflict issues, especially the ones that are also a high priority, but they might problem solve or even have a subcommittee of technical specialists work out a solution on the low-conflict issues.

Relate the Issues to the Overall Relationship

Linking the issues to the relationship should have a critical impact upon your negotiating strategy, yet many people never even think about it. They may get so wrapped up in winning the negotiation that they damage an important relationship. The opposite error is made just as often; people overemphasize the importance of preserving the relationship and accept a bad deal.

I vividly recall two of my relatives' spending tens of thousands of dollars on legal fees they could not afford, while damaging their working relationship and their partnership's reputation over a silly, symbolic conflict. Most families could tell similar stories.

Virtually every executive can tell stories about paying too high a price to get or preserve a relationship. In fact, some of them are just plain tired of hearing that they have to cut their margins, provide costly extra service, or make other sacrifices to satisfy certain customers, even though the relationship has never been really profitable.

To avoid these errors, step back and take a hard look at the issues and the relationship. Consider three factors: the importance of the issues themselves, the total amount of conflict on these issues, and the value of the relationship. The real importance of the issues is often hard to determine, especially when people are in a conflict. Substantively trivial issues often become important "issues of principle," over which people act stupidly. You should therefore be ruthlessly objective; ask yourself how important this issue is, not how strongly you feel about it.

If the issues are genuinely important (for example, if a great deal of money is involved), there is a lot of conflict, and the relationship is relatively unimportant, you should probably bargain hard. Conversely, if the issues are not important or there is relatively little conflict of interest (although there might be lots of personal conflict), and the long-term relationship is really important, you should not bargain hard, and you might even ask for help from a third party such as a mediator or mutual friend.

These extreme cases are relatively easy to decide. When the issues and relationship become more balanced, the decision is much more difficult. For instance, what should you do if the issues are important, there is a lot of conflict, and the relationship is really valuable?

The Preparation Questionnaire in Appendix 1 will help you to make these difficult decisions. It has the same structure as this chapter and should help you to define the issues, set your objectives, and so on. Please feel free to copy it and use it whenever you prepare to negotiate.

SET YOUR OBJECTIVES

Set an objective for each issue. If you do not know where you are going, it is pretty hard to get there. These objectives should be divided into essential and desirable. For your essential objectives, decide what you *must* get (your MSP's). For desirable objectives decide what you would like to get, but be prepared to make sacrifices on them to achieve your more important objectives.

Your MSP's

For relatively minor issues, you can set general objectives, but for the most important issues, you must be firmer and more specific. *You must set a firm MSP (minimum or maximum settlement point).*

My friend and associate, Kathy Terwilliger, does not like the term MSP because it is not very readable. As she said, "Minimum or maximum settlement point doesn't exactly have a ring to it. 'Walk away point' is better, and WAP is certainly a better acronym." I agree, but I'm stuck with MSP; our firm has used the term in hundreds of classes, and it is clearly identified with our work. So call it what you like, but make sure that you set it.

Do not overdo it. Set a firm MSP (or whatever you want to call it) *only* on your most important issues. If you set one on too many issues, you can easily create what mathematicians call a null set: No deal is possible because you cannot possibly achieve every MSP.

Many people confuse their MSP and their goal, but they are actually the opposite ends of the bargaining range (the distance between both parties' MSP's). Your MSP is the *worst* deal you will accept. Your goal should usually be the *best* deal you can get.

And what is that best deal? If there is a a deal on the table (i.e., if a deal is possible within both parties' limits), your best deal is the other party's MSP. In other words, *your MSP is your limit, while their MSP is your goal* (unless other factors, such as the importance of the relationship prevent you from trying to push them to their limit).

An MSP should be based entirely on your own situation—*your* economics, *your* political constraints, *your* alternatives. For the moment ignore the other party and ask a key question: If I do not make a deal in this negotiation, what will I do?

Naturally, your power determines how ambitious an MSP can be. If you have attractive alternatives and other kinds of power, you can set ambitious limits. If you are in a weak position, you should be willing to settle for much less.

The MSP should be the point at which another alternative becomes more attractive than this one. It is not an arbitrary number, nor is it carelessly set. It should be based on a careful analysis of your economics and alternatives, and you must sincerely believe in it. If you cannot buy Tom's Ford for less than $12,350, you would rather buy Barbara's Chevrolet. If Mary cannot work full-time on this project, you will assign it to Bob; he is not as talented as Mary, but you need a full-time person.

Normally, you will have only one MSP on an issue, but you can occasionally have two or more. If there are two (or more) sets of conditions, you can have more than one MSP. For example, you could have one MSP on your price for a cash deal and a different one if you have to accept payment terms. However, for each set of conditions, you should have only one firm, hard MSP.

Some people say, "We cannot set a firm MSP because there are too many variables. We just try to get the best possible deal." That approach can be very risky. In fact, *the most serious preparation mistake is to fail to set a firm MSP on your major issues.* Setting it provides four major benefits.

Preventing you from conceding too much

Once you start negotiating, your natural desire to make a deal will influence your judgment. You naturally tend to regard deals as victories, deadlocks as defeats. The longer you have negotiated, the stronger these feelings become. For example, if you have spent months trying to negotiate an important contract, neither party wants to tell their management that all that time, effort, and money were wasted.

You may therefore make one concession after another, trying for that elusive victory. Then, when the contracts are signed, you may realize that the victory was not worth winning, that you would have been better off without the deal. For example, the banks and many of their customers wish that loans worth billions had never been made.

An even more dramatic example concerns Rolls Royce. Its negotiators desperately wanted the engine contract for Lockheed's L–1011 airliner. Despite repeated warnings from their own engineers, they made concession after concession. They ended up with a contract that any rational engineer would know was ridiculous. They agreed to go well beyond the existing state of the art on a low-margin, fixed-price contract. When the nearly inevitable cost overruns occurred, they found that they were selling each engine for substantially less than it cost to build. This contract (and various other mistakes) literally drove Rolls Royce, a famous name and a fine engineering firm, into bankruptcy.

The Lockheed negotiators naturally felt they had negotiated very well. However, they had actually made an extremely costly mistake. By driving the price so low, they bankrupted a key supplier, could not meet their commitments to their own customers, and ultimately lost 2.5 billion dollars on the L–1011. The moral is quite plain—*if a deal is too good for either side, it is probably bad for both of them.*

A firm MSP would have prevented this disaster. Rolls Royce would have walked away, and Lockheed would have been forced to rethink its entire strategy. Instead of going forward on the optimistic assumptions that its engines would cost only $X and would be delivered on time, they might have re-analyzed the entire project. Perhaps they would have decided to abandon it; perhaps they would have budgeted more for the engines; but they certainly would not have rushed forward, hoping that, just this once, new technology could be developed and produced on a tight budget.

Preventing you from not conceding enough

A firm MSP can also prevent your making the opposite mistake—walking away from a good deal. Sometimes people become so angry or intent upon beating the other side that they insist on unnecessary concessions or even walk away from an objectively excellent offer. They say, in effect, "The price for everybody else is $15,000, but it's $18,000 for you. Take it or leave it!"

Increasing your power

A firm MSP will also increase your power. You will look and feel stronger. If you know that you will walk away rather than break your limit, you will become firmer as you approach it. Your concessions may become smaller, and your discomfort and resistance to moving further will increase. The other party will often sense this firmness and make concessions.

Increasing your comfort

Because discomfort has such negative effects, decreasing it will usually improve your results. With a firm MSP based upon your economics you will feel better and negotiate more effectively. A firm MSP creates a sense of purpose, limits the conflict, and makes it less personal. You are not trying to exploit the other side; you are just striving to achieve what you absolutely need to justify committing yourself and your organization.

Your Priorities

Of course, not all your objectives are equally important. You should therefore set explicit priorities. Which objectives are most important to you? What concessions will you make on other issues to reach your most important objectives?

The more clearly you understand your objectives and priorities, the more intelligently you can strive for them. In addition, as we noted earlier, differences in priorities create opportunities for profitable trades—but these opportunities are useless if you do not understand *both* parties' priorities. So set yours, and then focus on learning theirs.

ANALYZE THE SITUATION (FROM THEIR PERSPECTIVE)

After setting your objectives, shift your focus to the other party. At first you were concerned solely with your own situation: What do you need to get? Now focusing on the other side will help you to plan *how* to get what you need (and perhaps a little more).

The other side usually does not care about you or your company; you are usually a means to an end, not an end in yourself. Their objectives, priorities, and strategy will be based upon their own economics, politics, and perceptions. You must, therefore, try to understand how they see the situation.

Most people do not really try to do that. They are so concerned with their own objectives, their own problems, and their own strategy that they forget that the critically important information is on the other side of the table. Because this attitude is so common and so destructive, we are obsessed with overcoming it. In fact, if we had to summarize our philosophy of negotiations in just two sentences, we would say: *Don't be so interested in your own position. Focus on theirs.*

That focus should begin during your preparation, and continue throughout the entire negotiations process. Many people object that they do not have enough information to make estimates or predictions while preparing, but you often have or can easily get much more information than you expected. If you have negotiated with these people before, you should have some idea of their concerns and negotiating style. Or perhaps a colleague has negotiated with them or with other people from their department or company. Or you can ask people from other companies that deal with them. The information is usually available if you are willing to look for it.

First, study their objectives because they affect everything else. Then look at their perceptions of the situation, attitudes toward you, personality, authority, power balance, and probable strategy.

Their Objectives

Their objectives are the most important information. The more clearly you understand these objectives, the more effectively you can negotiate, regardless of whether you are bargaining or problem solving. When you are problem solving, understanding their objectives helps you to reach a deal that really satisfies them.

When you are bargaining, the party that more accurately assesses the other's limits normally gets most of the bargaining range. Our research indicates that the party making the more accurate estimate wins about 80% of the time. Why? Because they know how far to push and when to back off. In fact, in pure bargaining negotiations, your primary tasks are:

1. To determine the bargaining range (the distance between your own and their limits).
2. To maximize your share of that range (to get as close as possible to their limit).

These tasks *must* be done in order; you cannot maximize your share of the bargaining range if you do not know their limits. You cannot try to approach their limits if you do not know where they are.

Learning their priorities is only slightly less important than learning their limits. Every difference in priorities creates an opportunity for joint problem solving or value-adding trades. Remember, a good deal is one which satisfies each party's major priorities. You cannot put together that kind of deal unless you understand their priorities.

Therefore, regardless of the situation, your objectives, or your negotiating approach, *your most important task is to learn their objectives: What do they really want?*

That large question breaks down into a few smaller ones. What are they trying to accomplish? What are their priorities? How far can they go on each issue? Sometimes they will answer those questions, but usually you have to give tentative answers while preparing, then confirm or modify them as you acquire new information during the negotiations.

Let's refer to the sample negotiation in Chapter 1. George, a long-term client, has ordered $2 million worth of equipment. Without the higher productivity it will produce, his company cannot successfully compete in today's marketplace. The equipment will be delivered within two months, and must be used effectively shortly after it arrives.

George is polite and friendly, but a very tough negotiator, the purest of pure bargainers, a real games player. He just loves to get every dollar on the table. He even brags about how much he saved by bargaining on his office furniture. He has not told you if he is considering other consultants, but you suspect that he is not.

Your costs plus a fair profit would mean a price of $138,000, which you have set as your MSP. You will meet with George tomorrow to negotiate price. What should your opening offer be?

Our first point is that this question is premature. Before even thinking about your opening offer you should ask the critical question: What is George's MSP? Many people would not even ask that question. They would just assume that George would try to reduce any bid they made, then add a certain amount of "fat" to their MSP so that George could bargain them down to it or a little better price.

That is exactly the wrong approach. It starts from the wrong perspective (your MSP), and it almost guarantees that you will end near or at that limit (that is, with a barely acceptable profit). To start by trying to determine George's MSP would suggest that price is probably not that important. He has so much at stake that another few thousand dollars of profit for you could be almost irrelevant to him. He might be willing to pay $150,000, or $160,000, or perhaps even more.

When they had a near monopoly, Xerox used essentially that approach. Instead of computing their costs and then adding a fair profit, they based their prices on their value to the customer. If they did not use a Xerox machine, what would they do? Since typing with carbons, using photostat machines, and the other alternatives are very expensive and unsatisfactory in many other ways, Xerox made sensational profits while growing very rapidly.

This example shows how important it is to think of these issues while preparing. Once you are face to face, you may not see the issues so clearly. For instance, George might take a very hard line on the price, even pretend that the schedule can be slowed down, or minimize the importance of the government contract, but the facts clearly indicate that price is probably a relatively low priority.

So get in the habit of asking the critical questions: What do they really want? What is their limit on every major issue? How important is each issue? What trades are they willing to make? Give preliminary answers while preparing, then revise your answers as you get more information.

Even people who realize the importance of asking these questions may not begin doing so before the negotiations. But asking them while preparing will help you to plan a preliminary strategy and suggest specific questions to ask during the negotiations.

While analyzing the situation, ignore your own concerns and focus entirely on theirs. They will base their objectives, not on your costs and profits, but on their own motives, alternatives, and perceptions. So forget about yourself for the moment, and direct all of your attention to "getting inside their heads." Review your past conversations with them, consult other people, and do whatever else is necessary to learn their objectives. Your best cues are usually their alternatives, urgency, political situation, and budget.

Their alternatives

Their alternatives are the key to their objectives, and these alternatives are also the basis of their power. The central questions are: If they do not make a deal with you, what will they do? And what will it gain and cost them?

Perhaps they will do nothing at all, or they may do business with a competitor, or delay a project, or hire someone, or even go back to the drawing board. Set your prejudices and desires aside and analyze their alternatives as carefully as possible. What can they do? What do they really want to do?

Remember, during negotiations people often bluff, and many bluffs are successful. So look at the situation as objectively as possible. Study the competitors' prices, time limits, and so forth. You may find yourself in a very good position.

Some of the most outrageous—and obvious—bluffs have been made by professional athletes, and the gullible owners have fallen for them again and again. How many times have you read of an athlete who insists on renegotiating his contract or being traded. "If they don't do it, I won't play! I'll just sit out the year, or retire permanently."

Nonsense! The average career of a professional athlete is about five years. Their salaries are five, ten, even twenty or more times greater than they can earn at another job. Their contracts prevent them from playing for another team. Sitting out for a year will cost them a huge amount of money that they can probably never recover, yet countless owners have collapsed instead of calling the bluff: "OK, don't play. Call me if you get bored (or hungry)."

Their urgency

Estimate their urgency, the intensity of their desire for a deal. The more urgency they feel, the more they will probably concede to get a deal. This urgency can be based on economics, politics, or even personal anxieties. Its source is almost irrelevant; it is the urgency itself that influences them. You should therefore focus on how they feel, not how you think they should feel or how you would feel in the same situation.

Do they really want this deal? Why? Do they have any particular reason for wanting to make this deal with you? Or would they prefer to make it with someone else? Do they need to make it immediately, or can they afford to wait? Are they just shopping, or are they really serious?

Their political situation

Their political situation can greatly affect their objectives. At times, it can even be their primary concern. They may be more interested in certain people's reactions than in any economic factor because those reactions greatly affect their careers. Political factors may therefore cause them to choose apparently irrational positions or strategies.

For example, they may have to win concessions from you to prove their toughness or negotiating skill. If you do not recognize this need, your first offer may be too generous, thereby undermining their political position. They have to prove to management that they have *beaten* you down. If you are too soft, they may even reject a very favorable offer to preserve their reputation for toughness.

Union leaders are particularly concerned with politics. They know that they have to be re-elected periodically, and they all know of colleagues who have been ousted by militants. In fact, in some unions they cannot afford to appear too chummy with management; the unforgivable sin is to be seen as selling out to the bosses.

Intelligent management negotiators recognize the union leaders' problems and deliberately take unreasonable positions so that the union leaders can beat them. They may also engage in marathon negotiating sessions of 24, 36, or even more hours that help the union leaders to prove how hard they are working for their members. These sessions are sometimes little more than a ritual. People discuss hunting, fishing, baseball, and so forth, dragging things out to create tension, and then let the union negotiator triumphantly announce his victory.

Other political factors to consider are a negotiator's authority and political security. If you do not do so, you may waste time and give away your position by negotiating with people who cannot make a deal (i.e., junior people, or those in the wrong positions, or those with no credibility). You may then be forced to make additional concessions to get the decision makers' approval.

To minimize this problem, try to negotiate only with people who have both the authority and political security to make binding commitments. You may have to do considerable homework outside the negotiations because people exaggerate their clout; they claim to be decision makers when they have little or no authority. Do not take their word for it; ask other people; study the organization; learn how decisions are made and who makes them.

Go beyond formal authority and learn how secure they are. Politically secure people are usually more flexible, more willing to make concessions. Insecure people can be so afraid of their bosses' reactions that they dither or stonewall. They would rather lose a deal than make politically risky concessions.

Despite its obvious importance, many people ignore or minimize politics. They focus only on objective, economic factors and then do not understand why they lose deals. You should be more intelligent. Study their political situation and adjust to it.

Their budget

The other side's budget is, of course, a factor only in money-oriented negotiations, but analogous factors affect other negotiations. They may have only so much time to complete a project. Or they may have staffing or other restrictions.

They probably will not tell you their exact budget for money, time, people, or other things, but you can usually ascertain whether the budget is tight or loose, increasing or decreasing. You may also be able to find out whether it is tighter on one factor (such as time) than it is on another (such as price), which suggests that time is a higher priority than money.

Their Perceptions of Your Situation

They will react, not to your actual situation, but to their perceptions of it. You should therefore try to discover their perceptions and try to change them to fit your intentions. If, for example, they think that you are in a weak position, they may try to exploit you. You obviously should try to make them feel that you are stronger than they originally believed.

Learning their perceptions is far from easy, and you will often have to guess. Although it may be difficult, you should try to learn their perceptions of your objectives, situation, attitudes toward them, personalities, and probable strategy.

Many people object to trying to answer these questions. "Boy, this is complicated. You mean we have to guess at what they think we think?" I can understand their frustration, and it certainly is complicated, but I never said that negotiating was easy. In fact, it is quite difficult, but the more time you spend preparing, the more questions you ask, the harder you try to understand how they see things—including you—the better results you will get.

Your objectives

This perception is, of course, the most important because it will affect almost every action they take. For example, if they believe that your limits are considerably less favorable to them than they really are, they may settle for a little more than their own limit. You should therefore try to make them believe that your objectives are more ambitious than they really are. If, for example, they think that you will not sell your house for less than $200,000, while you will settle for $190,000, they could regard driving you down to $201,000 as a real victory, while you would be getting a very satisfactory price. If they believe a certain issue is your top priority, they will probably offer different trades than if they believe it is a low priority.

You should therefore learn what they think you want, then try to make them believe what you want them to believe. You certainly want to conceal your limits, and you may want to conceal your priorities. Conversely, if you want to problem solve, you may want to correct their misperceptions about your priorities.

You obviously cannot change their perceptions in the right direction until you know how they see you. So step back and try to look at yourself the way that they would; then decide if the picture you see is the one that you want. If not, make plans to change it.

Your situation

You should also try to learn how they see your situation. What do they believe are your prices, costs, authority, standard contracts, company policies, and so forth? Pay particular attention to their beliefs about the strength of your bargaining position.

Power comes from objective factors such as your alternatives, but its negotiating effects depend primarily upon people's beliefs about it. If they think you are strong, they will respond to your strength, even if you are in an objectively weak position.

This subject is so important that it is the central focus of Chapter 6, "Positioning Yourself." Now we will simply state that you should usually try to create a strong, confident impression. The stronger they think you are, the more likely they are to be conciliatory.

However, extreme weakness can occasionally help you. For example, Brazil and Mexico have gotten very favorable terms when renegotiating loans. Their economies are so weak, and they owe such awesome amounts that the lenders are afraid they will default, thereby ruining their banks. They are so weak that they are in a strong bargaining position. That sort of absurdity occurs more often than you think. Billy Sol Estes, a famous con man, once said: "If you owe a man enough money, you've got yourself a partner."

Attitudes toward them

What do they believe are your attitudes toward them? Does that belief support your intended approach? If so, reinforce it; if not, change it, but do so very carefully. For example, if they think you like them, and you want them to continue to think that way, you can easily work together on joint problems. But, if you intend to take a hard line, their perception may have disastrous consequences. They may be offended by your approach, or regard you as a manipulative phony.

Personalities

What kind of person do they think you are? If that image is consistent with your strategy, reinforce your image by acting as they expect.

If that image conflicts with your intentions, change it. For example, if they feel that you are devious and exploitative, and you want a joint problem-solving session, you must work hard to develop their trust. Conversely, if they regard you as a wimp, you probably cannot take a hard line unless you can create a credibly tougher image.

George Bush is a splendid example of how irrational factors can affect one's image. His career certainly did not justify the media's "wimp" label during the 1988 presidential campaign. During World War II he became the Navy's youngest pilot at the age of 18; shot down in combat, he won the Distinguished Flying Cross, a rare and very high honor. Many years later he served as the head of the CIA, an organization known for its machismo. Yet, because of a few journalists (most of whom had never fired a gun in anger), many people believed he was a wimp.

The same kinds of factors will affect your negotiations. You cannot isolate the next negotiation from your past relationship and general image, which can severely constrain your freedom. At times the past will flatly prevent you from choosing certain strategies or even negotiating some types of contracts.

You may therefore be forced to select a strategy that fits your personal history. A few minutes of socializing or a friendly problem-solving approach cannot overcome the effects of years of distrust, nor can a few "hardball" actions create a credibly tough image.

Of course, if your image conflicts too much with current objectives and plans, you may be forced to take extreme actions. Jimmy Carter tried to overcome his weakling image by sending helicopters to rescue the Iranian hostages. Unfortunately, partly because of his indecisiveness, the raid ended in disaster, which reinforced his image of impotence. If you want to change your image, make sure that your actions and their effects will really have the result that you want.

Probable strategy

Their expectations about your strategy are second in importance only to their perceptions of your objectives. Their strategy will usually be based, at least partially, on what they expect you to do. You should therefore try to discover those expectations in order to reinforce or change them.

That same principle applies to all their perceptions. You have to take the same three steps again and again:

a. Learn how they perceive your objectives, power, and so forth.
b. Decide how you want them to perceive the situation.
c. Plan ways to influence those perceptions in the right direction.

These three steps are neither easy nor enjoyable, but they are critically important. *The essence of negotiating is managing the other side's perceptions and expectations.* So learn what they expect you to do and plan ways to make their expectations support your strategy.

The process is quite similar to the way that governments, especially those of nations in conflict, act toward each other. Both are constantly trying to learn the other's intentions and to create a certain picture of their own plans. For example, during World War II the British and Americans went to extreme lengths to make the Germans think that we would invade the continent at Calais, not Normandy. Thousands of tons of bombs were dropped in the Calais area; reconnaisance patrols mapped the Calais beaches; false rumors were started; they even put "the invasion plans" on a corpse that they knew the Germans would learn about. It worked; the Germans were not ready for the Normandy invasion.

Their Attitudes toward You

Since their attitudes will affect every element of their strategy, try to discover how they feel. Do they want to do business with you, trust you, want to work out a mutually satisfactory deal, feel a strong desire to defeat you? Many of the cues to their attitude will not come until the negotiation starts, but you can often learn their general attitude before the negotiations.

For example, if they have returned your telephone calls promptly and answered your questions openly, they probably want to try to work out a deal. If they have been brusque and cold, you are liable to have a difficult negotiation. Go further; ask other people such as common acquaintances. You may find out that past problems or misunderstandings have created distrust, or that they respect you and value your relationship.

Their Personalities

Their personalities obviously affect the way they negotiate; in fact, this subject is so important that we devote Chapter 9 to the effects of personal styles. The more you understand them as people, the better you can predict how they will negotiate. This subject is so important that some professional negotiators actually keep extensive dossiers on key people. These dossiers were once referred to as Farley files, because Mr. Farley, a key advisor to President Franklin D. Roosevelt, kept such complete files on hundreds of people.

In addition to records of their past negotiations, these dossiers may cover their working habits, health, hobbies, religious beliefs, political attitudes, perhaps even their favorite foods and drinking habits. The professionals realize that apparently irrelevant information can give them an indispensable advantage at opportune moments.

Except, perhaps, for a few critical people, you should not do such extensive research. However, if you must negotiate important contracts with someone, it probably pays to study their personality and negotiating style. Whst kind of people are they? What do they really care about? How do they relate to people?

Do not assume that merely negotiating with them before has taught you all you need to know. It depends, among other things, on how the previous situations compare to this one. If this negotiation is much more important, or if you have greater conflicts than usual, they may act quite differently. You will have to make a thorough analysis of those past negotiations. Do they emphasize pure bargaining or joint problem solving? Are their opening offers realistic or outrageous? Do they tell the truth, blatantly lie, or just "fudge" a little? Are they more likely to be influenced by facts, friendliness, power, time pressure, or other factors?

If you have never negotiated with them, ask people who have done so. Start with your colleagues, but you might also ask people in other departments and vendors or buyers from other companies. They can probably tell you what to expect.

Their Authority

You clearly need to know people's negotiating authority. If you underestimate it, you may lose the deal. If you overestimate it, you may weaken your bargaining position.

It can be difficult or impossible to learn it during the negotiations. People often lie to inflate their egos or to gain a negotiating advantage. You should therefore try to determine their authority before the negotiations begin and confirm your judgment during the negotiations.

If someone does not have enough authority to negotiate a binding deal, try to avoid negotiating with them. Otherwise, you may make concessions to reach a deal, only to find that the other side rejects their negotiator's concessions and insists on additional negotiations (i.e., more concessions from you).

The Soviets have repeatedly used this technique. A westerner reaches an agreement with an apparently important person, and then is told, "Commissar Smirnov has been sent to Siberia for crimes against the people. We repudiate any agreements he has made, but will negotiate in good faith with all sincere parties."

This approach is a variation on the *salami technique*. You have a salami. If someone tries to take it all at once, you would fight or leave. But you will not fight that hard for just one slice of salami. So the first negotiators take a slice. Then their bosses take a slice. Then their bosses take a slice, and so on, until they have your entire salami!

If you absolutely cannot avoid negotiating with people who have limited authority, raise your MSP for that round so you save something for later concessions. If you do not do so, if you go to your final limits before the final round, you may be forced to choose between losing the deal and breaking your limits. For political reasons the negotiators of later rounds may need concessions that you simply cannot afford to give. They may even choose a less valuable deal with a competitor to preserve their political position and credibility.

The Power Balance

The combination of both parties' alternatives and their perceptions of the situation creates the power balance. How strong is each party? How strong does each feel?

When all is said and done, it is power that makes the difference. You may be charming, friendly, and reasonable, and your position may be absolutely correct, but power will usually determine who gets what.

Power should generally be analyzed in relative, rather than absolute terms, and the analysis should refer specifically to *this* negotiation. One party may be generally more powerful than the other, but relatively weaker in this negotiation. For example, a large corporation would normally be much more powerful than a moderately wealthy landlord, but it could be much weaker in a specific negotiation.

This particular corporation's headquarters was in an area that had really deteriorated. They therefore decided to build in a more fashionable location. Zoning and construction delays forced them to ask their landlord to extend their lease for six months. Since they knew that the landlord would have trouble renting their space, they assumed he would be delighted by their request.

The landlord astonished them by saying that the only way they could remain after the expiration of the lease would be to sign a new *ten year* lease.

When they berated the landlord for his unreasonable position, he replied, "If you don't like it, move."

"But we can't afford to move. We can't disrupt our operations, work out of boxes for six months, then move into our new headquarters."

"Tough. Either sign a new lease or get out."

They pleaded and threatened lawsuits, but the landlord was adamant. He could afford the loss of six months' rent much more than the corporation could afford to disrupt its operations. They ultimately signed the lease, then had to sublet the property at a much lower rental.

Power is partly objective, partly psychological. Objective negotiating power comes primarily from having attractive alternatives. Psychological power comes from both sides' beliefs. If you and they think you have power, you have it. Conversely, no matter how good your alternatives, if you believe you are weak, you may yield too easily; if they believe you are weak, they will probably react to your weakness.

Our research shows that people tend to underestimate their own power. For example, we have had people divide 100 percentage points between the parties. 50/50 would mean that the power is evenly balanced; 80/20 means one is much more powerful.

When we add both parties' estimates of their power, we get an average of about 85 rather than 100. Why? Because people are naturally aware of their own weaknesses. They know how badly they need a deal, or how poor their alternatives are, or how illogical their position is. However, they do not know the other side's weaknesses.

Sometimes, these weaknesses are extremely easy to see, but people may not even bother to look. For example, in the late 1970s the U.S. government panicked during an energy crisis and signed an agreement with Mexico to pay a premium price for natural gas. Any objective analysis would reveal that, since Mexico needed the deal much more than the U.S., the price should have been discounted.

Mexico had a nearly desperate need for foreign exchange and energy was their major export. More importantly, they had no other customers for their natural gas, while the U.S. could buy from many suppliers. Natural gas is the inescapable by-product of oil wells; it comes out of the ground whether one wants it or not. The Mexicans had only two choices: they could flare it (burn it as a waste product) or sell it to the U.S. at whatever price it chose to pay. The U.S. government ignored reality and paid an absurdly high price.

The moral is clear. If you carefully analyze the situation and the way the other side sees it, you will often find that you are much more powerful than you had believed.

Their Probable Strategy

Review the information from the other analyses so you can predict their probable strategy. What are they likely to do?

This question is certainly not easy to answer, but you may have several hints. For instance, based on the way they have negotiated in the past, their attitudes toward you, and your understanding of their objectives, you might expect them to be businesslike and moderately friendly, to make reasonable, but conservative offers, and to emphasize the importance of price and terms.

If your predictions are wrong, you have misread the situation, and must ask yourself why. For example, if they are extremely friendly, refer repeatedly to your long relationship, and make an offer that is surprisingly generous on price and terms, their objectives may be quite different from your expectations. Perhaps they really need this deal and are willing to be more flexible than usual.

Therefore, unless you are very confident that they will use your predicted strategy, consider alternative strategies that they might follow. Then plan ways to determine which strategy they are really using. What cues will reveal the one they have chosen? In our example, their friendliness and offer were the key cues; in other negotiations the cues could be the people sent to negotiate, the type of agenda, time spent on each issue, and so forth.

Try to find more active ways to learn their strategy. Think of questions or other probes that will quickly suggest the way they intend to proceed. The sooner you can recognize their strategy, the more effectively you can respond to it.

Organizing and Interpreting Your Information

If you carefully perform all of these analyses, you will probably have a confusing amount of information. You must therefore organize and make sense of it.

The Preparation Questionnaire in Appendix 1 can help you to clarify the picture. By forcing you to organize and answer questions on the information, it will help you to see the probable hard spots (the issues on which your objectives conflict sharply with theirs), the trading opportunities (the differences in your priorities), the effects that your personal styles will have on the negotiations, and so on. Completing this questionnaire is not easy, but it is worth the effort.

PLAN YOUR STRATEGY

Many people confuse strategies and objectives, but they are quite distinct. *Strategies are concerned with means, not ends*, with *how* you reach your objectives, not the objectives themselves. Good objectives and good situational analyses will not compensate for a poor strategy or vice versa. You need good objectives, a thorough analysis, *and* a good strategy.

Think of negotiations as a car trip. Your *objectives* are your destination, such as Atlanta, when you want to get there, and, perhaps, what you would like to see and do en route. Your *analyses* are similar to the study of the road maps and other information: Interstate I-95 will get you there the quickest, but the scenery is boring and a section of it is being repaired. The hotels along this route are overpriced. That great restaurant you read about is closed on Monday. The traffic in Baltimore is very heavy from 4 P.M. to 6 P.M. Your *strategy* is your plan to get to Atlanta. "We will leave on June 15 so that we can enjoy the weekend in Washington. We will take these highways on the first day. From Washington we will take Highway X, and stay overnight in Williamsburg. Then we will . . . ."

A good negotiating strategy contains several elements: the general approach, alternative approaches, questions, stage setting, the initial position, and probable concessions. Plan an initial strategy which contains all these elements, but be ready to revise it as you get more information.

The General Approach

Your first task is to select a general approach. You can attack, play a waiting game, rely on logical arguments, try to create a friendly, mutually accommodating atmosphere, and so on. Everything else should fit your general approach because consistency is the basis of credibility. For example, a friendly approach and an outrageous offer will create doubts about both your offer and your friendliness.

Your approach must also fit the overall situation. Each type of approach works only in certain situations. An attacking approach might be appropriate when trying to settle a bitter lawsuit, but it could anger everyone and create nasty political problems during a negotiation within your own department. You should therefore make a conscious, rational decision about your approach. What should it be *now?*

Many negotiators do not ask that question. They just do what comes naturally. "The important thing is to grab control; let them know who is boss." "No, a friendly approach is best; it makes people more flexible." Either approach works in some situations, but fails in others. If you always use the same approach, if you always attack, wait, or strive for a friendly atmosphere, you are responding to your own needs and tensions, not to the situation's strategic demands.

You may pay a high price for that temporary comfort. Your approach will frequently be inappropriate, and other people will predict and counter your moves. So break out of that rut! Each time you prepare, set aside your old habits and ask yourself: What approach fits *this* situation?

Alternative Approaches

Preparing only one strategy can be risky. If the other side acts in an unexpected way, you may be unable to respond effectively. You should therefore prepare alternative approaches, also called contingency plans, to counter each strategy they are likely to use.

Use the "what-if" approach that is so popular in many corporations. What if they take a much harder line than we expected? What if they ask us to renegotiate the compensation package? What if they want to tighten the negotiation deadline? Think of the changes they might make, and be prepared with at least preliminary plans to respond to them. Otherwise, you may be caught completely off guard.

The military calls this war-gaming. They develop counters to the most probable enemy strategies and specify the actions that identify each enemy strategy. They are then ready for almost anything. The war-gaming approach is equally valuable for negotiators. It protects you from having to make hurried strategic decisions in the middle of negotiations. If you have developed several strategies and know when to switch from one to another, you can act quickly and effectively.

Questions

Your analyses have almost certainly revealed that you lack important information. You should write down the information you need and make plans to get it.

Sometimes a direct question is best. At other times casual conversation, "the silent treatment," offers to make certain trades, excessive demands, or other probing techniques will get better results.

Most people do not ask enough questions, and they do not ask them in various ways. They ask a few direct questions, get vague answers, and never return to the subject. Make sure that you are more thorough. Ask those questions again and again in different ways until you get the real answers.

On the other hand, you must avoid the opposite extreme, cross-examining them. You do have to ask some questions several times to get a satisfactory answer, but you should not ask them in the rapid fire, repetitious manner of a cross-examining attorney. You are not Perry Mason, and they are not on the witness stand. Ask a question, listen to the answer, change the subject, and then ask it again in a little different way.

For example, the question, "Why are you selling your business?" is obviously important to a potential buyer, and many sellers will give evasive or waffling answers: "I'm ready to do something else."; "I've accomplished all I set out to do."; "We would like to retire."; "We want to move closer to our grandchildren."

Instead of insisting that they state the real reason for selling, you might, from time to time, probe with questions and comments, such as, "It must be hard to leave a business you have built up so nicely."; "My father loved retirement for the first three months, got bored, and went back to work. Have you thought about that?"; "The way living costs are going up, a lot of retired people are being squeezed." Then pause for a reaction.

The Initial Position

Chapter 3, "The Beginning Game," details the initial position. This section covers just a few general principles to consider while preparing.

Your first offer or demand is the most important (because it affects everything else) and the hardest one to make (because you have so little information). Any serious player can tell you that the same principle applies to bridge: The first card played can determine success or failure, but you often do not have enough information to make the right choice.

Because it is so difficult and important, your first offer should be planned well in advance. It is just too dangerous to "wing it," to wait until you start negotiating, and then offer whatever feels right. Of course, you should try to get more information before making that offer, and, if that information indicates that your plans are wrong, you should revise them and make a different first offer. But do not start negotiating without any idea of what your first offer will be.

If your opening offer is too generous, you may leave lots of money on the table, or raise their expectations to unrealistic levels, or have insufficient bargaining room. On the other hand, if you are too ambitious, they may reject your offer out of hand, become angry and rigid, or even break off the negotiations.

Because of their cultures, most Americans and Europeans care more about the second set of dangers; they are afraid of offending or irritating the other side. They may therefore make overly generous first offers. For example, they frequently submit proposals that contain only modest profits. The subsequent negotiations reduce this profit still further and may even drive the deal below the breakeven point. One way to reduce this danger is to get the other side to make the first offer. You then can see whether they intend to be realistic and reasonable. If possible, plan ways to get them to make that first offer.

Unfortunately, you will often have no choice but to make that first offer. If so, plan it carefully. Try to make it conditional and leave yourself plenty of bargaining room. You will rarely get more than you request or pay less than you offer, and a generous first offer can be well past their MSP.

In fact, my research and studies by Dr. Chester Karrass, indicate that, other things being equal, the first offer has more influence on the final deal than any other factor. People who make generous first offers get worse deals than people who make ungenerous ones.

So test their limits. Plan an ungenerous offer and observe their reactions. You may learn that you can get a much better deal than you had anticipated. However, since you may have misread the situation, plan an "escape route," a way to retreat without humiliating yourself. Countless negotiations have broken down because one party took an extreme position, but then did not know how to back down without losing face.

A conservative first offer also creates the bargaining room needed for the mutual concession ritual (you give a little; they give a little; you give a little, and so on). You may regard this ritual as silly, but many people insist upon it. If you do not perform it, they may feel that you are not negotiating in good faith. They may then become rigid or angry. In fact, they may even break off the negotiations despite your making an offer within their limits.

Even if you reach an agreement, they may feel defeated and want revenge. "OK, you got us this time, but we'll get even." They may then take a hard line on implementing the contract, paying their bills, or some other issue. It is far better for them to feel that they have defeated you, that they have driven you right to the wall. Lay the foundation for their victory with an initial offer that creates lots of bargaining room.

Concessions

Giving, receiving, and trading concessions are the central activities of the Middle Game, that is discussed in chapter 4. Now we will just deal with planning for the concessions you will have to make then. Understanding the principles and planning in advance will make that Middle Game go much more smoothly.

The most important principle is called the Iron Law of Concessions: *Don't give anything away.* In negotiations gifts are rarely appreciated, nor are most of them reciprocated. They often make people think, "If they can give it away so easily, it must not be worth much. We should have asked for more." They may then try for the concessions you "owe" them. They may also become suspicious: What is your little game?

Therefore, whenever possible, don't **give** concessions, **trade** them. Link your concessions to reciprocal compromises from the other side. I'll move here, if you will move there. Or, I will come down, if you will come up. Make sure they know that your movements are conditional, that you will withdraw concessions if they do not reciprocate.

Although you will probably not start trading until you enter the Middle Game, you should plan your trades well in advance. A good trade benefits both sides by essentially creating value. One side gives up something that is less valuable to them than it is to the other side and gets back something that is more valuable to them than it is to the other side.

You cannot make that kind of trade without planning well in advance. You must clearly set your own priorities and then learn theirs. Each difference in priorities creates a trading opportunity. You can trade a concession that is more important to them for one that is more important to you.

Let's refer back to the union-management negotiation that we discussed earlier. As management's representative you have decided that increasing productivity is extremely important to you, but not to them. Conversely, because of pressures from its members, maternity/paternity leave seems quite important to the union, but not to you. You might then decide to trade concessions on maternity/paternity leave for concessions on the work rules that affect productivity.

Of course, you cannot evaluate these trades without some way to compare specific concessions on different issues. In this example, what is the relative value of concessions on leave versus productivity? Leave may be less important to you than productivity, but there are limits. You could accept a one month unpaid leave for a specific change in the work rules, but not a three month paid leave for the same change.

To help you to evaluate trades you should prepare transfer equations. They essentially allow you to compare concessions on different issues. A concession of size X on issue A is approximately worth one of size Y on issue B. The equations can be objective or subjective. Objective ones simply use a standard such as dollars to compare concessions. For example, a labor negotiator would know that one additional holiday costs as much as a wage increase of X cents per hour.

Subjective transfer equations deal with the relative value of different concessions. For example, if you were very squeezed for cash, but needed to buy something, you might decide that every dollar reduction in the down payment is worth a three dollar increase in the total price.

Please note that both types allow comparability by expressing the costs and values of concessions in terms of a common standard—dollars. Sometimes, comparisons must be much more subjective and unmeasurable. For example, you want Barbara on the project and a completion deadline of August 15. Since Barbara is busy on another project, you would have to accept either a later deadline or a different person. The questions are: How much later? Who else can you get? How will having this other person alter the project's completion date?

The important point is to decide on your priorities so you can prepare equations to help you to evaluate trades before you have to make them. Then, in the higher pressure atmosphere of the negotiations you can act quickly and rationally.

One other subject related to concessions must be considered: the order in which you make them. Every concession sends a signal to the other side, and the first concession often sends the clearest signal. You should therefore make sure that your first and subsequent concessions send signals that fit your intentions. For example, if your highest priority is the down payment, your first concession definitely should not be on that issue.

That principle seems obvious, yet it is frequently violated. Many people simply do not think about the order in which they make concessions. They may move first on their most important issues, thereby confusing the other side.

Stage Setting

Support your strategy by setting the proper stage for it. Stage setting includes your image, the room, furniture, lights, drinks, calculators, paper, telephones, agenda, the size of your team, and many other factors that affect the negotiating atmosphere. Stage setting techniques will be discussed in chapter 3, "The Beginning Game," and chapter 6, "Positioning Yourself." We will now discuss the general principles.

Your image

The most important part of the stage is you—the way you shake hands, talk, listen, gesture, and all the other things that make up your image. Politicians, movie stars, and other people in the public eye know how important their images are. In fact, many of them pay huge fees to consultants to create or change their image. Perhaps the most successful campaign was the one that changed "Tricky Dick" into "The New Nixon." As Watergate showed, the substance had not changed, but his improved image allowed him to win two presidential elections.

You cannot and probably should not try for such a huge change, but you should certainly analyze your natural image, decide whether it fits the situation and, if necessary, change it. A Brooks Brothers' suit and financially sophisticated language would help you with a New York banker, but harm you with a midwestern farmer.

The idea of changing their image makes many people quite uncomfortable. They think that others will see right through their acts and regard them as phonies. However, you may be less transparent than you think you are, and the other people are probably not skilled behavioral analysts. So stop worrying about looking phony, and try to create the image required by your strategy.

Having said that, we must issue a warning: You cannot act completely unnaturally. People will not believe that Attila the Hun has become Mary Poppins, or vice versa. One reason Richard Gephardt was crushed in the 1988 presidential primaries was his flip-flops on many issues. The image you create must therefore be credible and consistent with the information the other side has about you. A little work and some objectivity will usually allow you to project a credible image that supports your strategy.

The stage itself

Make sure that the stage (i.e., the background) also fits your strategy. For example, a large team, a conference table, and a typed agenda can support a dominant or formal strategy, but prevent you from creating a relaxed, problem-solving atmosphere.

Stage setting always occurs, whether you like it or not. You always have to sit down, talk to each other, take notes, make calculations, and so forth, and both sides will be affected by the environment. The only questions are: Do you plan the stage setting or just let it happen? Does that setting help or hinder your plans?

Just letting it happen is a prescription for disaster. The vibes will often conflict with your strategy. It is far better to create a stage that gives off the vibes that fit your strategy. So ask yourself some questions such as: Should we meet at our place? My office? The big conference room? Their office? A restaurant? Which one? Maybe at the golf club?

DISCUSS YOUR PLANS WITH SOMEONE ELSE

Although our model contains only four preparation steps, a fifth step can be extremely helpful: Discuss your plans with someone else. Your plans may look great to you, but you are not completely objective.

Another pair of eyes may see problems or approaches that did not occur to you. The ideal reviewers are people who have negotiated with the other side. They can predict the other side's reactions and suggest better strategies. Your boss should usually be consulted, particularly for important negotiations. A higher level position can provide new information and perspectives.

Occasionally, you should go further and role-play the negotiation, particularly if the issues are especially complex or important. Professional negotiators often do so. They may even videotape the negotiations or role-play them several times, using different strategies. Role-playing and analysis are time consuming, but they are the ideal way to evaluate your plans. They will provide insights that you could not gain in any other way. In addition, practicing will increase your confidence and ability to execute your plans.

SUMMARY

Good preparation, both economical and psychological, is essential, but many people do not prepare thoroughly. They rush into the negotiations only to find that they have really rushed into trouble.

There are four distinct preparation steps: (1) define the issues; (2) set your objectives; (3) analyze the situation from the other party's perspective, and (4) plan your strategy. The Preparation Questionnaire in Appendix 1 will help you with all four steps.

First list all the issues. Do not be at all selective; just try for a complete list. Group them on one or more bases, such as by priority or amount of conflict. Then relate the issues to the overall relationship. If, for example, the issues are relatively unimportant, and you do not have much conflict on them, but the relationship is important, you obviously should not bargain hard.

After defining the issues, set an objective for each one. What are you trying to accomplish? For important issues set an absolutely firm MSP (minimum or maximum settlement point). The MSP is not your goal or your target; it is your bottom line, your walk-away point, the worst deal that you can live with. You will try for more, but you must get at least that much or you will not accept the deal.

Your MSP should be based on your alternatives. If you do not make this deal, what will you do? And how attractive are the other alternatives?

Failing to set a firm MSP is often the most serious preparation mistake you can make, and it a very common mistake. People just try to get the best deal they can, an approach which can lead to the two classic mistakes: conceding too much and not conceding enough. That is, you may go so far that you get a bad deal, or, because the other side upsets you, not go far enough, thereby walking away from a good deal.

Once you understand the issues and have set your objectives, shift your focus to the other side of the table. How do they see the situation? How do they define the issues? What are their objectives and alternatives? How strong do they feel? What kind of strategy are they likely to adopt?

Hardly anyone spends enough time on this step. We naturally concentrate on our own situation and concerns, even though the really important information is in the other side's head. Shifting your focus to the other side's situation and perceptions is the central theme of this book, and it comes up for virtually every negotiating step.

Only after you have thoroughly performed the preceding three tasks should you start planning your own strategy. As you do so, you will see holes and inconsistencies in your analysis. You then should return to the earlier tasks and do them correctly.

Your most important strategic decision is your general approach because it influences everything else. You might also select one or more alternative approaches (contingency plans) for use if the first one does not work, or you learn that your original strategy was based on an incorrect analysis.

You should also list the questions you intend to ask and the way you intend to ask them; decide upon your initial position and the way that you intend to communicate it; the general pattern of concessions, and the image you intend to create.

These four preparation steps can be time consuming, even boring, but they are usually more than justified. In fact, we suggest taking a fifth step: discussing your plans with someone else. They might be able to see inconsistencies or problems that you missed, and just explaining your plans to them will clarify them in your mind and help you to execute them well.

3

The Beginning Game

After preparing carefully, you are ready to negotiate. That is phase two of our model—the discussions, the time that both parties try to reach an agreement. These discussions can be divided into three parts: the Beginning, Middle, and End games.

The Beginning Game sets the stage and establishes the gap, the difference between both parties' positions. During the Middle Game both parties try to close that gap by moving toward each other. In the End Game they must make those final, painful concessions and close the deal.

Since the Beginning Game lays the foundation and affects every later stage, it is extremely important. Its demands are so different from those of later steps, that the Beginning Game is often separated from later sessions. People may meet in restaurants or at social gatherings to get to know each other. Ideas are informally explored without anyone committing to them. General questions are asked to feel each other out.

In more formal negotiations, such as those between governments, after exploratory talks both sides may present proposals or position papers that describe their demands and arguments. Only after thoroughly discussing both sides' positions—which may take weeks or even months—do they get down to serious, give-and-take bargaining. In fact, if the early discussions do not go well, they may never even start moving toward a deal.

Because the Beginning Game is so important and so different from later steps, our first principles are: (1) Take the time to prepare and execute the Beginning Game; (2) use a different approach for it than for later negotiating steps; (3) separate the Beginning Game from the later games if you think it would be helpful.

During the Beginning Game you have three major tasks:

I. Create the right atmosphere

II. Communicate your position

III. Learn their position

These tasks are normally interactive; each one affects the others. For example, your position and the way you communicate it will usually affect both the atmosphere and how much you learn about their position. If you take a hard line and make an attacking offer, the atmosphere will probably become adversarial or even hostile, and the other party may not communicate its position openly.

Your approach should obviously depend upon whether you are pure bargaining, problem solving, or some mixture of both. For example, a friendly atmosphere could weaken your bargaining position. You should therefore make sure that the atmosphere, position, and communication style fit your objectives and strategy.

Until you have accomplished the Beginning Game's tasks, you should probably not try to start the Middle Game (the time when you move toward a deal by creating, maintaining, and controlling momentum). Do not start moving until you have the right atmosphere, and both parties understand each other.

CREATE THE RIGHT ATMOSPHERE

The atmosphere created during the Beginning Game will usually set the tone for the entire negotiation. For example, starting with a friendly atmosphere may interfere with a power-oriented strategy, while a brusque, unfriendly opening can inhibit or even destroy a problem-solving strategy.

Minimize Your Own Comfort

Most people try to make themselves comfortable, rather than take actions that create the appropriate atmosphere. For example, dominant people often try to take control, even when it is inappropriate. Warm, friendly people strive—often to an extreme degree—to create a warm atmosphere, even when it makes other people think that they are weaklings or time wasters. Good negotiators are more controlled; they are essentially actors and can be friendly, formal or even hostile, depending on the situation.

Everything Affects the Atmosphere

You must work on the atmosphere, not just during the first few minutes of socializing, but throughout the entire negotiation. The atmosphere reflects your overall approach, demands and concessions, the way that you state your position, ask questions, listen to the other person, answer questions, and so on.

You may feel that you have created a friendly atmosphere by smiling, offering coffee, and making pleasant small talk, but that atmosphere will quickly evaporate if your opening offer is too demanding, or if you interrogate the other side, or interrupt them and refuse to listen to their position.

In addition, your past relationship and reputation will usually affect the atmosphere. You must therefore try for an atmosphere that fits your past; otherwise you will not be credible. If you have always been friendly and welcoming, acting cold and distant would probably confuse people or appear contrived. Therefore, if your strategy for this negotiation requires a colder atmosphere, you might explain, directly or indirectly, why you are acting this way. You might, for example, tell a mutual friend that you feel that the other party has taken advantage of your friendship (then hope that they communicate that message).

Trust Is Very Fragile

Trust is usually hard to build during negotiations. Conflicting interests and the essentially adversarial nature of negotiations cause most people to be rather suspicious. This underlying suspicion will often cause people to interpret actions negatively. For example, many people have felt that they were conciliatory and friendly, only to learn that they were seen as aggressive hard-liners.

Trust is also easy to destroy. A careless word can overcome weeks of painstaking work. So remember that suspicions are natural and work to reduce them. Watch your words and your actions, and remember that almost anything you do can be interpreted in the most negative way.

For example, many people make large concessions or are extremely open to create a trusting atmosphere, but the other side doubts their sincerity and wonders, "What is their little game?" In fact, during negotiations, *frequent reactions to large concessions are suspicion and greed.* People often doubt the value of those concessions or decide to demand even greater ones.

Trust is so important and so fragile that many of our recommendations throughout this book focus on it. These recommendations are often surprising, even cynical. You may not like them, but they are based on wide research. Perhaps people should be more trusting, but, alas, some of them are naturally suspicious. Perhaps they should respond more positively to large concessions (and some people do respond that way), but many people will regard those concessions as signs of weakness. You must therefore base your actions, not on how you wish people would react, but on how *this* person will react.

Types of Atmospheres

Atmosphere can be described in a variety of ways—distant, businesslike, aggressive, tea party, and so on. We will simplify our analysis by dealing with only five main types: friendly, formal, indifferent, adversarial, and hostile. These types form a crude continuum from friendly to hostile, but there are many other dimensions.

Since each type has its advantages and risks, you should carefully select the main type and adjust it to fit the situation. Pay particular attention to the other side. If they are not responding as you wish, or if they clearly want a different kind of atmosphere, you should probably change your approach.

The friendly atmosphere

Most people prefer at least a moderately friendly atmosphere. We feel more comfortable with it and believe that we can get more done.

How can you create it?

It is easy to create a superficially friendly atmosphere, but it often takes a great deal of effort to overcome the natural suspiciousness, competitiveness, and power emphasis of many negotiations. So work a little harder, but go a little slower than you normally would.

The first step is obviously to avoid getting down to business too quickly. Take a few minutes for social amenities, such as coffee or small talk. Adjust the topics to fit your audience, and watch for signs of boredom and impatience. If they seem bored or impatient, drop the subject.

Your manner must be friendly throughout the entire negotiating process, not just during the first few minutes. Communicate with your words, voice, and body language that you value your relationship and want an agreement that is fair for both of you.

Take reasonable positions and state them in ways that show your flexibility. No amount of smiles, friendly words, or social amenities will overcome the negative effects of extreme demands or hard line tactics.

Finally, show respect for the other side and their positions. Answer their questions openly and frankly. Listen carefully; concede the point when they are clearly correct. Let them win a few points. Nearly everyone feels friendlier to those who treat them respectfully.

When should you create it?

A friendly atmosphere is useful in many negotiations.

1. *When you are trying to solve joint problems.* It helps to build that essential trust. It also relaxes many people, causing them to open up. For example, if your equipment is not working properly in a customer's factory, you certainly want a friendly, joint problem-solving atmosphere. You need their input to solve the problem, and you definitely do not want them to make extreme demands, such as, "Get that garbage out of here." So defuse the tension by being as friendly as possible.

2. *When you are in a weak bargaining position.* The weaker you are, the less emphasis you want on power. Friendliness may make them less willing to use their power against you. If, for example, this vendor is absolutely essential to your company, become friends with the sales rep. Buy a few drinks or a lunch; go out of your way to be friendly and reasonable. Then, when the inevitable problems occur, when the sales rep has to decide who gets the fastest and best service, you have a friend where it counts.

3. *When you are negotiating with a friendly person.* Friendly people prefer a friendly atmosphere, yet an astonishing number of people ignore that obvious principle. They are so wrapped up in their own concerns that they ignore or reject attempts to create a friendly atmosphere. They may say, "No thanks," to offers for coffee, or dismiss questions about personal issues, or insist that they get right down to business. The net effect can be to turn a potential friend into an adversary.

4. *When you want to build or preserve a long-term relationship.* The importance of the relationship should usually be the primary determinant of the atmosphere. The more important that relationship is, the more you should move toward a friendly atmosphere (unless this person dislikes such an atmosphere).

Since I work all over the world, I am constantly "putting my foot in my mouth" on relationship issues. In New York, friendliness and small talk are regarded negatively. In fact, anyone who answers the standard question, "How are you?", is clearly from out of town.

Conversely, in Japan, Quebec, and many parts of Europe, getting down to business too quickly is ill-mannered. I vividly recall my Montreal associate, Raymond Dubois, telling me that I had irritated a prospect by selling during lunch. In Montreal (and many other parts of the world) well-mannered people do not discuss business while eating. (What do I know? I grew up near New York!)

You must therefore decide how important this relationship is to you, and, if necessary, take the actions that will build or preserve it. In New York you might have to be briefer and more businesslike than you wish, while in other places you may have to slow down and make small talk.

Incidentally, the small talk you make should depend upon the people you are meeting. Football interests most American men, but bores some of them and nearly all women and non-Americans. Politically contentious issues interest some people, but infuriate others. So plan in advance the subjects you will discuss, and make sure that your plans fit these people. If you do not know what to talk about, start with neutral subjects, the weather, traffic, cost of living, and then follow their lead.

What are the risks?

There are serious risks in being friendly, especially if you are too friendly.

1. *Creating distrust.* Friendliness can increase the natural suspicions. This danger is particularly great when dealing with very dominant, competitive people. Since they "play games," they naturally suspect that other people play the same games. Therefore, open, friendly actions actually increase their natural (and perhaps paranoid) suspicions.

2. *Appearing weak.* Some people, particularly dominant ones, regard friendliness as a sign of weakness. They may feel your position is weak or that you lack personal toughness.

Wealthy, self-made men are especially likely to feel this way. They tend to put people into two categories, good guys and others. The good guys are tough enough to stand up to them, and the rest are wimps, too weak to bother with. They test everyone—subordinates, vendors, colleagues, even customers and prospects—by acting rudely; they just want to see how you react.

The lesson to you, especially if you are relatively young, is to watch out for tests. If you feel that they are testing you, stand up to them. Do not grovel because people who test your toughness do not respect wimps.

3. *Alienating very dominant or very detached people.* These people are so uncomfortable with friendliness and other tender emotions that a friendly approach can actually have a boomerang effect. Instead of relaxing and opening up, they may regard you as weak or become more aggressive or distant.

The formal atmosphere

Formal negotiations are emotionally neutral, neither friendly nor unfriendly. The negotiators relate to each other, not as friends or enemies, but as people with clearly specified roles. Agendas are often explicit and may be written. Detailed, written proposals are exchanged. People may address each other formally, perhaps even using titles, such as "Mr. Secretary" or "Madame Chairperson."

How can you create it?

Creating this sort of atmosphere can be quite simple. Just stick to the business at hand, minimize emotional actions, establish formal procedures, and emphasize factual, logical, and detailed communications, including written proposals.

Of course, it may not be that simple. The other party or even your own team may object to your bureaucratic manner or demand a more relaxed approach. You may be forced to compromise, to accept an atmosphere that is essentially formal, but is also a little looser.

When should you create it?

This business-like atmosphere fits most negotiations, but it is particularly appropriate in the following situations.

1. *When you are unsure of what to do.* Because it is emotionally neutral, formality is a low risk approach that offers considerable flexibility. You are not committing yourself. You can begin formally, and stay that way or shift toward friendliness, aggressiveness, or almost any other attitude. Because friendly or adversarial atmospheres are not neutral, switching can confuse or irritate the other side.

2. *When dealing with detached people.* They respond best to this kind of atmosphere. They like its neatness, clarity, and control. They also dislike all emotions.

3. *When the negotiations are between teams.* Interteam negotiations generally require some formality. Without clear procedures, the negotiations can easily get out of control. Everyone will talk at the same time; interruptions will occur repeatedly; issues will become confused, and so on. A formal atmosphere, with clearly designated spokespeople and a written agenda can keep the negotiations "on track."

4. *When the issues are complex.* Some formal elements improve communications. For example, formal agendas help to ensure that all subjects are covered. Written proposals clarify both sides' positions. The more complex the issues are, the more valuable these formal elements become.

Unfortunately, complexity often causes people to become more informal. They essentially say: "These subjects are too complex for formal negotiations. We have to 'let our hair down' and explore all the alternatives."

That approach is fine if the other side reciprocates, but it can be suicidal. If their natural caution is intensified by your relaxed manner, or if the informality creates confusion, the negotiations can break down.

It also increases the danger of misunderstandings. Ronald Reagan has even dismissed translators when meeting heads of foreign states. Since neither of them was fluent in the other's language, serious misunderstandings have occurred.

5. *When the parties are hostile to each other.* When a friendly atmosphere is clearly impossible and a hostile one could cause a deadlock, formality may be best. It saves face while allowing both sides to communicate. For example, diplomatic negotiations between hostile countries are nearly always quite formal.

The Arabs and the Jews hate each other. The Vietnamese and the Chinese feel the same way. But, when they meet at the UN and other places, the extremely formal rules of diplomacy prevent them from being too rude to each other, thereby allowing them to negotiate.

To a lesser extent, these rules apply to business. Joe and Suzanne may despise each other, but they are required to act politely. Once again, I must tell a personal story. Mr. X and I loathed each other. I thought he was an incompetent fraud, and his opinion of me was even more negative, but neither of us could afford a confrontation.

Our jobs forced us to meet from time to time, and insensitive people might have thought that we were the best of friends. "Hello, Al, how are you doing?" "Fine, how's the family and your golf?" More perceptive people would have realized how we felt about each other because our greetings were too hearty and we were too polite to each other, and our negotiations were actually quite formal. We could not afford to be openly hostile, nor could we pretend indifference. We needed each other—despite our personal feelings. We therefore used written proposals, formal agendas, and so forth to minimize the effects of our personal feelings. We never became friends, but we did some mutually profitable business.

What are the risks?

1. *Limited exploration of other alternatives.* Formality can cause people to stay close to their positions, thereby overlooking new and better options. In general, the more formal the negotiations are, the less exploration will occur. Formality naturally causes people to be constrained and somewhat inflexible. This inflexibility is less than you would see with an indifferent, adversarial, or hostile atmosphere, but it can still be a serious problem.

You must therefore make a strategic choice. If you want some freedom to explore other alternatives, but wish to stay fairly close to your original position, a formal atmosphere might be appropriate. If you want to explore a wide range of options, relax the rules and loosen up. If you prefer to restrict the discussion to a few alternatives, a more adversarial atmosphere might be better.

2. *Alienating dominant and friendly people.* Dominant people tend to dislike formality because they like to confront issues personally and directly. They may also regard it as a sign of bureaucratic rigidity. If you seem too formal, they may regard you as a mere bureaucrat.

Friendly people usually feel that a formal atmosphere is cold and impersonal. They want to deal with a warm, understanding human being, not a computer. If you seem cold and bureaucratic, they may become withdrawn.

The indifferent atmosphere

An indifferent atmosphere can greatly increase your power. The other side may make concessions because you do not seem to care about reaching a deal.

Financial officers in major corporations are often quite skilled at appearing indifferent. When bankers and other vendors of financial services call on them, they say, directly and indirectly: "You are the fourth banker I have seen this week. I have heard it all—every sales story, every claim that you are original, creative, and customer-oriented. Go ahead, try to sell me, but I'm really not interested.... Oh, by the way, do you mind if I sign some letters while you are talking?"

How can you create it?

You can be formal or informal, friendly, cold, or even hostile. The specifics hardly matter as long as your manner and positions communicate indifference about the deal.

You can, for example, communicate that you have other attractive alternatives. Or you can make an ungenerous first offer, or refuse to make concessions because you don't want the deal anyway. Or you can act as if the entire subject does not interest you. The critical point is that the other side must *believe* that you really are indifferent.

When should you create it?

It is appropriate only when you are primarily pure bargaining *and* have some of these other conditions. It conflicts with virtually all problem-solving actions, and you should act indifferent only when the situation favors that approach. For example, if you do not have any alternatives, and you desperately need this deal, an indifferent approach is extremely risky.

1. *When you really are indifferent.* This atmosphere can easily result in deadlock. You usually cannot take that risk unless you really are indifferent. If, for example, someone wants to buy a business that you do not want to sell, you can afford to act indifferently because you really are indifferent. Your indifference puts you into a powerful position.

Shopping for a new car is another excellent illustration. You can just wander around the showroom, looking a bit bored, asking general questions. Since the car dealer's people know that you can easily go someplace else, they have to chase you, offering discounts, rebates, and improved warranties.

2. *When the other side is eager for the deal.* The more they want it, the less chance there is of a deadlock. They may not like chasing you, but, if they really want the deal, they will do so. You can therefore increase your power by appearing indifferent. "I would like to sell it to you, but so many people want to buy it that I do not know what to do."

Again, buying a car (or almost anything else) is a a good example. At least ninety percent of the time the buyer can appear less eager than the seller. We call that imbalance the Buyer's Natural Advantage. Vendors almost always want to sell, and their sales force is paid to make sales, usually without regard to whether those sales are profitable. Several executives have told us: "If we let our sales force do what they like, they would give our products away—and pay for the shipping!"

Buyers can pretend that they are just testing the market, even when they desperately need a vendor. In normal circumstances sellers cannot pretend. Everyone knows that they want the business. For example, a rep usually gets a commission, even if the company loses money on the sale.

At times the sales force's eagerness has grotesque results. For example, because its customary vendor could not meet its commitments, a major aerospace contractor urgently needed a large computer, and none were available within the tight deadlines of their government contract. Without the right kind of computer they would default, losing millions.

In desperation, top executives flew to the headquarters of the only possible supplier. They literally begged for help, offered an enormous amount of future business, and clearly stated that the price was almost irrelevant. The computer company's salespeople checked everywhere and finally found a computer that could be made available by juggling production schedules and creating many other problems for their company. Then, after promising prompt delivery, they sat down to negotiate the price and sold it for a discount! I find the story as unbelievable as you do, but it actually happened.

3. *When your interests clearly conflict.* Indifference and other power-oriented approaches should be restricted to pure bargaining because they inhibit working together on joint problems. Relationships between staff and line departments often show how indifference inhibits working cooperatively.

Presumably, both sides should be working together toward common goals, but they often see each other as adversaries who are indifferent to their own needs. The line may be infuriated by "those bureaucrats in head office" who do not understand the critical importance of production schedules, and so forth. Staff is equally frustrated by the line's arrogant attitude toward their need for information, the importance of their role, and so on. Therefore, instead of working together, they act as adversaries, to everyone's cost.

4. *When you are bluffing.* Occasionally it pays to bluff. If you are very weak, you might try to hide it by being indifferent or adversarial. Do not bluff unless you are a very good actor. The risks are just too high.

What are the risks?

Indifference, especially extreme indifference, can easily discourage or turn off the other side, causing the negotiations to break down or forcing you to change the atmosphere abruptly (which can damage your credibility). The risks increase dramatically if any of the following conditions occur.

1. *Overestimating their eagerness or your strength.* If you do so, the negotiations can easily deadlock. This sort of error is quite common; optimism is often stronger than judgment.

2. *Alienating a dominant or dependent person.* Dominant people intensely dislike anything that implies that they are weak. In fact, rather than chase an apparently indifferent person, some of them would walk away, even if they objectively need the deal.

Dependent people can easily feel rejected. This risk can be reduced (but not eliminated) by clearly communicating that you are indifferent to this specific deal, not to them as people.

3. *Missing joint problem-solving opportunities.* An indifferent atmosphere can inhibit trust development and information sharing. Building trust is always a problem, and an indifferent atmosphere intensifies that problem.

The adversarial atmosphere

Now we are moving into a risky, high tension area. An adversarial atmosphere can frighten the other side or make them lower their expectations, especially if they really need the deal, but it can also anger them or create other problems.

An adversarial atmosphere does not necessarily mean that people are rude or aggressive. For example, courtrooms are completely adversarial, but their rituals are extremely formal and polite (despite what you see on television). The critical point is that everyone understands that their interests conflict, and each side protects its own interests. There may not even be the pretense that people are trying to work out a mutually beneficial deal.

How can you create it?

It is not easy to create an *effective* adversarial atmosphere. You must communicate that you are adversaries, while allowing the other side to save face. Many people do not understand that distinction, especially ones who have previously been too soft. They equate toughness with nastiness and act as obnoxious boors.

Such an overreaction might be necessary for them personally; they may have to try the extreme before stepping back to a more balanced approach. That is the way most of us learn. But, if possible, evade that intermediate step. Clearly communicate that your interests conflict and that you intend to strive for the best deal, but avoid excessive rudeness, nitpicking demands, interruptions, and so on. Let them know that you have the power and are willing, if necessary, to use it, but do not make them eat too much crow. They may just get stubborn. Even if circumstances force them to concede, they may resent you and thirst for revenge.

When should you create it?

An adversarial approach has the same power emphasis as an indifferent one, and most of the same conditions apply. A few other situations also favor this atmosphere.

1. *When it is a normal part of the game.* Some cultures expect or even demand an adversarial atmosphere. For example, most negotiations involving attorneys require some fencing; they have to prove to their clients that they are earning their fees.

In parts of the New York Garment District, people expect personal insults, interruptions, and so forth, and no one takes them personally. In fact, the person who acts too politely is almost automatically distrusted. I can remember the good old days, before air conditioning, when garment dealers' negotiations sometimes occurred outside the offices. People would literally yell at each other, and nobody cared who heard.

"Harry, that price is outrageous. Where do you get the nerve to ask for $27 a dozen?"

"Jim, I can't believe that you object to such a wonderful price. My own brother couldn't get such a price. But, because I like you, I'll let you have it for $26.50."

"$26.50? You've got to be kidding. You're robbing me. I'll never do business with you again; you're a crook. You're taking the bread from my children's mouths."

"Me? I'm the best friend you ever had. I'm losing money on this deal, but I'm trying to help you."

"All right, Harry, I'll let you rob me this time, but I'll never buy from you again."

"See you next Tuesday, and you buy the coffee."

"Okay. I'll get some Danish too."

That sort of conversation would make most people feel extremely uncomfortable, but in the garment district it was quite normal.

2. *When dealing with a very dominant person or a bully.* As we noted earlier, these people tend to put others into two classes: good guys and others (lightweights). They often make that choice on how well the other stands up to them. They feel contempt for anyone they can dominate.

If you feel that the other side is testing you, get tough. Do not be rude or confront them, but make sure they realize that you have power and are not afraid to use it.

3. *When you are in a powerful position.* Since this atmosphere creates risks, you should not use it unless you do not need the deal.

What are the risks?

An adversarial atmosphere has virtually all of the risks of an indifferent one, plus some additional ones.

1. *Creating emotional resistance to compromising with you.* The other side may become rigid and perhaps even irrational. Saving face can easily become more important than reaching a deal.

2. *Creating later implementation problems.* If they feel defeated, the other side may not implement your agreement properly.

3. *Reducing the prospects for future agreements.* If they feel defeated, they may decide to take a harder line in future negotiations. They may even refuse to negotiate with you again.

The hostile atmosphere

A hostile atmosphere fits only a few kinds of situations, and nearly everybody is extremely reluctant to create it, even when it is appropriate.

How can you create it?

It is very easy—just be hostile. The degree of appropriate hostility depends, of course, on the situation. Sometimes the hostility should be blatantly obvious; usually it should be somewhat subtler.

Some insurance adjusters are openly hostile: "We know you are trying to cheat us, and we are not going to let you get away with it. In fact, we are ready to spend as much as it takes to keep you and other chiselers like you from ripping us off. So let's go to court." By itself, such an approach could easily be self-defeating, but, when supported by the insurance company's power, it can be extremely effective.

When should you create it?

This atmosphere fits only a few situations, but for these situations, it can be quite valuable.

1. *When you must dramatically change the other party's perceptions.* Sometimes their perceptions prevent the negotiations from progressing. Hostility may wake them up. For example, a banker was trying to work out a loan that was months overdue, and the borrower kept insisting on being treated as a valued customer. Finally, the banker got fed up and said, "You aren't a valued customer. You're a deadbeat, and I'm here to get our money!"

2. *When the other side has taken an outrageous position.* The more outrageous their position is, the more outraged you should be. Make sure they understand your anger. You do not want them to feel that you regard their outrageous position as a legitimate starting point for the negotiations.

For example, if your asking price for your house is $300,000, and they offer $180,000, do not say: "That's a little low." Doing so would just undermine the credibility of your asking price. Get mad, scream, throw them out of your house, or do anything else that communicates that their offer is insulting.

A hostile reaction is particularly necessary if the person making it is a games player. These people often take an outrageous position to test you. If you react mildly, they may conclude that you are weak and take a harder line.

What are the risks?

The risks of a hostile atmosphere are the same as those of an adversarial atmosphere, but they are much more extreme. A hostile atmosphere can create extreme resistance to compromising or even cause people to refuse to negotiate with you. The emphasis shifts from working out a mutually satisfactory deal to beating you or repaying you for your insults.

You should therefore create it *only* when it is absolutely necessary, and *only* as a last resort.

Atmosphere and the Type of Negotiation

In chapter 2 we noted that pure bargaining and joint problem solving are near the ends of a continuum, with many other approaches in between them. The atmosphere you create should be consistent with your position on that continuum. A friendly atmosphere helps when joint problem solving; adversarial, indifferent and hostile atmospheres support pure bargaining. A formal atmosphere is neutral. The following diagram illustrates that relationship. Please note that (1) the distance between *friendly* and *formal* is much greater than that between *formal* and *indifferent*, and (2) *indifferent, adversarial*, and *hostile* are quite close to each other.

Friendly	Formal	Indifferent	Adversarial	Hostile

JPS				PB
Building Trust				Building Power

COMMUNICATE YOUR POSITION

We will consider two communications dimensions: *content* and *process*. Content is the information, while process refers to the way you communicate it. If content and process seem too academic, think of them as facts and psychology. You should distinguish between what you want to communicate and the way that you communicate it.

Process can be broken down into three subdimensions: *clarity, confidence, and flexibility*. Can they understand you? Do you seem to be sure of what you say? And how willing are you to negotiate? Clarity and confidence are essential, and in most situations increasing them is desirable. Flexibility is more complex. If you seem too rigid, the negotiations may never get started. If you seem too flexible, the other side may perceive you as weak and become greedier and more demanding. You must therefore communicate the *right* degree of flexibility, and it varies according to the issue and your strategy.

Your emphasis upon bargaining versus problem solving affects both content and process. Because bargaining is a power-oriented process, you might withhold or distort some information, while expressing your positions firmly. For instance, you might evade or ignore a question about why you want to sell your business because a frank answer would weaken your position; you might, for instance, insist: "This business is a gold mine. I would not even consider selling it if my wife's business was not growing so rapidly that she needs my help."

When problem solving, you might be more open and speak more tentatively to suggest a readiness to explore other possibilities. In the earlier example of possibly selling your business, you might say, "You're right; the competition is tough, and it is getting tougher. We do have the right products, but we just do not have enough capital to compete with such powerful competition. That's why we are looking for a well capitalized partner. How can we work together?"

Of course, you may bargain on some issues, problem solve on others. Your communications should therefore vary from issue to issue, but the overall pattern should depend upon your general strategy.

Although this chapter focuses on the Beginning Game, most of these principles apply during the entire negotiation, and these principles are so general that they should be modified to fit your situation.

Help Them Understand Your Position

Understanding is the primary goal of communication. Unless the other side understands your position, you probably cannot work out a deal. Of course, you may sometimes want to conceal some parts of your position, but the other side must understand the information that you do decide to communicate.

Nonetheless, some people deliberately create confusion, while others inadvertently do so. Confusion is particularly destructive during negotiations. First, it increases the underlying suspicion; the other side will wonder: "Why are they trying to confuse me?" Second, confusion causes projection.

Projection is the natural tendency to believe what one wants or fears. The more ambiguous a situation is, the more likely people are to project. For example, the Rorschach is a projection test: people look at meaningless inkblots and say what they see. Their responses are caused by their hopes, fears, and other emotions.

If your position is ambiguous, they may misinterpret it. They may expect concessions that you cannot possibly make or feel that you are trying to cheat them, or they may just blame their confusion on you and decide to do business with "people who speak my language." A few simple principles can greatly reduce these dangers.

Keep it simple

Complicated positions, convoluted sentences, strange words, and lengthy speeches often confuse and irritate people.

Years ago, when I was a business school professor, a group of Ph.D's and MBA's were planning a major presentation to a billionaire, a legend. It was the group's big chance, and the presentation had everything we wanted: Discounted cash flow charts, four-color transparencies, lots of numbers and other details, even payback projections—exactly what you would need to get an A from a business school professor.

While we were congratulating ourselves on our wonderful presentation, someone who knew the billionaire said: "If you talk to him this way, he will turn you down." We looked at him in amazement. "What way?"

He responded: "That man is a peasant. He likes to put his finger to his nose and say: 'I have a nose for a deal.' If he cannot write the deal on the back of an envelope, he will not do business. Because your proposal is so complicated, he will throw you out."

We laughed. This poor fool obviously did not have the benefit of our superior training.

But, sure enough, the next day the presenters were interrupted in midsentence. "Thank you very much for your painstaking research. My associates will study your proposals and get back to you." In other words, please leave and let me talk to someone I can understand.

Don't make our mistake. Follow the old KISS formula, "*Keep It Simple, Stupid!*"

Make clear offers

Your offers are the most important part of your position. Make sure that they understand *exactly* what you are offering. Vague offers can destroy your credibility, produce a deadlock, or even cause a lawsuit. For example, *after* the closing, disagreements often occur over what is included in the sale of a house. The sellers believe that they can remove a chandelier or gas grill, while the buyers are just as convinced that these items are included in the sale.

Clear offers reduce this problem. Just making sure that the realtor's listing clearly states that the chandelier and gas grill are not included in the house's price will prevent most problems, while stating that fact in the final contract will usually end all discussions.

Write down your offers

In complex negotiations most offers should be made or confirmed in writing. Despite what you think you said, they may hear something entirely different. In addition, you may forget what you have offered, especially if the negotiations take several weeks. The inevitable misunderstandings can create serious problems, and your attempts to correct them may be seen as reneging on your earlier offer.

In some situations written offers can also appear more credible. You may, for example, feel embarrassed about an offer. Perhaps you regard it as unreasonable, even outrageous. Or your associates may want to be much more generous, making you think that you are too demanding. Since your feelings are likely to show, a written offer may be more credible than a spoken one.

A variant on this approach is to use one visual aid—one blackboard, one flip chart, or one piece of paper. Engineers and trainers use this technique, and it can really reduce confusion. Both parties work at the blackboard or flip chart, crossing out items, drawing lines linking trades, and otherwise making sure that both parties have the same perception of the situation. This technique reduces the endemic confusion caused by both parties keeping separate notes.

You have your notes; I have mine. Each set of notes is based partially on hopes and fears. When the inevitable conflicts occur, we are both likely to insist that our notes are correct, or even that the other party has acted in bad faith. Using one visual aid allows us both to see the conflicts before they occur, and to resolve them while believing that we are all acting in good faith.

Subtly communicate your priorities

Negotiating an agreement about several issues is often a process of cutting and fitting until you reach a deal that matches both parties' priorities. In fact, some people regard it as analogous to fine carpentry; we keep cutting and fitting until the deal is just right. We cannot find that kind of deal unless we both understand each other's priorities.

Stating your priorities too openly or too quickly could give them an advantage; as knowledge is power, they would know more than you do. You should therefore balance your need to communicate your position with your need to protect yourself. Make sure that you do not go much faster than the other side.

Communicate your priorities, but do so subtly. Give them hints before and during the Beginning Game about the general nature of your priorities (*not* your MSPs), and then see whether they state or hint at their own priorities. Both sides' perceptions of each other's priorities should slowly become clearer as the negotiation progresses.

For example, in the Beginning Game you might say, "On this issue, I'm going to be very, very firm." On another issue, you might say, "We would like to have such and such." That pattern suggests that the first issue is more important. Your later signals, especially the pattern of concessions, should clarify your priorities and limits for each issue.

Identify the deal-breakers

A *deal-breaker* is something absolutely essential. Without it, there is no deal, period. For example, a subsidiary may have been told by its parent corporation that it will not guarantee its loans in any way whatsoever. Bankers naturally want such guarantees, and the company's officers must let the bankers know that they cannot possibly get them, and that they have to structure the deal in some other way.

Please note that this principle of identifying the deal-breakers directly contradicts the previous principle of communicating priorities subtly, and implicitly contradicts other principles that make it easy to compromise. It therefore applies only in extreme cases, when something is simply non-negotiable.

Obviously, something should be regarded as a deal-breaker only if it is supremely important. Do not take a substantively insignificant demand and elevate it to deal-breaker status because it is a matter of principle.

However, if something really is a deal-breaker, if you sincerely cannot accept anything else, let the other side know it, and the sooner the better. "The parent company has told us that they will not provide any sort of guarantees. If you absolutely must have such guarantees, we cannot possibly do business."

Taking such a hard line can make you feel uncomfortable, but it is much better than wasting time in negotiations that cannot possibly lead to a deal or being pressured to make an unacceptable concession. If bank A will not even consider a loan without guarantees, talk to banks B, C, and D. If no bank will consider it, change your plans or go back to your parent company, but do not waste your time on pointless negotiations.

Answer legitimate questions openly and cheerfully

Many of their questions will be legitimate and reasonable. Answer these questions as openly and cheerfully as possible. For example, prospective buyers might ask:

"What did you pay for your house?" Since they can get the information from other sources (such as the recorder of deeds), evasion or waffling gains nothing and reduces your credibility. Just say, without embellishment, "I paid $143,000 when I bought it four years ago."

Evasive answers create distrust and resentment. If they can get the information anyway, give it to them in the most cheerful and open manner. An open, cheerful answer makes them more likely to believe your answer, while increasing your overall credibility.

Use their language

Using their language greatly improves communication and trust. For example, when their satellites met in space, the Americans spoke Russian and the Russians spoke English. Both sides knew that speaking the other's language reduced communications problems and increased trust. The same principles apply to many business negotiations.

For example, let's say that you are buying a business, and the seller will take a mortgage for part of the purchase price. Your key priority may be the monthly payments, while the seller may be more interested in the interest rate. Negotiate the interest rate, not the monthly payment. You can easily convert it into monthly payments, but negotiating the interest rate may make the seller more comfortable and flexible.

"OK, if you insist, I will give you another half percent if you will increase the repayment period from five to six years." That trade could actually reduce your monthly payments, while making the seller happier. The seller receives a higher total amount, while you have smaller monthly payments.

If necessary, ask them what language they would prefer. If you are selling, ask the customer what type of bid they want. Do they want a great deal of details? Should the bid be organized in a certain way? Large buyers, such as the U.S. government, have a standard format. Smaller organizations rarely have formal requirements, but they might still prefer one sort of format or language. If you know how to present your bid, they will understand and perhaps become more receptive. In addition, by reducing confusion, using their language helps both parties to concentrate on the important issues.

Use your weapons judiciously

You will usually have a limited number of "weapons" (facts or arguments that will strengthen your case, put the other side off balance or give you a tactical advantage). Use them judiciously. If, for example, you are making excellent progress with a friendly atmosphere, do not nakedly show your power. However, if you feel that a power-oriented approach might be necessary later, subtly let them know that you do have power and, if you are forced to do so, you would reluctantly use it.

Get all the issues on the table

Both sides can usually negotiate more intelligently if they put all the issues on the table. You both need to see the entire picture. Otherwise, you may reach agreement on one or two issues and then find that you are so far apart on an important issue that you need the trading leverage of the settled issues to close the gap.

This last point relates to a common, but often inappropriate, negotiating strategy. Many people use an "easy first" strategy: They settle the easy issues first and then focus on the important and more difficult issues. Sometimes this strategy works, but it is often disastrous. By settling the easy issues first, the negotiators have essentially reduced the negotiations to a one-issue negotiation on which they are very far apart. At this point negotiations can be almost impossible to settle; neither side is willing to make a large enough move to make a deal possible.

It is usually, but certainly not always, better to keep several issues on the table. In fact, a good general rule is that *the farther apart you are on one important issue, the more issues should be on the table, and/or the farther apart you should be on those issues.* Then you can trade a concession on issue A for one on issue B. You have trading leverage.

Putting everything on the table can also reduce the danger of agenda bargaining or dominance contests. One or both sides say, in effect, "I won't tell you my position until you do something" (such as make a concession or accept my position on a certain issue). This sort of condition often leads to a deadlock.

There are, however, exceptions to this rule. They will be discussed in the section on timing your communications, especially your offers.

Send very clear rejection signals

If the other side makes an unreasonable offer, reject it very clearly and forcefully. Earlier, we said to become outraged by outrageous offers. The same general principles apply to offers that are out of line, but not outrageous. Of course, your reaction should be less extreme, but they must understand that you do not like their offer. Several simple rules will make your rejection signals clearer or more forceful.

Do not say, "That is a little steep."

Do not imply that the offer is close to your range. Tell them it is not worth considering: "I will not even consider it." Then be sure you don't discuss it; it simply does not deserve your attention.

Support your words nonverbally

Support your words with your body language. Do not hesitate before rejecting an offer. Just a few seconds' hesitation can suggest that you are willing to consider it seriously. A quick, firm rejection is much more effective.

If their position is really outrageous, get angry; bang your fist on the table, rip up a written offer; or stand up and start to leave. You may feel inhibited about over-acting, but ignore those inhibitions. Make sure the other side realizes that their offer is an insult.

Do not change the subject after an offer

Changing the subject after an offer can make the other side believe that you are tacitly accepting their offer on this issue. Your first reaction should be a firm rejection; then you can change the subject.

Lay on the guilt

People with a strong need to be liked are particularly vulnerable to the guilt approach. When they make a bad offer, don't get angry; act hurt. You might say, for example, "I am really surprised by your offer. I thought you were serious and that we could do business on a reasonable basis. I am sorry we can't."

Support your words with a hurt expression and tone of voice. Make them feel guilty for giving you such an offer.

Verify their understanding of your position

Since they may misunderstand you, check to see how they perceive your position. Tactfully ask them to summarize your position. Their answer may surprise you. They may have an entirely different belief from what you expected. They may, for example, think that you desperately need a deal, when you are really just "testing the market."

Do Not Give or Demand Information; Trade It

An unbalanced flow of information is undesirable. If they know more about your situation than you know about theirs, they have power over you, and you may distrust them. If you know more than they do, power and trust are reversed. You should therefore strive for a balanced communications pattern. You give them some information; then they give you some. You ask a few questions; then you answer a few.

The way that you handle this issue can dramatically affect the atmosphere. If you are evasive, they will naturally distrust you. Excessive openness can have the same effect. Asking a few questions and saying, "I'm sure that you have some questions," can create a better balance of information, and a more trusting atmosphere.

Trading information helps both substantively and psychologically. Both sides need information to reach a mutually satisfying deal, and the process of trading information builds that essential trust.

Make It Easy to Compromise

Compromise is the essence of negotiations. To reach a mutually satisfactory deal, both sides must move from their initial positions. In fact, one could say that *the central problem in negotiations is creating, controlling, and ending movement toward a mutually satisfactory agreement.* Although the actual movements come later, some actions during the Beginning Game will facilitate later compromises.

State issues in divisible terms

Issues should almost always be expressed in ways that allow compromise. You should violate this rule only when absolutely no compromise is acceptable; at all other times, leave the door open to some intermediate position.

The difference between positions that allow and do not allow compromise is very easy to see. For example, if you say "7" and I say "4," we can compromise on 5, or 6, or some other number. But if you say, "Our policy demands using our contract language," and I say the same thing, compromise will be difficult or impossible.

It is even more difficult if you treat something as an issue of principle. You do not want to compromise on your principles; neither do other people. Therefore, keep principles out of the discussion; express issues in ways that allow both sides to make concessions without violating their principles.

Focus on goals, not the specific means for reaching them

It is usually easier to agree on goals than the specific steps toward reaching them. Then, after agreeing that a deal should satisfy both parties' goals, you can work out a plan for reaching them. This procedure encourages both parties to explore ways to reach both parties' goals, and they may find that the best arrangement is considerably different from either side's original plan.

Proposing a specific way to reach your goal will often result in a counterproposal. Then, instead of exploring a variety of approaches in a problem-solving manner, you bargain or argue about which proposal is best, and both sides stay close to their original positions. We saw this process in the sample negotiation between Jack and George. Instead of focusing on their goals—Jack's concern for quality control, George's desire to develop Joan—they discussed involving Joan in win-lose terms. Both parties' objectives could have been met if they had shifted their focus.

Some union management negotiations also illustrate this principle. Unions naturally resist "going backwards,"—reducing wages or benefits. Demands that wages be cut or that work rules be changed to increase productivity are almost always rejected. However, Republic Air Lines, U.S. Steel, and several other companies have made such changes by beginning with an agreement on an extremely important goal: the survival of the company.

Once both sides agree that this goal is threatened, the specific changes become much easier to negotiate. In fact, there are several examples of the *union's* proposing wage and benefit cuts! They know that survival comes first.

Briefly explain your position

Say why you are taking a position, particularly if the other side objects to it. These explanations must be made in a sincere, nonaggressive way. Do not talk down to them or insist that they accept your position. Just help them to understand why this problem forces you to take certain positions.

But keep those explanations brief! Long explanations can actually weaken your position. You can give away too much information, appear unsure, or even apologetic about your position. Explaining your problem can also facilitate joint problem solving. Instead of focusing only on "my position versus your position," both sides may consider other alternatives.

Allow plenty of bargaining room

You should create bargaining room with your first offer, then *slowly* move toward their position. Many people dislike this approach. They would rather offer their best deal and then refuse to budge. Doing so violates the very spirit of compromise. The other side has to feel that they have gained something by negotiating. If you do not build bargaining room into your original position, you cannot make those essential concessions.

At times you cannot create bargaining room on some issues. For example, you usually cannot quote higher than list price, and you may be unable to give discounts. You may then have to create bargaining room by making false demands. Then you can trade them for the other side's acceptance of your price. For example, your first offer might be for all cash. You could then remain firm on the price, but offer increasingly generous credit terms.

There are several additional reasons for making ungenerous first offers. First, you may make the other side doubt their position. They may become afraid that a deal cannot be reached, or question their own objectives. They may even change their MSP.

Second, their anxiety about reaching a deal may help you learn their limits. At first you can see they are unsure that a deal can be reached. Later, after you have made some concessions, they may visibly relax. This relaxation suggests that you are approaching or are even within their range. You can then slow down or stop your concessions because you have a good estimate of their bottom line. You probably could not make such an accurate estimate if you had made a more generous first offer. Neither the early tension nor the later relaxation would have occurred.

Third, an overly generous first offer can raise their expectations. They may then take a harder line, trying to maximize their share of the perceived bargaining range. In fact, some negotiations end in a deadlock, even though a deal was possible, because the opening offer made the other side too greedy. They concluded there was more "money on the table," and the other party was being unreasonable about additional concessions.

For all these reasons make sure that your original first offer gives you plenty of bargaining room.

Communicate that you are willing to move, if they do so

Compromise is a two-way street. They will probably not move unless they expect you to do so. You should therefore communicate that you are willing to make concessions *if they will do the same.* That condition is essential; if they think that you will move unilaterally, they will have no incentive to make concessions. They can stonewall and wait for you to move.

You must therefore walk a fine line between appearing too rigid and too flexible. Either extreme is undesirable, and both have the same effect: They make the other side less willing to compromise.

Establish trading value

Trading value is the value that the other side will give you in return for a particular concession. Two factors determine trading value: the value to them, and the cost to you, of that concession.

If a concession seems to cost you nothing, they will probably give you little or nothing in return. Let's return to our earlier example of trading credit concessions for their acceptance of your fixed price. If you act as if those credit concessions cost you

little or nothing, they will probably refuse to move very far toward your price. Therefore, create trading value by indicating that your position is a serious one, and any
concessions will be costly to you.

Do not sell too hard

The harder you sell, the less they may believe you. Their natural suspicion may
increase, or they may think there is something wrong with your offer.

Let them sell themselves

Sometimes, they will make your points for you. They will say how much they
want to do business with you, or how much they like your products. Do not interrupt
them or try to emphasize their points. They are much more likely to be persuaded by
their own words than by yours. So keep quiet, and let them sell themselves.

Avoid preconditions to negotiating

Preconditions are actions that the other side must take before you will negotiate
with them. For example, people often insist they will not talk or make any kind of
offer until the other side makes a reasonable offer.

Diplomatic negotiations offer extreme examples of the stupidity of preconditions. For example, while trying to settle the Vietnamese war, the Americans insisted that they would not stop bombing North Vietnam until the Viet Cong
negotiated about South Vietnam, while the VC insisted that they would not negotiate
about South Vietnam until the Americans stopped bombing North Vietnam. Similar
absurdities have occurred between the Israelis and Arabs, the Iraqis and Iranians,
and in countless other diplomatic negotiations. Both sides say, in effect, "We will
negotiate, if the other side surrenders first."

Preconditions often cause the other side to lose face. For example, replacing
their current offer with a reasonable one implies that their first offer was unreasonable.
Since no one wants to lose face, preconditions inhibit negotiations. They should therefore be avoided. *Do not insist on preconditions unless saving face is more important
to you than reaching a mutually satisfactory deal.*

Encourage them to make concessions

Many people actively discourage concessions by taking positions which essentially punish the other side for yielding. For example, they say, directly or indirectly, "Take
it or leave it." The visceral reaction is usually, "I'll leave it." You should therefore take
positions which allow the other party to concede gracefully and look like a winner.

You should also communicate that they can benefit from negotiating, that compromising will produce better results than stonewalling. Many people do just the opposite; they say, in effect, "Don't negotiate because you will not gain anything by it."

The classic example was the World War II Allies' insane insistence on uncon-
ditional surrender. Since Germany and Japan knew they had absolutely nothing to gain
by negotiating, they continued fighting long after they were beaten. We wasted bil-

lions of dollars, killed countless people, and allowed Russia to take over eastern Europe to fulfill an absurd commitment. Hard-liners and public relations people may force governments to act stupidly, but you should be more sensible and flexible. Make the other side want to compromise.

Avoid Excessive Details, Especially About Price

The more details you provide, the more ammunition you give them to shoot at you. You cannot possibly justify every detail in a long proposal, and they will naturally concentrate on your weakest points.

Let's say that you offer a package of a computer, software, maintenance, and programmer training for $1,500,000. Your package might be $200,000 less than your nearest competitor's, but your training costs could be 50 percent higher. Will your customers thank you for saving them $200,000? Of course not! They will demand that you lower your training fees in order to match the competition.

State Your Positions Confidently

People tend to do what they feel is expected of them. If you act as if you expect an offer to be rejected, they will reject it. If you communicate a lack of confidence or a readiness to improve your offer, they will demand concessions. Your offers and arguments will be taken more seriously if you apply a few simple principles.

Avoid weak, vague terms

Terms such as "asking price," "about," "around," "in the range of," and "first offer" imply that your offers are not really serious, that you are just starting the negotiating process.

Speak in a confident, but normal tone

Do not state a position as a question or put a nonverbal question mark after it. Do not hesitate or speak slowly. On the other hand, do not speak so quickly that you appear eager to get it over with. Just communicate your confidence by speaking in a normal voice at a normal speed.

Look them right in the eye

Avoiding eye contact can reduce your credibility; overly intense eye contact can have the same effect. Just look them in the eye in a comfortable, natural way.

Do not ask: "What do you think of my offer?"

That question invites criticism and rejection. It also suggests that you do not think much of it.

Time Your Communications, Especially Your Offers

Timing can be critically important, especially for your offers. If you speak when they are not receptive, you will probably waste your breath, and you can undermine your position.

Timing your initial offer is particularly important. If you make it too soon, you may seem too eager. If you wait too long, they may become confused about your intentions or doubt your authority. You must therefore listen sensitively, speak when they are receptive, and make your initial offer at just the right time.

The best time is usually after they have made and explained their initial offer. It will help you to understand their expectations and priorities. You can then adjust your offer and the way that you present it.

The first offer is the most difficult one because you know so little about their position. You do not want to offer too much or too little. Four simple rules can help you.

Try to get them to make the first offer

In addition to providing valuable information, having them move first can directly improve your deal. They may offer you much more than you would dare demand. You can accept it or bargain for a better deal.

Maneuver them into requesting what you want

In adversarial, pure bargaining negotiations this principle can be useful. It generally should not be used in any other situation.

Even if the other side will not make a complete offer, you can sometimes maneuver them into demanding things you would like; then you can trade cost-free concessions for ones that benefit you. We call that technique "creating a bargaining chip out of thin air." It has also been called the *briar patch strategy.*

Earlier generations were raised on the "Brer Rabbit" and "Brer Fox" stories. Brer Fox's great ambition was to kill and eat Brer Rabbit, whose ambition, quite naturally, was to stay alive and free. One day Brer Fox caught Brer Rabbit and was going to eat him. Brer Rabbit, knowing he was in desperate danger, decided to trick Brer Fox.

He complained and complained about the terrible briar patch, then said that Brer Fox could do anything he wanted, skin him alive, cook him and eat him but, please, please, please "don't throw me in the briar patch."

Since he wanted to punish Brer Rabbit for all the tricks he had played on him, Brer Fox threw him into the briar patch. Of course, Brer Rabbit promptly ran away laughing.

How does a child's bedtime story relate to business negotiations? Quite closely. Sometimes you can get the other side to demand things you both want, then get what you want, *plus* another concession. For example, as a seller you and the buyer might want to delay the closing of a house purchase for three months. If you ask for a delay, a shrewd buyer might refuse, then trade the delay for a concession on another issue. If you can maneuver them into making the request, you may get a trade that favors you.

If they ask for a delay, you probably should not say, "Fine, that is what we want too." You might instead reply, "That would really create problems for me." Then probe to find out how badly they need the delay. The more they need it, the more you can get when you trade it to them.

Analyze their offer before replying

If they do make the first offer, analyze it before countering it. Analysis is especially important if their offer is considerably different from your expectations. Large differences suggest that you have misunderstood the situation; correct your misunderstandings *before* replying.

Make your first offer a bit at a time

If they will not make the first offer, make part of your offer and wait for a reaction before offering the next part. Their reactions can help you to adjust the offer. In other words, if you see a negative reaction, you can make the rest of the offer more generous. Conversely, if they seem pleased by the first part of your offer, you may decide to be less generous. In addition, after you have made part of your offer, they may make part or all of their offer.

Piecemeal offers can also overcome certain emotional reactions. For example, your basic price can be quite moderate, but you slowly add on profitable extras. New cars are usually sold this way. The dealer advertises a low price to bring people into the showroom and then adds on delivery costs, dealer preparation, power steering, radio, and so on. Accessories have much higher profit margins than the basic car, and the reaction to the rising price suggests how much the customer is willing to spend.

This approach has been called the *wince pricing system*. Keep raising the cost until the customer winces. It is most frequently used for blind items (ones which have no standard price). Eyeglasses are an excellent example; exactly the same glasses can cost between $50 and $200. Some opticians charge whatever the traffic will bear.

"How much are these glasses?"
"$50."
If the customer winces, that is the price. If not, they say, "For the frames. The lenses are another $50."
If the customer winces, the cost is $100. If not, the optician says, "...each."

Even though you would not want to act like an unethical car sales rep or optician, you should decide whether you will communicate your entire position during the Beginning Game. Certain points might be held back for a more opportune time. You might not take a position on the down payment before learning the other side's position on total price.

To give an example, it occasionally pays to hold back an important demand until the rapid momentum of the End Game. As the deal comes together, you may be able to slide an important demand right past the other party. For example, you might be selling under extreme time pressure. If they realize it during the Beginning Game, they can exploit your weak bargaining position. You might do better by avoiding the timing issue until the end.

After settling the price and terms, you can casually say, "Why don't we close this within two weeks?" They may not realize how important timing is to you and agree. Even if they realize its importance, most people would not reopen the negotiations of the price and the terms; they would just negotiate the closing date.

LEARN THEIR POSITION

Learning the other side's position is the most important Beginning Game task. Otherwise, you may make concessions that are costly to you, but nearly valueless to them. Or you can take a hard line when they feel indifferent and powerful. Or you may try to structure a deal that does not fit their priorities.

This subject is so important that we shall devote chapter 5, "The Feedback Loop" to it. We will now discuss only a few general principles.

Do Not Be So Concerned with Your Own Position. Focus on Theirs

Those two short sentences summarize our philosophy of negotiations. The absolutely essential step toward negotiating effectively is to shift your focus from your own position to their position.

Unfortunately, most people focus nearly exclusively on their own position. Their actions say, in effect, "If I could just get them to understand *my* facts and *my* logic and *my* needs, they would make the concessions I need." Unfortunately the other side is saying exactly the same thing.

They therefore have parallel monologues instead of a genuine dialogue. Both sides repeat themselves again and again, hoping to convince the other to accept their position. But eloquence is no substitute for understanding, and you cannot gain that understanding without shifting your focus and sincerely wanting to understand the other side.

Learn Their Entire Position, Especially Their Entire First Offer

You have not completed the Beginning Game's tasks until you have learned their entire first offer. You do, of course, want to learn many other things, but their first offer is critical. Without it, you cannot plan the rest of the negotiation.

Learn How They Feel about Their Positions

Try to discover what they really want and expect. You may find that they feel sure of some points, but are unsure of, or even embarrassed by others.

For example, you might find they are confident about delivery dates, but avoid eye contact and speak hesitantly when they discuss the price. This pattern suggests it will be easier to get concessions on price than on terms. You might also take advantage of their embarrassment by comparing their price to a competitor's.

Do Not Talk Too Much

Talking too much has several disadvantages. First, it gives away information. Since information provides power, you essentially give away power.

Second, it prevents you from acquiring information. Sam Rayburn, the former Speaker of the U.S. House of Representatives, had a favorite saying: "You ain't learning nothing when you're talking."

Third, it can make you look eager for the deal.

Fourth, it irritates many people, which can make them unwilling to compromise.

Decide Whether to Discuss the Total Package or Its Separate Parts

There are no firm rules for making this decision, but there are a few general principles.

If you are receiving money, discuss item by item

You can often get more by taking one issue at a time. First you get a little on one issue, then add a concession on a second, then a third, and so on. This approach is a variation of the famous "salami" tactic.

If you have made a detailed proposal, discuss the total package

A detailed proposal almost invites them to attack its weak points, even if the overall offer is quite generous. Blunt their attack by keeping the focus on the entire package.

If you are more knowledgeable or have a faster mind, discuss item by item

Conversely, if they are faster or more knowledgeable, negotiate the total package. Item-by-item negotiations can be confusing, particularly if you do not fully understand a subject or prefer to think slowly. The total value of all concessions can easily be lost in the mass of offers and counteroffers.

During item by item negotiations the faster or more knowledgeable person can see the entire deal, while the other person may be completed confused. Car salespeople exploit their edge by making their deals as complicated as possible. The poor customer watches dazedly while the salesman manipulates the price of the car, delivery, dealer preparation, radio, automatic transmission, taxes, license, and so on. The customer could minimize the salesperson's edge by insisting that they negotiate only for the total price.

SUMMARY

The Beginning Game lays the foundation for the entire negotiation. If it is not executed well, it can interfere with every later task.

Its three main tasks are to (1) create the right atmosphere; (2) communicate your position; and (3) learn their position.

Instead of planning the atmosphere, many people just act naturally to make themselves comfortable. We recommend deciding which atmosphere fits your strategy, and then deliberately creating it. We described five atmospheres—friendly, formal, indifferent, adversarial, and hostile. The friendly atmosphere fits joint problem solving. The formal atmosphere is neutral, and the other three are primarily or entirely for pure bargaining.

The principles for communicating your position apply to most parts of the negotiation process. We considered both the content and the process of communications, and further divided the process into clarity, confidence, and readiness to negotiate.

We considered six general communications principles: (1) Help them to understand your position; (2) do not give or demand information—trade it; (3) make it easy to compromise; (4) avoid excessive details, especially about price; (5) state your positions confidently; and (6) time your communications, especially your offers.

The discussion of learning their positions was quite short because this subject will be covered in chapter 5, "The Feedback Loop." We briefly covered a few general principles: (1) Do not be so interested in your own position. Focus on theirs; (2) learn their entire position, especially their entire first offer; (3) learn how they feel about their positions; (4) do not talk too much; and (5) decide whether to discuss the total package or its separate parts.

Applying these principles will prepare you for the Middle Game. You will have a solid foundation for moving toward a good deal.

4

The Middle Game

The Beginning Game establishes the gap, the distance between both parties' positions. You should both know: "We are here; they are there. Therefore, the distance between our positions is …."

Closing that gap is the Middle Game's major purpose. You must both move from your original positions, without moving toward a bad deal. The initial positions often create such a large gap that one or more parties feel that a deal is impossible—the gap is not bridgeable. During the Middle Game both parties must move far enough so that the gap becomes small enough to be bridged. The final moves to close the deal occur during the End Game.

The Middle Game's central tasks are therefore creating, maintaining, and controlling momentum. These tasks are often quite difficult because both parties naturally dislike making concessions. This chapter will show you how to start and continue moving, without losing control.

There are two dangers: (1) not creating or maintaining momentum; (2) losing control of the momentum. Because people naturally dislike conceding, one or both sides may *stonewall* (insist that the other side make most or even all of the concessions). The other extreme is that you may get swept up by the momentum and concede too much or concede on the wrong issues, thereby moving toward a poor deal.

You must therefore balance movement and control. Get both sides moving toward a deal, but make sure that you do not move too far, too fast, or in the wrong direction. This chapter contains three major sections, one for each task.

   I. Create Momentum

  II. Maintain Momentum

 III. Control Momentum

Because momentum is so important to negotiations, some of the principles and tactics discussed here are also covered in other chapters.

CREATE MOMENTUM

Since you cannot reach a deal without momentum, your most important Middle Game task is to start both parties' movement. Inertia is as much a factor in negotiations as it is in physics. Overcoming that inertia is like trying to push your car by hand; the hardest task is to start moving.

Your task is complicated by the fact that there are at least two parties involved, and both must start moving. Again, extreme approaches are undesirable. Insisting that the other party move first violates the essential spirit of compromise and often increases their stubbornness; they would rather lose the deal than lose face by moving first. Moving yourself without demanding that they reciprocate can encourage them to stonewall; since you are essentially rewarding them for being rigid, why should they act flexibly?

I call the strategy of rewarding intransigence with concessions "the Jimmy Carter school of negotiations." He never understood that giving things away and appealing to the better nature of the Russians, Iranians, Panamanians, and others could not possibly work. They had absolutely no incentive to compromise, and every reason to make additional demands.

George Kennan, former ambassador to the Soviet Union and a top-level advisor in the State Department, has pointed out that the pattern of unilateral concessions started long before Jimmy Carter. When Kennan was a relatively junior diplomat, he was so frustrated by the American government's negotiating strategy that he sent a full-rate telegram of several thousand words to the State Department. Books on diplomatic history call it "the long telegram."

He got their attention and very forcefully argued that the Russians see unilateral concessions not as something to be reciprocated, but as signs of weakness that should be exploited. Alas, later generations of U.S. leaders have probably never even heard of "the long telegram."

They do not realize that some people will not move without an incentive to do so. Furthermore, simply getting both parties to move is not enough. You want to move toward the *right* deal, and the first moves can determine both the speed and direction of the momentum.

In simple, pure bargaining negotiations, the right deal for you is easy to define: It is the one near the other side's limit. There is therefore little danger of moving in the wrong direction, but there is an extreme danger of moving too slowly or too rapidly. If you move too slowly, the other party may decide that you are not negotiating in good faith and become angry and rigid. If your concessions are much larger than theirs, you may end up close to your own limit. In fact, you may run out of bargaining room and be unable to make those critically important final concessions, thereby losing the deal.

In multiple-issue, mixed negotiations the right deal is the one that benefits both parties. It should match their priorities, and the first concessions can determine the direction of later moves. For example, if your key priority is price, and delivery is almost irrelevant, your first concession should be on delivery, not price. A price concession signals that it is a relatively low priority, and gets you started in the wrong direction. You should therefore carefully examine both side's initial positions, decide in which direction to move, and then try to create momentum in that direction.

Creating the right kind of objective momentum is hard enough, but you have one additional task: creating the *feeling* of momentum. Both parties should feel that they are making progress toward a deal. Substantive movement usually affects this feeling, but other factors also influence it. For example, both sides could make concessions, yet feel that "we're getting nowhere" because they regard the other's concessions as meaningless. Conversely, even without concessions, people can feel that they are making progress; they are starting to understand and trust each other.

The atmosphere usually causes differences between feelings and substance. If it is positive and constructive, feelings of progress are likely. Conversely, a negative atmosphere can cause people to doubt quite substantial concessions.

The techniques for creating momentum obviously depend on your strategy. Some of them will work with almost any strategy or situation; others must be used more selectively. For example, a best seller[1] once taught people to "win through intimidation." That approach works only with people who are objectively or psychologically weak. With most people it will usually backfire.

Cooperation works better in most business negotiations. Emphasizing your common interests and readiness to trade concessions will usually start the momentum. However, there are lots of people, including the believers in winning through intimidation, who would regard that strategy as a sign of weakness, and become even more demanding. You must therefore base your strategy on a thorough analysis of the situation and the other people.

The following techniques will be helpful in many situations, but they must used judiciously.

Understand the Obstacles to Momentum

There are three major obstacles in most negotiations: the fear of conceding too much, the fear of losing face, and the belief that "We are more reasonable than they are." The first two are obvious, but the last one requires an explanation.

This belief is based on egotism (of course, we are more reasonable than they are) and by the natural tendency to feel that our position is correct, while they have taken theirs because they are irrational or want to gain a bargaining advantage. This belief also affects perceptions of concessions; ours were real, while theirs were just "cutting away fat."

Understanding these fears and beliefs can help you to reduce their effects, but you can never completely eliminate them. You should therefore continuously analyze your own and the other side's actions, and try to determine why certain actions are being taken so you can deal with the underlying causes.

For example, if fear of losing face is preventing movement, ease those fears. If you believe that you have been more reasonable than the other side, calmly explain your beliefs and listen respectfully to their reply. Perhaps they are more reasonable than you first thought.

Complete the Beginning Game's Tasks

If you do not have the right atmosphere and understand each other's positions, you have little chance of creating controlled momentum toward a good deal. In addition, many Beginning Game tactics, such as stating issues in divisible terms and focusing on goals rather than means, help you to get things moving.

These points seem too obvious to merit discussion, yet they are repeatedly ignored. Again and again we have seen people make or demand concessions without fully explaining their own position or understanding the other side's position. They remind me of those bad jokes about people who hate heavy traffic so much that they turn off busy highways when they see an empty side road, and roar through the countryside saying: "We may not know where we're going, but we're moving fast."

Revise Your Analysis and Strategy before Moving

During the Beginning Game you should have learned a great deal about their positions, negotiating style, concerns and so on. Use that information to revise your strategy. For example, if their priorities seem different from your expectations, you might offer different trades. If they seem surprisingly weak, you might become more power-oriented.

Chapter 5 will suggest specific techniques for revising your analysis and strategy. Now the critical point is that this revision should be done *before* you start moving. Otherwise, you may commit irreversible errors.

Avoid Silly Symbolic Conflicts

The fear of losing face is particularly intense before the first concession. For both strategic and face-saving reasons, neither party wants to move first. The longer the impasse continues, the more important face becomes. Both sides may feel that moving first would be a form of surrender.

They can then get involved in a power or macho conflict, trying to prove their toughness. If the contest continues long enough, we have "trench warfare," a term that originated in World War I when both sides stayed in heavily reinforced trenches and shot artillery at each other, killing millions of soldiers without benefiting either side. They even coined a term for it—"a war of attrition"; both sides were bleeding to death, hoping the other side would be the first to run out of cannon fodder.

Business people can be just as silly. They may stubbornly refuse to make concessions, even on trivial issues such as where the negotiations will take place. "I'm not going to their office. Insist that they come here." The emphasis essentially shifts from "Let's make a mutually satisfactory deal," to "Beat the SOB!"

Four steps can help you to avoid this type of conflict. First, avoid silly positions. Before taking a position ask yourself, "Do I really need that, or am I just trying to show my power or toughness?"

Second, don't involve face on minor issues; focus on the important issues, and avoid making trivial matters issues of principle.

Third, whenever possible, create an escape route that allows you to concede without losing face. For example, "We have found a new supplier who will cut our costs, thereby allowing us to cut our price."

Fourth, do not involve the other side's face unnecessarily, and leave them an escape route. If they give an obviously false explanation that lets them climb down from a position, graciously agree with their reasoning and thank them for their concession.

Do Not Insist That They Move First

Of course, you benefit from their moving first, but insisting on it could create a silly symbolic conflict. Both sides could demand a surrender on the symbolic issue of who moves first.

Preconditions to negotiations are a particularly destructive example of this principle. One or both sides state that they will not negotiate unless the other side takes some action first. The precondition itself is often so important that accepting it would mean losing the negotiation, and the mere fact that one has yielded to it implies surrendering. For example, Iran repeatedly said that they would negotiate an end to their war with Iraq if Iraq would essentially surrender before the negotiations! Their specific conditions were that the Iraqi president be deposed and tried as a war criminal and that Iraq agree in advance to pay massive reparations.

The American-Vietnamese peace negotiations offer an example of an essentially irrelevant precondition. For months they refused to negotiate substantive issues because both sides stated absurd preconditions about the shape of the table!

Whether they refer to serious or symbolic issues, preconditions almost always inhibit the momentum. Avoid stating them, and try to step around any that the other side presents.

Offer Conditional Concessions

To create momentum without surrendering, offer, explicitly or subtly, to move if they will reciprocate. You can, for example, say, "I'm willing to negotiate, if you are." Or, "If I improve my delivery time, can you come up on the price?" Or, "I'll cut my delivery time by ten days, if you will raise your price offer by 2 percent." These examples were increasingly explicit. You might use the vaguest one first and then become more explicit.

Try for Agreements on Principles

Since it is usually easier to agree on principles, start with them, and then work out the details. For example, when loaning to businesses, banks normally want certain covenants such as a minimum amount of cash or some maximum amount of indebtedness. Negotiating these covenants can be very difficult. The language issue is particularly difficult because the banks want to use their standard contract language while the customer's attorney wants to change it.

This sort of disagreement often degenerates into a macho contest between attorneys. They try to show how smart they are and how hard they are fighting for their clients' interests by arguing over irrelevancies. In fact, attorneys' squabbles have destroyed countless deals that could have been easily negotiated without them.

The obvious solution is to keep the attorneys in their place. First, agree on general principles such as too little cash or too much debt harms everybody. Then agree on the amounts needed to protect both sides. After agreeing on the substance, tell the lawyers to write a contract that formalizes the agreement. This procedure is faster, more efficient, and better for your relationship than letting the lawyers argue endlessly over meaningless details.

Respond to Their Priorities

Doing so gets you moving in the right direction—toward the deal that fits both sides' objectives. If you offer trades that give them what they really need, they will probably concede what you really need (if your priorities do not conflict sharply).

For example, if price and after-sales service are your key priorities, while they need a quick delivery and prompt payment, offer to concede on their priority issues in return for concessions on price and service.

Send Consistent Signals

Confusion is usually undesirable, and inconsistent signals create confusion. You may send them deliberately or accidentally. For example, you might want to conceal that you desperately need this deal, but you should do so by acting in a consistently indifferent way. Acting indifferent one minute, mildly interested the next, and eager the next will just create confusion and distrust.

If you want the others to understand your priorities, send consistent signals that fit those priorities. For example, if you want them to know that the price is critically important, make sure that your words, body language, and offers all send that message. Your offers are particularly important. If you keep saying that price is your key priority, and then make your first concession on price or offer to trade a price adjustment for something else, you will confuse them. Your words say that price is most important, but your offers say exactly the opposite. Since people usually pay more attention to your offers, they can easily conclude that price is not that important to you.

The same principle applies to your strategy, power, and so forth. Consistent signals reinforce each other. Inconsistent ones raise doubts about both the issue and your personal credibility. So decide on the picture you want to present, and make sure everything you do supports that picture.

Make Your Concessions Appear Painful

If your concessions seem painless, the others will probably not reciprocate. Yet many people devalue their concessions by acting casually or making remarks such as: "I'll throw in six months' free service" or "I'll come down a little," or "I'll knock off $350." Such phrases essentially say: "I'm not giving you anything I value." So why should the other side give you anything in return?

Your words and actions should say that your concessions hurt you. You are not coming down a little; you are coming down a lot. You are not casually throwing in something; you are reluctantly making a significant concession. Do not overact or make a long speech. Just let them know that the concession hurts, and that you expect them to reciprocate.

Ask Vendors for Additional Goods or Services

Because they cost less than equivalent price cuts, most vendors would rather give you more goods or services than lower their prices. Providing them also seems more professional and businesslike than price cutting. They can feel that they are not haggling; they are just living up to their professional obligation to serve the customer.

This approach works particularly well with professional people. Most lawyers, doctors, or accountants regard haggling as beneath their dignity. They are professionals, not tradesmen. Requesting a price discount violates their dignity, but they might respond positively to this sort of approach. "I really appreciate your legal help with this real estate deal. Since it cost a little more than I expected, I wonder if you would mind reviewing my old will to make sure it is up-to-date."

Shift Issues at Impasses

If you cannot make progress on one issue, discuss another one. This common sense principle is violated very frequently. Both sides stubbornly insist that a certain issue must be settled before they will even talk about another subject.

Shifting issues can facilitate movement by reducing the tension. You may also learn that you can get a good overall deal even if you concede on the contentious issue. For example, you might gain enough on the new issue to offset concessions on the contentious one.

Make Small Concessions

Many people feel that large concessions will create momentum and encourage the other party to reciprocate. Even Henry Kissinger made that mistake. In *White House Years*,[2] he said:

> In the negotiations I conducted I always tried to determine the most reasonable outcome and then get there rapidly in one or two moves.... Thus in the many negotiations I

undertook—with the Vietnamese and others—I favored big steps taken when they were least expected, when there was a minimum of pressure.

Only someone as blindly arrogant as Dr. Kissinger could brag about his strategy for a negotiation that he unquestionably lost. The agreement won him the Nobel prize, lost us a war, and ended with our routed troops fleeing Saigon in helicopters, deserting our allies. The North Vietnamese correctly concluded that his large voluntary concessions signaled weakness, and they took advantage of it.

Exactly the same principle applies to many business people. If you move too much or too fast, they can easily become greedy, unyielding, or suspicious, particularly if there is not a strong foundation of mutual trust.

Small concessions are better than large ones for several reasons. First, by giving away less bargaining room, they help you to reach a better deal. Second, they communicate firmness; they say that you are not going to move very far or very fast. Third, they support the credibility of your previous position, while a large concession suggests that it was not a serious position. Fourth, they may cause the other side to doubt their own limits. They may feel that a deal is impossible and reevaluate the entire situation. They may even change their MSP.

Fifth, small concessions increase the time pressure on the other side, particularly if they have not set a firm MSP. If they believe that they cannot reach a deal at this pace, they may try to speed things up by making larger concessions. Sixth, they help you maintain the momentum. You can obviously make small concessions more frequently than large ones. In fact, negotiations can deadlock if you start by moving so quickly that you run out of bargaining room and have to "slam on the brakes." You may not be able to make those essential final concessions.

The moral is clear: *Do not make large concessions; make a series of small ones.*

Move on Only One Issue at a Time

Moving on several issues at once has the same general effects as making a large concession, but these effects can be more extreme. The other party may even believe that you are collapsing and take an extremely hard line. Moving on several issues also confuses them about your priorities; they cannot tell which issues are most important to you.

The combination of the last two points and an earlier one about starting with an ungenerous offer makes some people fear that they will not reach an agreement. That fear is quite legitimate; they may make fewer deals. However, the ones that they do make will be more profitable.

In addition, the last section of this chapter, Controlling Momentum, will show you how to reduce the risk of missing a deal. An important rule for controlling momentum is to start moving early. Then you have enough time to move in a slow, controlled way toward a *good* deal.

Remember, your objective is not to rush into any deal; it is to reach a *good* one. Rapid movement may cause you to make unnecessary concessions or miss opportunities to restructure the deal to both parties' advantage. So start moving early, and continue in a slow, deliberate way toward a good deal.

Demand Reciprocity

You may feel that we have belabored the point that *both* sides must move. After all, can't you always get things moving by making a concession? No!

Sometimes you will get a concession, but you will frequently get exactly the opposite result. They may feel that their intransigence is paying off and decide to become even tougher.

Do not fall into the trap that destroyed Jimmy Carter, but don't stonewall either. Make concessions, but insist that they reciprocate. If they refuse to do so, withdraw your concessions. Either both sides move, or nobody moves.

MAINTAIN MOMENTUM

You obviously must maintain the momentum to reach a deal, and it becomes more difficult as the negotiations progress. The early concessions usually just cut away fat, but the later ones become progressively more painful. Each move is a little more painful, a little more costly, than the one before.

All the reasons for resisting concessions continue to operate, and most of them become more powerful. Both sides feel that they have been more reasonable and moved more than the other. Both fear losing the negotiation. Both worry about the reactions of their bosses and other people.

Long impasses may therefore occur, forcing you to recreate the momentum again and again. This uneven, rather jerky, process is so stressful that it can easily cause a deadlock; one or both parties may decide that the deal is not worth so much time and trouble.

There are, however, two mitigating factors: inertia and information. Inertia makes it easier to maintain momentum than to create it; for example, when pushing your car by hand, it is much easier to keep it moving than it is to start moving it. The information you have acquired about the other side's situation, objectives, and strategy helps you to keep moving toward a deal.

A few simple techniques can help you to keep things moving in the right direction.

Emphasize Agreements, Not Disagreements

Emphasize your progress, not your problems. For example, if you have agreed on three issues, but have yet to settle ten, summarize the agreements and say, "We are making progress, but have a long way to go. Let's try to build on our progress."

Say "Thanks" for Some Concessions

Do not be effusive about it; just show your appreciation, even if their concession is a small one. Doing so essentially rewards them for moving, and people usually repeat rewarded actions. A thank you can be particularly valuable after a long impasse. If you thank them and reciprocate with a concession, most people will make additional concessions.

Conversely, you can inhibit momentum by essentially punishing them for making that concession. "That's not good enough!" or "Is that all you can do?" Since they have been punished for conceding, their natural reaction is to refuse to move again. Unfortunately, these punishments are quite common. Because they are disappointed by a small concession, people often attack the person making it. It is far better to swallow your disappointment, then encourage more progress with a thank you and a concession.

Make It Easy for Them to Concede

Forego words or actions that might hurt their pride. For example, do not say: "Take it or leave it." Many proud people would reject the offer, even if it were attractive. Do not ask, "Is that your final offer?" because any answer creates problems. Since saying: "No, it is not my final offer," opens the door to more concessions, most people would say, "Yes." Then, to preserve their credibility, they might refuse to concede further.

Avoid positions, words, or nonverbal actions that seem disrespectful. Face is so important to many people that they would rather lose money than lose face. The history of diplomacy clearly illustrates the importance of face. Again and again nations have gone to war over trivial issues rather than lose face by backing down. Two Latin American countries even fought a war because of a soccer game!

Face is almost as important in business negotiations because people are the same everywhere. Countless deals have been lost because somebody thought that an essentially trivial concession would make them look weak or foolish.

So make it easy for them to move toward you, and avoid the words and actions that could make them put their backs up. Create an atmosphere that makes mutual concessions seem natural and comfortable. Then support that atmosphere with your own concessions.

Avoid Premature Finality

During the Middle Game do not say "final offer," "best offer," or "as far as I can go." Those words change the game from "let's both keep moving toward a deal" to "take it or leave it." You have essentially announced that you will make no further concessions, and that the only way they can get a deal is to surrender. People do not like to surrender, even if the surrender terms are quite attractive. They may therefore refuse to make additional concessions.

Premature finality also undermines your credibility. You will probably have to make concessions after this "final offer." Then, when you really are at your limit, making your final offer, the other side may not believe you and push for additional concessions.

Briefly Justify Concessions

Without a justification, they may believe that you just cut away meaningless padding or that you are weak and eager. Either belief reduces their motivation to reciprocate.

A plausible justification suggests that your concession is meaningful. You have made a specific concession for a specific reason.

For example, if your original bid was $272,454, do not just knock off $5,000. Round numbers suggest that you are just giving away "smoke." Instead, reduce your bid by $3,568.14 because you have found a subcontractor who can reduce your costs.

This kind of move tells the other party: "I am not just cutting off fat, nor am I giving you 'smoke.' My original bid was economically justified, and I am making a real concession because I have found a way to cut my own costs."

Avoid Consecutive Concessions

Unless absolutely necessary, do not make two or more concessions in a row. Insist that they move before you move again. Consecutive concessions suggest weakness and reduce your bargaining room, thereby hurting you in two ways. Of course, like all rules, this one will occasionally have to be broken. Sometimes they simply will not move. If you can afford it, and it is absolutely necessary, make another *small* move, and try to make it conditional; "I'll move if you will."

Don't Debate, Negotiate

Many people try to score debating points by criticizing the other side's errors and inconsistencies. They may win the debate, but lose the negotiation because the other side becomes defensive, aggressive, or unyielding.

There is an absolutely critical difference between a debate and a negotiation. In a debate both sides appeal to third parties, the judges or the audience. The worse you can make the other side look, the better score they will give you. "Look at how ridiculous their position is. The evidence clearly indicates that they are illogical, perhaps even dishonest." That sort of talk may win you points in a debate, but destroy you in a negotiation.

During negotiations there is no third party, no judge, no audience. The crucial decision—whether to make another concession—is made by the other side. A concession would essentially say: "You are right, and we are wrong." Therefore, the better debater you are and the worse you make them look, the more rigid they may become.

So avoid sterile debates and try to understand and adjust to their concerns rather than belittling them. Make them want to move toward you. *Trade concessions, not insults.*

Use the "Salami Technique"

Relatively few people use this technique (you take a slice, then another, and another, ...). They prefer to ask for everything at once, but doing so rarely works. The other side naturally refuses to make such large concessions. For example, people often present several arguments, perhaps even their entire case, at one time, hoping that the other side will accept their position. When the other side does not collapse, they do not know what to do. They have essentially used all of their ammunition and they have nothing left to encourage specific concessions. It is usually better to move them *slowly* toward your position. Make points one at a time, and try for a concession for each point.

For example, a larger corporation once offered $15,000,000 for a small firm, but the price was "subject to inspections." So they sent in inspectors, one after another. After each inspection they negotiated. First, they found about $1,800,000 worth of questionable receivables; they negotiated a price reduction of about $1,300,000 for them. Then they found some worn out or obsolete equipment. They asked for a $600,000 price reduction, then "graciously" agreed to "only" $425,000. They did the same thing again and again, and they were always reasonable. Each reduction was justified by objective facts, and they always compromised. They saved over $4,000,000, which is much more than they could have gotten in one negotiation.

Use Silence Judiciously

Silence makes some people so uncomfortable that they will talk or even make a concession just to break the silence. A few people have even learned the value of silence from lucky accidents. For example, while negotiating for a new job by telephone, a man had an uncontrollable coughing fit and covered the telephone mouthpiece.

> "We'll start you at $45,000."
> He wanted to say, "Fine," but could not stop coughing.
> After a minute or so, the other person said, "Well, we could probably go to $46,000."
> Cough, cough.
> "$46,500 is absolutely the best we can do!"
> Cough, cough.
> (Angrily) "You are really holding us up....It's against company policy, but this one time we could start you at $47,000, but not one penny more!"

Silence must, however, be used selectively and tactfully. If it looks as if you are using it as a pressure tactic, they may become rigid. So create a "friendly" silence. You are just thinking or allowing them to think.

Never Interrupt an Offer or a Prelude to One

An offer is the best thing they can give you. In fact, the key to momentum is getting the other side to make offers. A good offer obviously improves your position. Even a bad offer might contain some good parts. Besides, any movement, no matter how slight, maintains the momentum.

Interrupting an offer can delay or even prevent its being completed. You may change subjects and never receive the offer they started to make.

The same principle applies to preludes to offers, signals that an offer may be made soon. "My partner and I have carefully considered our position...." "We were wondering if it might be possible to...." "We might be able to work something out along the following lines." "If you lower the price, we could probably...." Preludes can also be nonverbal. Calculations by an individual or discussions among a team can mean that an offer is being prepared. They might even be deciding whether to accept your last offer!

Whenever you hear an offer or a possible prelude to one, *be quiet*. Let them make the offer.

Make Their Implicit Offers Explicit

Implicit offers do not commit them to any specific action. They suggest a concession without explicitly defining it. For example, they might say, "We might compromise on the price for better terms. How much can you reduce the down payment and interest rate?"

You might make significant concessions but get only a few dollars on the price. To reduce this danger ask them to make their offer explicit: How far will they go on price?

If they will not make an explicit commitment, be as vague as they are. Trading vaguely defined concessions has been called *trading in principle*. You agree in principle to swap concessions on price and payment terms. Discussing this sort of trade helps both parties to shape the deal by learning each other's general priorities. Later trades can be more specific and explicit. You should therefore trade in principle, but make sure that both sides are about equally explicit.

Nail Down Concessions

Vague concessions should be defined and nailed down to prevent later misunderstandings and ensure that the concessions are not modified or withdrawn later. For example, a supplier might say, "We might cut shipping costs about 3 percent." If you do not clarify that concession, it may disappear later. The other side could easily believe that they have not made a firm concession, or simply forget it, or deliberately forget it.

Nail it down by visibly computing the exact dollar value of 3 percent, and making their commitment explicit. "Let's see now, you said that shipping costs would be $24,670? Three percent would be $740.10; round it off to $740. Then our shipping costs would be $24,670 minus $740 equals $23,930. Is that correct?"

Do Not Let Them Withdraw Concessions

People often try to withdraw concessions. Sometimes they will present justifications: "Because freight rates are going up, we cannot take off that 3 percent we mentioned yesterday...." Sometimes they will deliberately misstate their position or simply forget a previous concession.

Gently remind them of their concessions. Do not imply that they are doing anything wrong; they might then deny ever making a concession, or become more adamant about withdrawing it. "Oh, no, we never committed to do that; we just said that we might consider it."

If, after having been reminded, they still try to withdraw a concession, get tough. Insist that they honor their commitments. If necessary, accuse them of not bargaining in good faith. Doing so is, of course, risky, which demonstrates the value of nailing down concessions to avoid this risk.

Unless it is absolutely unavoidable, do not let them withdraw a concession. Doing so undermines both your position and your credibility.

Time Your Breaks Carefully

Depending upon their timing, breaks can help or hinder the momentum. If you are at an impasse, it may help to take a break, think things over and let people cool down. Conversely, if you are making good progress, a break (particularly a long one) can destroy the momentum.

Every experienced sales rep can tell horror stories about inopportune breaks. "The deal was almost closed. All we had to do was work out a couple of minor details, but he had to rush to an important meeting. When I went back the next day to work out the details and close the sale, and he told me, 'I've had a chance to think about it and decided that your price is too high." Then the whole negotiation process has to begin again, or perhaps the deal is completely dead.

Therefore, time your breaks carefully. If you are not moving, take one. If you are moving along nicely, avoid unnecessary breaks and keep all breaks quite short.

Manage Walkouts

Walkouts can occur at any time, and they are usually very disruptive. Both sides become more rigid, and neither wants to lose face by reopening the negotiations. Most walkouts are unnecessary, and nearly all of them are poorly managed. Instead of thinking about the long-term consequences, people simply yield to their anger or desire to escape from tension.

If you want to walk out

First and most important, think carefully. A walkout is a powerful and dangerous weapon, and all weapons should be used judiciously. Before leaving, ask yourself whether you are responding to your head or your stomach. Are you leaving for a strategic purpose, or are you just reacting to inner tensions? Will walking out advance the negotiations or help you in some other objective way (such as allowing you to work with other vendors), or will it just make you feel better?

That is, ask yourself: "What will I gain and lose by walking out?" Answer the question honestly. Many times you will see that your real reason is emotional: you want to punish them or relieve some pressure on yourself. You may pay a high price for yielding to your emotions. Unless you have a clear, rational reason for walking out, don't do it.

Second, if you must walk out, do it slowly. Make it very easy for them to stop you. The typical walkout is much too abrupt. Suddenly, with no warning one side storms out. The other side may want them to stay, might even grant concessions to keep them there, but they are too surprised to respond.

It is much better to leave slowly. Warn them that you will not stay unless they alter their position. Wait a few minutes. Pack up your papers, slowly. Wait another few minutes. Make your verbal warnings clearer and stronger. Wait a few more minutes. Stand up and remain there for a moment. Then walk slowly to the door.

Third, don't slam the door. Leave in sadness rather than anger. You had hoped that the negotiations could succeed, are sorry that they have failed, and still hope that you can work something out.

Don't say or do anything that increases the already formidable difficulties of reopening the negotiations. Above all, avoid personal insults. "I don't know why I have wasted so much time dealing with jerks like you."

Do not insist that you will not talk to them unless they make another offer. Do not even insist that they must telephone you or come to your place. Make it as easy as possible for either side to contact the other.

Fourth, if possible, maintain some personal contact. If you are negotiating as a team, have the friendly person stay a few moments and express the hope that you can all get back together. If you have social contacts, keep them up. For example, if you are members of the same club, make a point of saying hello or having a drink or round of golf together. That is, make them realize that you reject their negotiating position, not them as people.

If they walk out

Your natural reaction might be to lock the door behind them, to say or do things that make it very hard for them to return. "Don't let the door hit you on the way out." Although this reaction is natural, it is quite destructive. Instead, keep the door open as wide as possible. Make it easy for either side to reopen the negotiations.

First, try to avoid the need to reopen the negotiations by keeping them from leaving. Do not lose your dignity or weaken your position by grabbing their arm or begging them to stay, but clearly communicate that you are sorry that they are leaving.

Second, if they insist on leaving, graciously escort them to the elevator or parking lot. As you walk there, make small talk or, suggest a round of golf, or a lunch, and do other things to defuse the confrontation.

Escorting them also creates opportunities for the negotiations to continue. Do not press. Above all, do not beg. But, if they indicate a little softening of their position, respond positively. Remember, they probably do not want the negotiations to end. They may even regret having said that they were leaving. Make it easy for them to keep talking.

Third, at their car or the elevator, clearly express your regret that the negotiations have broken down and your hope that they can be reopened. Do not grovel. Just say, "I'm sorry we can't work anything out today, and I hope we can get together soon." You might even suggest a specific time and place, preferably one that is neutral or gives them a small, symbolic victory. "I'll probably see you at the club Saturday night," or "I'll be in your neighborhood next Wednesday. Perhaps I should stop by."

Fourth, sometime during the parting process, let them know that, even though you could not agree on this deal, you hope to work together in the future. Do not let the breakdown of this negotiation destroy a valuable relationship.

Fifth, after they have left, communicate directly or indirectly that you would be glad to talk. For example, let common friends know that you hope to reopen the negotiations. Be friendly and gracious to them if you meet socially. You might even arrange accidental social encounters and let your friendly manner communicate that you would be glad to talk.

Sixth, avoid preconditions to reopening the negotiations. Above all, do not insist that they apologize or eat crow. "I won't talk to them until they apologize, submit a better offer—in writing, admit that they lied...." Preconditions prevent flexibility at the best of times, and their effects are particularly strong after a walkout because people are usually oversensitive.

Reopening the negotiations

If you do get together, tact is essential. Both sides are normally so sensitive that they overreact to insults, including unintentional ones.

Meet on neutral turf because both sides may feel that visiting the other implies surrendering.

Focus on rebuilding the relationship. Apologize or at least express regrets for the unpleasantness. Do *not* apologize for your offers or demands; it would weaken your bargaining position. But do clearly express your regrets about the unpleasantness and, if you can do it sincerely, accept some responsibility for it. "I should not have been so abrupt." or "I guess I got carried away by my own eloquence." or "My wife has often told me to be more tactful."

One of my professors once said, "Any conversation that includes an apology can't be all bad." If you apologize, most other people will reciprocate. And even if they don't, what have you really lost?

Do not interrogate them. Of course, you have questions, but you should defer asking them until after you have at least patched up the relationship.

Above all, do not demand they move quickly. Even if they want to do so, responding to your demand could be too humiliating.

Keep Lots of Issues on the Table

In Chapter 3 we said "Get all the issues on the table." Then you should keep them there. The logic for keeping them there is the same as we proposed in Chapter 3. A very common error is to settle every issue except the hardest one, hoping the momentum will help to settle it. However, this approach can kill the momentum because both sides hold firm on the hard issue and have nothing to trade for concessions on it.

With several issues on the table, you have that trading power. In addition, if you reach an impasse on the hard issue, you can restart the momentum by changing the subject.

If you can't move on issue A, discuss issue B. If you can't move there, shift to issue C. If you can't move on any single issue, offer to trade a concession on C for one on A.

Demand Reciprocity

This principle applies throughout the entire negotiation. Do not hope for reciprocity—demand it. Once you start moving, make sure that both sides continue to move. If they will not do so, stop moving, and perhaps even withdraw your previous concessions.

CONTROL MOMENTUM

There is an unavoidable conflict between your need for momentum and your desire to get the best possible deal. If you move too quickly, you may concede too much. If you move too slowly, the momentum may disappear. You must therefore control the momentum so that *both sides* move, but you do not move too far.

We have already described trench warfare, negotiations in which neither party moves. At the opposite extreme is surrender: You move a great deal, while the other side concedes little or nothing. The best pattern falls between these extremes. *Both* sides move, and they do so in a deliberate and controlled way.

THE MOMENTUM CONTINUUM

little or none	mutual and controlled	too much or too rapid
trench warfare	ideal	surrender

The earlier discussion should help you to avoid trench warfare. Now we will consider ways to avoid a surrender. There is inevitably some overlap with earlier points.

Let's take another look at the sample negotiation that we first encountered in chapter 1. You may remember that they could not start any momentum toward a deal because the atmosphere became so adversarial, and Jack did not understand why George wanted Joan to do the training.

Jack discussed the situation with his partners, and they agreed that he had been too rigid and uninterested in George's position. They also studied Joan's resume and decided that she had the right kind of training and experience to teach the seminars. However, since she did not know their approach and systems, they were concerned about quality and control problems.

The next meeting with George started rather unpleasantly because he was still annoyed. However, after Jack apologized and said that he would consider using Joan, George loosened up and explained why she was so important.

Tadmar, George's company, had a chance for a critically important government contract. If they got it, George would probably get a large promotion *if* there was someone to take over his job. Joan was the only logical candidate, and she had been with Tadmar for only two years. Higher management would not promote her unless she could demonstrate her competence in a highly visible way, such as teaching these seminars.

Once Jack understood the situation, it was easy to work out a mutually satisfactory solution. Joan would do the training, but Jack's company would train and supervise her to ensure control and high quality.

After reaching this agreement, George leaned forward and said, "Now... with Joan involved, we get a break on the price, right?" His words and manner clearly signalled that problem solving time was over; they were starting to bargain.

> Unfortunately, Jack misses the message and continues his problem-solving manner. "Sure. Let's see. Our original proposal was for $150,000."
>
> George interrupts, "But you said the cost of your trainer was $10,000. So that brings us down to 140."
>
> "No, we have to put in the cost of training and supervising Joan, about $5,000. So it really only saves you about $5,000."
>
> "So, your current bid is $145,000?" George's manner shows that he is not too dissatisfied with the price. He would just like to get a better deal.
>
> "Yes."
>
> "Come on, Jack. I've been doing a little checking, and I figure that your costs are running between $110 and $115,000."
>
> Jack looks surprised because George's estimate is quite accurate. "Really...."
>
> George jots down a few figures, then says, "A fair profit would be 10%. Let's see... add 10% to 115 and we get... 126.5. That's a fair price for the job."

Jack is flabbergasted. Since he had expected George to respond positively to his flexibility on the training issue he does not know how to respond to this attacking offer. Jack has, in fact, forgotten that George loves playing the bargaining game.

> "That's impossible. There is no way that we can do the job for that."
>
> George looks skeptical and says, "I know that you've got a lot of room there. How much do you think you can take off?"
>
> "Well, there's a little room, but not much." He pauses, then continues, "If Joan is as good as you say, we could probably shorten our time for training and supervising her." After using his calculator, he says, "I guess I can reduce the price to $142,000."
>
> "Jack, you're trying to make about $30,000 profit on this deal." Shaking his head, he adds, "That's too much profit for a contract like this."
>
> "George, 142 is a very competitive price for the quality we deliver."
>
> "Your group does a good job, Jack. And I'm willing to pay for that. Hmm... how does 129 sound?"
>
> "That's totally out of the question, George."

"Well, so is 142." George's statement indirectly acknowledges that his offer of $129,000 is unreasonable, but Jack does not pick up the signal.

After jotting down a few figures, Jack says, "I can go to 139.5, but that's pushing it, George."

"That's a little better, but it is still not a price that I can live with."

"Well, I have come down a lot, George."

"I realize that—and I'll return the favor. He pauses, thinks, then says, "I'll go to... 131, and that's a darn good price, Jack."

Jack just shakes his head.

After a moment of silence George asks, "Can't do it?"

"Can't do it, George."

"Well, what can you do? We have to reduce the costs somewhere."

"I don't know how we're going to do it. 139.5 is a very good price."

"Well, it is still a little too steep for me."

Jack hesitates, calculates a few numbers, thinks carefully, then slowly says, "Well... I can shave another $2,000... to 137.5. But that's juggling a lot of numbers!"

George leans back in his chair, arms behind his head, clearly very comfortable. He is obviously satisfied, but still tries for a little more, "That is still too much. Can't you do better than that?"

"I don't see how."

George smiles because he is obviously winning; his entire manner says that he is satisfied, but trying for a few more concessions. "Well, Jack, you are looking at the end of the road here. My pockets aren't lined with gold."

Jack misses George's nonverbal signals and responds only to his words. He makes a concession. Since George has not responded to his last offer, it is his second in a row. "George, my partners aren't going to like this, but I'll go as far as I can possibly go— 136."

Realizing that Jack's offer is not really a final one, George counters with, "Okay, and I'll match your concession.... For 132.5 the contract is yours."

Jack shows that he feels pressured. Shaking his head, he says firmly, "Sorry, George, I just can't do it."

"Well, what can you do? I've got to have a price that I can live with."

The pressure is obviously affecting Jack. He looks like he just wants to get up and leave. He furrows his brow, thinks it over, then slowly, but firmly says, "I can do it for 134.5, but just barely!"

George shows no signs of tension because he is having a great time. He enjoys the game, and is certainly winning it. Therefore, instead of grabbing an exceptionally attractive deal, he tries to squeeze just a little more out of Jack. "

"Well, I can see that you're trying, and I'm trying too. So let's settle at 133.5 and get down to work."

Jack's face is flushed because he is so frustrated. He very firmly states, "Absolutely not, George. I've got to get more than that."

Because he still wants to squeeze out a little more, George hesitates, strokes his chin, and pretends to think, "Well, we are only $1,000 apart." He looks at Jack, hoping that he will make another offer.

Jack ignores his signals and states very firmly, "It looks that way."

George, magnanimous as only a winner can be, casually makes an offer, "I'll tell you what. Let's split the difference. That is fair to both of us."

Jack pauses a long time because he is uncertain of whether to make that final $500 concession. If he does so, he would be just barely higher than his MSP, and both he and his partners had expected a much more profitable deal.

The silence unnerves George. He knows that this deal favors him, and he wants to lock it up before it gets away. He leans forward and eagerly presses for a decision. "Come on, Jack. It's a fair price for both of us." He offers his hand while saying, "Let's shake on it."

After a brief hesitation, Jack accepts the handshake and says, "Well, George, you'd better introduce me to Joan. It looks like we're going to be working together."

Normally, the haggling over the price of this size contract would take longer, but we have compressed the process. However, despite the artificiality, we can see that Jack did some things very well, but made some serious mistakes.

First and most important, he got a mutually satisfactory deal. His company can live with the price, and George is delighted with it; the training arrangements give Joan the visibility George wants, while providing the quality and control that concerned Jack and his partners.

He got the deal because he corrected his earlier mistakes. He turned a negative atmosphere into a positive one by apologizing, communicating flexibility, and listening to George's position and concerns. He learned why Joan's involvement was so important, then worked out mutually satisfactory training arrangements. Because he performed the Beginning Game's tasks so well, he could create momentum, then maintain it until they reached a deal.

Unfortunately, that deal was at an unnecessarily low price. He missed numerous signals indicating that price was not really that important to George, then made unnecessary concessions.

If he had thought about it, he would have realized that price was not one of George's top priorities. George had ordered two million dollars worth of equipment. The staff had to be using it properly within two months to enable Tadmar to get a critically important government contract, which could gain George a nice promotion. George had apparently not requested bids from any other consultants, and his whole manner communicated that he was not really concerned about the price.

Jack also made the very common error of continuing a problem-solving approach when George had clearly shifted to bargaining. This shift occurs in many negotiations. People work collaboratively to analyze and solve problems, then bargain over how much each party contributes to the costs. Since Jack did not follow George's lead when he shifted to bargaining, Jack was almost certain to lose the bargaining part of the negotiation. That is, even though the deal is mutually acceptable, George got most of the money on the table.

Failure to shift to bargaining was particularly harmful, because George loves the bargaining game. Jack knew that before the negotiations began, but forgot it. George's attacking offer and other signals should have reminded him, but he never really understood that the game had changed and that he had to change with it.

Jack probably should have asked for a concession in return for the important concession he had made on Joan. Since involving Joan clearly benefitted George and could create a wide variety of problems for Jack's firm, he should have asked for something in return, perhaps even a higher price.

He should have objected to George's estimate of his costs. Instead, he tacitly accepted George's estimate, which weakened his position.

During the bargaining itself, his concessions were always larger than George's. This pattern shows that George was quite clever; he did not refuse to make concessions because doing so could have broken the momentum by making Jack stubborn and rigid. By making smaller concessions, George kept up the momentum and got most of the money on the table.

Jack also made two concessions in a row, and he did so at exactly the wrong time. George was sitting back, obviously comfortable, indicating that no concessions were needed.

Jack also communicated finality prematurely and ineffectively: "I'll go as far as I can go—136." Since he was making his second concession in a row, and George's last offer was only 131, his finality was not credible; George knew that he could go further. Premature finality undermines the credibility of later, more serious final offers, which is one reason that George kept pushing for and getting concessions.

The net result was that Jack ended up very close to his MSP. His firm will make an acceptable profit, but it could have done a lot better.

This example shows the close link between controlling momentum and the Feedback Loop. Jack would have had more control if he had picked up George's signals about the limited importance of the price issue and his satisfaction with a higher price. Just computing the relative size of both parties' concessions (the past ROM) would have shown Jack that he was moving faster than George and that continuing this pattern would result in a deal close to his own MSP.

Although the negotiating session described in chapter 1 and the one we have just read seem quite different, Jack made essentially the same mistake in both sessions: He did not pick up and adjust to George's signals. In the earlier session, he did not try to learn George's reasons for wanting Joan on the project; then he did not really try to learn and aim for George's MSP.

We all make this mistake again and again. We are so intent on our own positions—our needs, our priorities, our bottom line—that we forget that the really important information is on the other side of the table. We have to overcome that natural tendency and focus our attention on the other party. What do they want and how far will they go? Then we can put together a deal that satisfies both parties, but give us most of the bargaining range.

Avoid One-Way Streets

A surprising number of negotiations are essentially one-way streets. One side makes demands, the other makes concessions. The demanding side nearly always wins. In fact, the only question is usually: *How much* will they win?

The Russians use this approach brilliantly. Their general strategy is: "What's ours is ours; what's yours is negotiable." For example, there have been countless negotiations about West Berlin; can you remember a single one about East Berlin? Since they have East Berlin, it is not a subject for negotiation.

They have applied the same principle in Vietnam and Korea, and we have fallen for it. We have negotiated about South Korea and South Vietnam, but never about the north of either country. The same pattern has occurred in Ethiopia, southern Africa, and many other places.

From time to time they become less demanding, and the gullible media applaud their reasonableness and attack our intransigence, our refusal to make more concessions, to move further down that one-way street. They cannot see what the Russians so clearly see—that a little bit here, and a little bit there, adds up, over a long enough time, to a substantial victory. If you doubt that assertion, just look at a map of the world. Color the area controlled by Russia in 1945, 1960, 1975, and today. It is slowly but surely getting bigger.

The effects of one-way streets have also been demonstrated in union-management negotiations. For many years, in nearly all Western countries the unions demanded excessive improvements in wages, benefits, and working conditions, and then graciously made concessions (reduced, but still clearly excessive, demands).

Management rarely made any serious demands and, when they did, the unions screamed "bad faith." They insisted that negotiations must be a one-way street. That pattern led inevitably to a loss of competitiveness. Many American and European products simply were too expensive. Production fell; unemployment rose.

Because American managers have accepted unpleasant realities, and American unions are rational and nonideological, union-management negotiations have become a somewhat more two-way street. Management demands, often called give-backs, have been accepted; wages or benefits have been reduced, changes in work rules have increased productivity, and unemployment has fallen substantially.

In Europe, where most unions are much less rational and more ideological, wages have continued to rise, and changes in work rules to increase productivity have been strenuously resisted. Therefore, European unemployment, which has historically been much lower than America's, is now much higher.

The lesson could not be clearer. *Avoid one-way streets, even if they seem to be going in the right direction.* Management clearly lost by allowing the unions to get away with such a one-sided approach, and the unions did almost as badly. The unions once thought that one-sided negotiations were in their interests, that constantly getting more for less was good for them. But they ended up with millions of members on the unemployment lines, an enormous reduction in their total membership, and an equally great loss of political influence.

We would all be better off if both parties had looked down that street and asked: "Where does it end? Do we want to go there?" Management should have granted wage increases, improved pensions, and so forth, because an improved standard of living is generally desirable. Management should have demanded, and the unions should have agreed to, changes in work rules, and so forth that would have made a higher standard of living affordable. In simplest terms *both* sides should have been making and conceding to demands so that they would move toward *mutually* satisfactory, and economically sustainable, agreements.

This first rule for controlling momentum focused on the direction of movement; the remaining rules focus primarily on the speed.

Start Moving Early

A common pattern is to avoid moving until the deadline approaches and then closing the gap by moving together too quickly. My friend, Doug Lind, once compared negotiations to sex between strangers. "There is a long period of flirtation, when nothing much happens. The pace slowly increases. The final few minutes are wild, with both people tearing off their clothes, frantically eager to consummate the deal."

This pattern is exceedingly dangerous. You do not have enough time to evaluate offers or to fit together the right trades. You may also get caught up in that final momentum and make unwise concessions.

To minimize this problem, begin moving early and keep moving throughout the Middle and End Games. Do not move too quickly or on too many issues, but do move—and insist that they do the same. The sooner you start the momentum, the more controlled it will be.

Avoid Making the First Concession

Earlier in this chapter, we argued that you should not insist that the other side move first. Doing so can easily create a silly, symbolic conflict. However, if you can avoid making the first concession without creating an emotional or symbolic problem, by all means do so.

The person who makes the first concession generally makes the most concessions. Yielding first provides a poorer basis for the "splitting the difference" ritual. More importantly, it communicates weakness; it says that you want the deal more than they do, and no message can do more damage to your position.

Move Slowly

Speed is the natural enemy of control. The faster you move, the greater the danger that you will lose control. Tactics discussed earlier, such as making small concessions, moving on only one issue at a time, and demanding reciprocity, cause slow, controlled movement; the next few tactics have the same general effect.

Think before Acting

We all occasionally act without thinking. We may even believe we are making a mistake, but go ahead anyway, rationalizing that we have to do something. Nonsense! Negotiations are not a Scrabble game with a timer on each player. You can almost always take a few minutes to think before acting.

If you need time to think, but dislike silence, ask questions to keep them talking. Or agree beforehand that a colleague will take the floor when you make a subtle signal. If you need more time, take a break. One way or another, create time to think before you act. A quick, careless action can ruin you.

Watch the Ratios of Movement (ROM)

There are two ROMs. The *Past ROM* tells you the relative speed of both parties' past movements (concessions). The *Future ROM* tells you how fast both sides will have to move to reach a deal within your bargaining range. The Past and Future ROMs will be discussed more thoroughly in chapters 6 and 7. Now we shall just cover the basic principle: If either ROM is unbalanced, you can be heading for trouble.

The past ROM

First, calculate the Past ROM. Let's say that both sides have made three price concessions. Your concessions total $20,000, while theirs total $16,000. The Past ROM is therefore 5:4; you are moving $5 for every $4 that they move.

Second, determine where you will end up if you continue that pattern. For example, if you are still $90,000 apart, continuing that pattern will cause you to concede $50,000 to their $40,000.

Third, ask whether you want to end up there. For example, if conceding an additional $50,000 would cause you to break your MSP, you obviously cannot continue a 5:4 ROM.

Fourth, if necessary, change the ROM, and the sooner the better. The longer you wait, the less room you have to maneuver.

The Past Rom in the negotiation between Jack and George favored George. His concessions were always smaller than Jack's and Jack made two concessions in a row. George therefore got most of the money on the table.

We have used price negotiations as our example because an ROM can be computed more easily, but the same general principles apply to negotiations on almost any subject, even contract language.

Please note that you cannot compute the past ROM without accurate records of both sides' offers. Record all offers and look for patterns. How far has each side moved? Are they moving faster or slower now than they did earlier? If the present trend continues, where will you end up? If that trend would result in a poor position for you, slow down.

The future ROM

The Future ROM ratio is much easier to compute. Just look at the relationship between both sides' most recent offers and your own MSP. For example, if your offer is $100,000, your MSP is $110,000, and their offer is $125,000, the Future ROM is 3:2. To reach an acceptable deal, they must move $15,000, while you can move only $10,000.

That ROM may not sound too bad, but it should warn you to be cautious. First, $110,000 is your MSP, your bottom line, the worst deal you can live with. You would like to do better, but to get a better deal, the ROM is even higher. For example, to end up at $105,000, they would have to move $20,000, while you moved only $5,000 (so the ROM would be 4:1).

Second, any ROM above 1:1 is potentially dangerous. The other side can easily object to moving more rapidly than you do. You can also run out of bargaining room. The negotiation can break down because you cannot make these critically important final concessions. Even if you do make a deal, it will be at or near your limit, meaning that the other side will get most of the money on the table.

Again, a look at the negotiation between Jack and George is instructive. Jack did not consider either ROM until it was too late. He should have realized sooner that he was moving faster than George, and was running out of bargaining room. He then could reduce the size of his concessions to get a better deal.

Withdraw Overly Generous Offers

If you see that your offer has been too generous (for example, if it is obviously more than they expected), withdraw it immediately. Find some excuse, however transparent, but get that offer off the table—fast! "Wait, that isn't what I meant to say. I meant.... " or "I'm sorry. I can see now that I made a computational error. I really should have said...."

If you do it quickly and politely enough, the other side will probably allow you to withdraw an offer. But after a few moments they will probably insist that you leave it on the table. The longer it stays there, the more damage it will do.

Firmly Reject Their Offers

The more firmly you reject an offer, the less likely they are to push you. Conversely, if they sense weakness or hesitance, they may keep pushing. A lukewarm rejection (e.g., "That sounds a little low") can be seen as partial acceptance. Longwinded comments often suggest weakness. The shorter and crisper your answer, the firmer you appear. Good answers are, "I couldn't consider it." or "That's ridiculous." or "I wouldn't think of it."

Your voice, gestures, and other actions should support your words, but many people do exactly the opposite. They smile as they say, "That offer is an insult." They say, "We won't even consider it," then discuss it at length. They threaten to leave, but do not even pick up their papers.

The other people are not fools, nor are they blind. If your mouth says, "No," while your body says, "Yes," or "Maybe," they may feel that you can accept their last offer or a slightly better one. So support your words with actions. If you say that you will not consider something, flatly refuse to talk about it. If you say that you are leaving, start to do so. First pack up your papers. Then stand up. Then start walking toward the door. Do it slowly so that they can stop you, but back up your words with actions.

Beware of Rapid Momentum

Rapid momentum can easily get out of control, and it might mean that you are going in the wrong direction. You might be like the motorist, speeding along, delighted that there is no traffic. The reason for the lack of traffic is that he missed the sign that said, "Danger, bridge out." So he zips around a turn and drives into the river.

If the other side is conceding too rapidly, you may be falling into some sort of trap. Perhaps you are pushing them in exactly the direction they want to go. In football, they call it a *draw play*. The offensive line deliberately lets the defenders push them aside, so a runner can take advantage of the defenders' position.

Even if neither side is trying to trap the other, rapid momentum often occurs just before a deadline. The mood shifts from pessimism to optimism; both parties expect to reach a deal. Suspicions are replaced by a desire to maintain the momentum. Rock-solid positions crumble. Potential problems are ignored. Concessions are made without thoroughly analyzing their consequences, sometimes with disastrous results.

For example, any operations manager can tell you about sales reps who have made excessive commitments to customers, and then pressured operations to fulfill these commitments, regardless of the cost. "I know that you have a huge order backlog, and usually cannot deliver in less than three months, but the only thing preventing the deal was their insistence on immediate delivery. We had settled everything else, and they had really been reasonable. Can't you do it for me, just this once?"

When you see rapid momentum, beware! Stop and think before acting. If you let the mood infect you, you can easily make unnecessary, even catastrophic, concessions. You may even know that they are unnecessary, but justify them as the only way to maintain the momentum.

By all means maintain it, but give away no more than necessary to keep the ball rolling. If they move $5,000, move $1,000 or $2,000. If they offer to split the difference, take their concession, and offer to split the remaining difference. If they concede on a big issue, yield on a little one.

Clarify Their Offers

Make sure you understand offers before responding to them, especially during periods of rapid movement. Countless problems have been caused by people's responding to an offer and then learning they have misinterpreted it or its consequences. By then it may be too late to protect yourself. So, if the offer is at all complex or ambiguous, clarify it.

Ask questions. Summarize your understanding of what they have said. Compare it to their previous offers so that you know exactly how far they have moved (or whether they have moved at all). Obviously, you cannot make that comparison without clear notes of their previous offers.

Establish and Maintain Linkages between Issues

By emphasizing trades, linkages reduce the danger of moving without getting something back. If, for example, you say, "I will make a concession on issue X, if you make one on issue Y," you have established a clear linkage. Either both sides move or neither one does.

Linking issues not only causes both sides to move, but it also nearly automatically forces you to move toward the right kind of deal. Both sides will normally be most flexible on their lower priorities issues, firmer and more demanding on their higher priorities. The pattern of concessions should therefore lead to movement toward a deal that satisfies both parties' higher priorities, with sacrifices on the less important issues.

Demand Reciprocity

The reciprocity principle is critically important for all three Middle Game tasks. You cannot create, maintain, or control momentum unless they reciprocate, and many people will not do so without your insistence. When you make a concession, demand one in return. Watch the ROM and ensure that both sides are moving at balanced speeds. Make conditional concessions, and withdraw them if the other side does not fulfill the conditions.

If you demand and get reciprocity, you should both move toward a mutually satisfactory deal. Conversely, if you do not do so, you may move too far, or too fast, or in the wrong direction.

SUMMARY

The Beginning Game creates the gap, the distance between both parties' initial positions. The central purpose of the Middle Game is to close this gap by creating, maintaining, and controlling momentum. Both substantive and psychological momentum are needed. People have to believe they are making progress, and their beliefs depend upon both the substantive movements and the atmosphere. They may be pleased by the progress despite relatively little movement or feel that nothing is happening despite substantial concessions.

Creating momentum is often difficult because both sides may fear that moving first will cause them to concede too much and to lose face. Many actions can reduce these fears such as avoiding silly symbolic conflicts, not insisting that the other side move first, making conditional concessions, and trying for agreement on principles.

Maintaining momentum is a more complex task, particularly in the later stages of the Middle Game. By then most of the fat has been cut away, and the concessions hurt. Inertia ameliorates this problem, but impasses are still quite common. Restarting the momentum after an impasse, particularly a long one, can be much more difficult than creating the original momentum. The parties may distrust each other or feel committed to their last position or be so annoyed at the other's refusal to compromise. Therefore, try to prevent impasses or at least keep them short. Have the inertia work toward a deal rather than against it.

We discussed many techniques for maintaining momentum, such as focusing on agreements, saying thank you for some concessions, avoiding debates, and using the salami tactic.

Controlling momentum is often extremely difficult, especially in the final moments. People can be caught in the final momentum and make concessions without fully understanding their implications. However, overemphasizing control can cause the momentum to disappear, thereby leading to a deadlock. You must therefore balance movement and control.

To control momentum, you should avoid one-way streets, start moving early, move slowly, think before acting, and follow several other recommendations. The most important recommendations are to make sure that the Past and Future Ratios of Movement (ROM) are balanced, and to demand reciprocity. These recommendations are, of course, interrelated. A favorable Past ROM indicates that both sides are moving toward a satisfactory deal for you, while an unfavorable one indicates that they have not fully reciprocated your concessions. You must then insist that they do so or withdraw some of your own concessions.

Above all, you must consider both the speed and the direction of the momentum. Try to move in a controlled, deliberate way toward a mutually satisfying deal.

5

The Feedback Loop

The Feedback Loop is absolutely essential. As the negotiations progress and you learn more about the other side, you must adjust your strategy. Alas, most people do not use the Feedback Loop properly.

They may intellectually accept the need to adjust their strategy to fit the situation, but they may not probe thoroughly, or ignore evidence that conflicts with their assumptions, or continue strategies long after they have proved their ineffectiveness.

To avoid those mistakes, you must shift your focus from yourself to the other side. This shift is not easy. It requires a fundamental change in your attitude; you must genuinely want to understand them, and most people do not really have that motivation. They want to talk, not listen, to force the other side to accept their position, not to try to understand "where they are coming from."

This shift in attitude is the heart of our philosophy of negotiations. Although we have stated it before, it is worth repeating: *Do not be so interested in your own position. Focus on theirs.*

If you focus on their position, the rest is fairly easy. Conversely, if you focus on your position—your objectives, your facts, your strategy—our other principles and techniques will not help you very much. Your attitude and motivation are much more important than any specific techniques.

A poker playing analogy may be useful. Poor players squeeze their cards. They shuffle them around and open them slowly, hoping that this silly ritual will improve their hands. Good players quickly look at their hands, and concentrate on the other players. Guess who ends up with the money? If you spend your time talking, studying your papers, and mentally rehearsing your arguments, you are essentially squeezing your cards, and you are probably going to lose.

Once you make that mental shift, you should take four steps.

1. *Acquire information*. Listen, observe, and probe.
2. *Interpret that information*. What does it mean?   How does it change your original estimates of their objectives, power, strategy, and so on?
3. *Use that information to revise your strategy*. What should you do differently?
4. *Implement that new strategy well*. No matter how good your new strategy is, it will not help you unless you implement it well.

Problems can occur at any step. You may not get enough or the right information, or misinterpret that information, or revise your strategy incorrectly, or implement your revised strategy poorly. To succeed you must perform all four steps well.

Although these steps occur in order, the relationship among them is often circular. When you are working on interpretation, you may realize that you need to acquire additional information. While revising your strategy, you may realize that your interpretation is incomplete or incorrect and that you have to acquire and interpret additional information.

Because understanding the other side is the heart of our philosophy, there is considerable overlap between this and other chapters. For example, the analytic dimensions and many general communications principles have already been mentioned; now we will reconsider these subjects from the perspective of revising your analysis and strategy.

Because implementation is extensively discussed elsewhere, this chapter contains only three sections.

I. Acquire Information
II. Interpret Information
III. Use the Information to Revise Your Strategy

ACQUIRE INFORMATION

This is the essential first step. If you do not acquire information, you obviously cannot interpret or use it. We will discuss three subjects: the information you need, the general principles for acquiring it, and the three main techniques for acquiring it—listening, observing, and probing.

Information Needed

Because most negotiations contain a bewildering amount of information, you must be selective and resist your own natural biases. You are probably much more sensitive to other people's moods and attitudes than you are to their negotiating objectives and strategy, even though the latter are almost always much more important. You may therefore overlook cues to their MSP or priorities, or even be misled by their feigned anger or friendliness.

Of course, you should try to understand their feelings, but you should usually emphasize other factors. Chapter 2, "Getting Ready To Negotiate," described many of these factors—their objectives, perceptions of your situation, attitudes toward you, personalities, authority, and negotiating strategy.

Their objectives and strategy are especially important, and you should focus on them. While preparing, you should have made and recorded preliminary estimates of all these factors. During the negotiation you should search for information that will improve those estimates.

The Feedback Loop Questionnaire in appendix 2 will help you to acquire, interpret, and use information during the negotiations. Take a copy with you and consult it during any important negotiation.

General Principles

A few simple principles can improve your results. These principles are not at all sophisticated or hard to understand, but most people do not apply them well. Why? Because they really do not want to understand the other side. Remember, techniques are almost meaningless until you make that shift in motivation—from wanting to express yourself to a sincere desire to understand the other side.

Make them want to communicate

If they want to communicate, your job is half done. That motivation is often quite easy to create. If they trust you and believe that you sincerely want to understand them, they will probably communicate rather openly.

Most people are starved for understanding. When they sense that you really want to understand them, they will often be extremely open. They may even tell you things that obviously weaken their negotiating position. "I probably should not tell you this, but we just had a cancellation of a large order." or "I really need this job because...." or "My boss doesn't like your competitors because...."

Conversely, if they doubt your sincerity, or feel that you are not listening, or believe that you are trying to exploit them, they will naturally close up or even lie to you.

Therefore, if it fits your overall strategy, strive for a comfortable, conversational atmosphere in which sharing information seems natural. Note the word "sharing." If you try for a one-sided information flow, most people will naturally suspect your motives and clam up. So ask a few questions, then answer a few. Volunteer some information and encourage them to reciprocate.

And listen while they talk! Nothing makes people more willing to communicate than an attentive listener.

Take your time

Hurrying can make them nervous, noncommittal, or even evasive. It can also cause you to overlook important information. If, for example, you ask several questions in a row, they may feel that you are cross-examining them. Rapidly changing the subject can prevent some thoughtful people from giving complete answers because they need time to think. Rushing can actually prevent you from getting the very information you need!

So, slow down and let them tell their story in their own way. Remember that with people, the shortest distance between two points is often not a straight line. They need to digress, tell stories, provide apparently irrelevant background. If you let them do so, you will often find that the apparently irrelevant information is more important than the answers to your direct questions!

Psychologists learned that principle literally by accident. One part of the famous Hawthorne research included interviews about workers' satisfactions and frustrations. (The Hawthorne research project[3] is best known for its work on the relationship among lighting, group dynamics, and productivity. It was, however, a much larger, and longer-term project). An early phase of the research used highly structured interviews with checklists, and so forth.

Because the researchers were dissatisfied with the data, they experimented with nondirective techniques: They simply asked very general questions, such as, "What do like about working here?" Then, they listened carefully and visibly to the answers. They encouraged people to keep talking by nodding their heads, restating their positions, and asking very general follow-on questions such as, "Why do you feel that way?"

The results were literally amazing. First, they learned much more than they had learned with the structured interviews. In fact, they learned that some of the conclusions drawn from those interviews were clearly incorrect (workers were much less satisfied than it had appeared). Second, many people became more positive about the company even though no substantive action had been taken.

"Thanks for talking to my foreman. He has been a lot more reasonable lately" (nobody had talked to the foreman). "I'm glad you got them to improve the service in the cafeteria" (but the service had not changed). That is, having a chance to express their frustrations had eased those frustrations.

The Hawthorne research and work in other settings ultimately led to America's major contribution to psychotherapy—the Rogerian or nondirective approach. What does psychotherapy have to do with negotiations? Much more than you may think. Both are concerned ultimately with changing people, resolving conflicts, and working out problems. The critical foundations of both are understanding other people and making them want to change their positions!

Take notes

Note-taking slows you down, imposes discipline, broadens your data base, sharpens your perceptions, and helps you to see patterns. It also tells other people that you are taking them seriously.

You should usually ask permission before taking notes. Most people will not object, and your polite request will reduce their discomfort. In formal negotiations, you need not ask; people expect you to take them. But during informal negotiations, taking notes without permission can cause evasiveness or caution. If they reject your request or accept it very reluctantly, put your pad away (but write your notes immediately after the session).

Your notes will be most useful if they are well organized. Do not just write random comments or mix your notes with calculations and other information. Organize your notes; date and number each page and then keep them in order.

Take particularly careful notes of both sides' offers because they are the most important information. Record each offer carefully and note when it was made. Otherwise you cannot see where the pattern is leading, the kind of deal they want, the relative priority of each issue to them. In fact, without good notes, you might even offer them something that they have already conceded to you! The Record of Offers form in appendix 3 will help you to see the overall pattern.

In team negotiations appoint an observer

The speakers miss many signals because they naturally focus on their own position, strategy, and arguments. They are too busy planning their own words to pick up the other side's signals. A quiet, observant, and perceptive person should therefore act as observer. This subject is so important that it is discussed in detail in chapter 10, "Negotiations Between Teams."

Separate observations from inferences

When we ask people what has happened in a negotiation, nearly every answer is an inference, not a description of people's actions: "He has shown weakness." "They are going to leave." "She will accept the offer."

When we ask for explanations, people usually answer, "It's obvious," or "I just feel it," or "Can't you see it?" Only after several questions do we learn what people actually *did*: "He looked away, lowered his voice, slowed down his rate of speech, and paused several times."

Making inferences without explicitly relating them to observations can prevent you from improving your ability to understand other people. You are essentially acting on hunches or intuitions, and you can remain on that level indefinitely. Some of your hunches may be excellent, but some may be absolutely wrong.

The meaning of any action depends upon the person and situation. You should therefore record people's actions and relate them to their past, present, and future context. Ask yourself: What did they do? What did they do before and after? Is my interpretation consistent with their previous patterns?

Unless you use this approach, you may not have enough confidence to act upon your conclusions. For example, you may think that your last offer passed their MSP, but not be sure enough to refuse to make additional concessions. With the proposed approach your inferences will become much more accurate, and you will gain confidence in them. Then you can act decisively.

A note-taking system can help. Make two columns: "observations" and "comments." In the observations column, record whatever you see and hear: their proposals, the way they make them, their reactions to your offers, disagreements within their team, and so on. In the comments column, record your thoughts and questions. What do you think their actions mean? What questions should you ask? This system separates their actions and your thoughts. The next example illustrates the kinds of observations and comments you might make. Note that there may be no comments, one, or more comments for one observation. These notes are not at all complete or in order; normally, there would be many additional notes between them.

OBSERVATIONS	COMMENTS
Very friendly greeting	Want JPS? Eager for a deal?
10:40 A.M. They offer X	Concession larger than expected. Is he in trouble?
11:15 A.M. I offer to trade X for Y. They firmly reject it	Did I misread their priorities?
11:25 A.M. I offer Y. They relax, seem satisfied	Have I passed their MSP?
Despite considerable pressure, I refuse to concede.	
12–12:45 P.M. Pressure continues and intensifies. Nobody moves.	Perhaps I misread previous relaxation.
12:45 P.M. They make a large concession, Z, and say it is their final offer.	Does not sound final. Should I use a bargaining chip to close?

Separating observations and inferences helps you to see patterns, especially when you review your notes. In fact, because things are happening so fast during the negotiating session, I often cannot understand the overall pattern until I review my notes. So take notes like this and review them regularly, looking for patterns.

Listen Carefully

Listening is one of the very few actions that helps you with both pure bargaining and joint problem solving. It increases your power (because knowledge is power); it builds trust (because people tend to trust those who listen to them); and it eases tension and reduces harmful emotions (because people relax when they believe that they are being heard).

Despite its obvious value, most of us do not listen well. We usually know that we should do so, but cannot resist the temptation to open our mouths.

Listening has three major objectives. First, to hear the information that people are sending to you. Second, to encourage them to speak freely. The more intently you listen, the more freely most people will talk. Third, to build their receptivity. If you listen carefully to them, they will probably listen to you and be more responsive toward your proposals. The Hawthorne research cited earlier clearly proved that listening well contributed to all three objectives. A few simple rules can improve your listening skills.

Do not appear to judge them

Of course, you have to be skeptical during negotiations, but do not be too obvious about it. No one likes to be judged, especially not by an openly skeptical person. They will speak more freely if they feel that you are trying to understand them, not trying to decide how wrong or dishonest their position is. So emphasize understanding, not evaluation; be a friendly, sympathetic listener, not an adversary who judges their position in right-wrong terms.

Clearly communicate that you are trying to understand

Even during an adversarial relationship, it is hard to get angry at someone who is trying to understand. If, for example, you ask sincere questions to clarify their position, people may feel that you are not particularly intelligent, but they will appreciate your motivation. They may therefore speak more openly.

Ignore your natural reluctance to ask them for clarification. You may dislike admitting your confusion, but doing so can improve both your understanding and your relationship. It is particularly important to clarify their offers because confusion there can cause extremely serious problems.

Don't talk too much

The popular stereotype is that top negotiators are fast-talking, persuasive wheeler-dealers. In fact, many of them are rather quiet. They listen rather than talk. They ask questions and wait respectfully for the answers. They create conversations and avoid speeches. They try for a dialogue and avoid monologues.

For example, the investment bank Drexel Burnham Lambert is famous for its wheelers and dealers, but Fred Joseph, the CEO, regards himself as a listener, preferring to let other people do most of the talking while he concentrates on listening, on learning what the clients really want.

Encourage them to talk

This encouragement should be both verbal and nonverbal. Most questions should be open-ended. Closed-ended questions can be answered in a few words: "What is your list price?" ($279.95) "How many people will you assign to this project?" (four professionals, one clerical) "When do you expect to complete this job?" (March 14) Note that the questions are often longer than the answers, and that the questioner is learning only the specific facts, not how the other side thinks.

Open-ended questions encourage a longer and broader response: "Would you explain your pricing policy?" "What do you think of our proposed schedule?" "Why do you feel that you need so many people?" In addition to producing more information, this sort of question helps you to understand the other side's thoughts and concerns.

Once they start talking, ask follow-up questions to get more information. "Could you explain that, please." "I'm not sure I understand you; do you mean...?" "How is that pricing policy related to your proposed schedule?"

Your manner and actions can be more important than your words. If you are clearly uninterested in what they are saying, they will probably stop talking or become argumentative. Conversely, if you seem sincerely interested, they will usually keep talking.

Communicate respect

Even if you disagree completely, listen respectfully to their position. Remember, your primary objective is not to score debating points; it is to understand their position. The more respectful you are, the more openly they will communicate.

Show that you understand

Listen actively, not passively. Play back what you think they mean. Explicitly link points made at different times to clarify the bigger picture. Summarize regularly. And take these actions in a tentative, interrogative way. Instead of saying, "You have three concerns," say, "You seem to have three concerns." The first comment can cause an argument; the second one invites them to clarify or to offer additional information.

Active listening greatly reduces repetitious speeches. People repeat themselves, often with raised voices, because they feel misunderstood. In fact, in many repetitious, sterile arguments both sides are essentially saying, "Since you were too stupid to understand my position the last time I expressed it, I will repeat it, more loudly and in simpler language, so someone of your limited intelligence can understand."

Conversely, when people feel understood, they have less need to repeat themselves. Your restating their position therefore allows them to move on to other subjects. It also clarifies issues in your own mind and encourages them to correct misunderstandings. They may even offer additional information. "Oh, I forgot to mention one other point...."

Observe Their Actions

People's actions are often much more revealing than their words. Nearly everyone can control their words better than their gestures, voices, and facial expressions. Even professional negotiators (hired guns) occasionally give themselves away. Alas, most people miss many cues, including quite obvious ones.

Observe and record their nonverbal actions

The next section will help you to interpret "body language," but you cannot interpret it unless you see and record it. Look for movements, gestures, facial expressions, intonation, hesitation, and so on. Record your observations; then look for patterns and links to their words and later actions.

Look for negative cues

Negative cues are actions they did not take, and these cues can be even more revealing than positive ones. For example, if you make an outrageous offer, and they do not get angry, your offer may not be so outrageous after all. Their limit may be much more favorable to you than you originally expected.

If you offer a concession on one issue, and they switch to another issue without discussing your concession, you may have passed their MSP on this issue. For example, if you reduce your price by 2% and they immediately shift to maintenance costs, they may have tacitly accepted your price.

Negative cues are much subtler and harder to read than positive ones. You will miss most of them unless you observe carefully, take complete notes, and use the hypothesis-testing approach. Before you act, predict their reactions. Remember Sherlock Holmes' famous dogs that did *not* bark. If they react differently from your expectations, ask yourself why. Nonaction is no more random than action. If they did not act, there is probably a reason. Since the dogs did not bark, Holmes inferred that they had not been disturbed by anyone. Learn that reason, and you may have the key to their position.

Probe for Additional Information

Listening and observing are valuable, but passive. You must supplement them with more active methods. You must probe, even if it makes you uncomfortable. People tend to think that probing is just asking direct questions, but there are many other probing techniques, and you should use all of them.

Ask direct questions

The simplest way to get information is to ask for it. Do not be afraid to ask questions such as: "Who else is bidding?" or "How soon do you need it?" or "How much do you want to spend?" Most people do not ask enough questions. They forget to ask some and are reluctant to ask others.

Forgetting to ask questions

The forgetting problem is easy to remedy. Before negotiating, list all your questions. During the negotiations add to your list. Then check them off as they are answered. But do not accept just any answer. Try for a complete and accurate one. For example, during negotiations to purchase a used car, the following exchange often occurs.

Buyer: "Why are you selling it?"
Seller: "I don't need it anymore."
Buyer: "OK, what is the mileage?"

The buyer may feel that he has asked an important question, but the answer is so vague and general that it means nothing. The buyer should have asked follow-up questions to learn the specific reasons for selling the car, such as, "Do you now have two cars and only need one?" or "Do you take the train to work and have no need for a car anymore?" or "Are you so short of money that you are desperately raising cash?"

Reluctance to ask questions

Reluctance to ask questions is a much more difficult problem. It can be caused by many factors such as embarrassment about one's ignorance, fear of offending, and expectations that they will not tell the truth anyway. None of them is a valid excuse. Ignorance may be embarrassing now, but not asking enough questions can cause a bad deal and make you look really foolish.

Fear of offending the other party is another inhibition that you must learn to ignore. You are not trying to start a love affair; you are trying to negotiate a good deal, and you need information to get it. Ask those questions, even if the other side resists answering. You have been taught since birth not to ask rude questions, and, consciously or unconsciously, you may avoid subjects that make the other side uncomfortable.

For example, a couple who were interested in buying a house requested an exterminator's inspection. After consulting the sellers, the realtor told them, "They are insulted that you would want such an inspection. What kind of people do you think they are?" Embarrassed, the buyers withdrew their request.

Do I need to tell you the rest of the story? Probably not, but I will anyway. They bought the house, moved in, and discovered that it was infested with rats. Disgusted with the sellers and angry with themselves, they sold out immediately, losing about $20,000.

They had acted in the trusting way that matched their social training, but had ignored the fact that negotiations are essentially adversarial, with different rules from other relationships. One of those rules is: The less they want to talk about a subject, the more you should focus upon it. The critical information is likely to be right there.

Evasions and lies are less of a problem than you may think. Many people will tell you the truth, particularly if your question is worded and timed well. Some people will lie, of course, but most people do not lie very well. Their voice or manner may give them away.

An obvious lie may be more helpful than the truth. If you can infer the truth from their manner and other information, you may actually learn more than you would have learned from a truthful answer. Their lying suggests that this issue is important to them, which tells you something about their priorities and suggests that they are hiding something significant.

You might then ask yourself: "Why are they avoiding subject A and lying about subject B? Perhaps they are under extreme time pressure. Therefore, if I ask '....,' they will probably.... I can also check with Joe; he usually knows about this sort of situation."

Probe gently

Gentle probes are questions, statements, or actions that relax people and open them up. They create a natural, conversational atmosphere that reduces both your discomfort and the danger they will become offended. For example, if you act sympathetically, they may tell you their troubles, including ones that weaken their case.

Gentle probes are particularly effective outside the negotiations because the climate is more relaxed. If you create a good relationship and then probe gently, you may learn exactly what you need to know, while making them like and trust you.

As with so many other lessons, I learned the power of gentle probes accidentally. My wife and I had been very carefully searching for a new home during a buyers' market. We had all the time in the world and we must have looked at over 50 houses. I loved one of them, but could not sell it to my wife.

One pleasant Sunday, because I had nothing to do between appointments to look at other houses, I stopped in to chat with the seller. As we walked along the street, enjoying the fine weather, part of our conversation went like this.

> "It really must be boring to spend every Sunday trying to sell a house."
> "I hate it."
> "So would I."
> "You have no idea what it's like. I work hard, six days a week. You know, you've been in my restaurant. On Sundays I want to relax. Instead, I'm stuck with this damned house. It's not my house. It's my mother's. When Dad died, and she moved out, I told her to price it realistically, but, no, she listened to the other children. But what do they do to help? Nothing! *My* wife cleans the place. *My* children cut the grass. *I'm* here every Sunday! Well, I'm fed up. Last week we had a little 'family council' meeting, and the others finally agreed that we would take whatever price is necessary to move this damned thing!"

Never could I have learned all that information by direct questioning. My gentle, conversational manner—which was caused, not by cleverness, but by knowing that my wife would not buy the place—opened the floodgates, releasing extremely valuable information. I wish I could claim that I whipped out my checkbook and made a great deal. Alas, I could not sell that house to my wife at any price. A few years later it had tripled in value. Oh well, live and learn.

Pause after probing

Whenever you probe, pause to give them plenty of time to respond. Any other action has undesirable effects. If you explain or expand a question, you give them time to think of a clever or deceptive answer. Their first reaction is likely to be more revealing than one they have carefully considered.

If you allow them only enough time to make a brief answer, you may cut them off before they finish answering. In fact, the important information often comes last. Many people start to answer with banalities, then, after they have gotten over their own inhibitions, they say what really matters.

If you change the subject or ask additional questions, they may feel cross examined and become stubborn or evasive.

Pauses give them time to answer, allow the power of silence to work for you, and communicate your respect for their desire to think. They may then talk more freely.

Make probing offers

Probing offers test the other side's reactions. For example, to learn if their limits are more favorable to you than the situation suggests, you might make an outrageous offer. If they do not object strongly, perhaps your offer is not so outrageous; it may be closer than you expected to their limit (or even past it). Perhaps, because of unknown factors they are desperate for a deal.

Offers to trade can help you understand their priorities. *In the early stages you should trade in principle* (e.g., "Will you give us a discount if we pay promptly?"). Note that we did not say how large a discount or how promptly, because our objective is to learn their general priorities and situation. A positive response to that offer would suggest that, within limits, prompt payment is more important than price, implying that they may have a cash flow problem. A negative response suggests the opposite.

Let's say that they responded positively. The next step is to become more specific. How much of a discount will they trade for how prompt a payment? Will they give, say, two percent for 30 days? For 10 days? For cash?

You will normally learn more by first trading in principle and then becoming more specific than you would learn by starting with specifics. For example, if you started by asking for a two percent discount for 30 days, they might bluntly reject your offer, thereby causing you to think that they are not concerned about cash flow. Trading in principle and then negotiating the specific amount might result in, perhaps, a one percent discount for payment in 10 days, an excellent return on your money.

Follow up your probes

Most people do not follow up their probes. They ask a question, get an uninformative answer, then drop the subject. They may even drop it when people's reactions suggest that their probes have struck a nerve. For example, if a question upsets the other side, they may politely change the subject—even though the reaction suggests that this topic is critically important.

Most people will not admit their weaknesses openly, nor will they tell you their objectives and strategy. You must probe for that information, and this probing should normally be done in two distinct phases: exploratory and intensive.

First, explore all the significant issues. Look for reactions to your probes that suggest the sensitive areas. For example, evasiveness or embarrassment suggest sensitivity. Insistence that a subject is not relevant suggests that it may be very relevant indeed. A later section of this chapter lists many other cues and their possible meaning.

Then intensively probe the sensitive areas. You may ask direct questions, probe gently, offer trades, threaten, and so forth, but do not drop the subject. Stick with it, then return to it again and again until you are sure that you understand it.

Intensive probing can be unpleasant because you must often focus on subjects the other side wants to avoid. But, as we noted a few moments ago, the more they want to avoid a subject, the more you may gain by probing into it. If you see signs of sensitivity about a subject, keep probing until you know why they feel that way.

INTERPRET INFORMATION

Information is useless unless it is interpreted correctly. You should use the new information to revise your original analysis. Focus primarily on their objectives, power, and strategy, but also consider their personalities, perception of you, and other subjects. This section discusses three topics:

A. General principles
B. The pattern of offers
C. Reading their script

General Principles

In this section we discuss a few general rules for interpreting information. All these principles must, of course, be applied judiciously. They fit some situations, but not others.

Look for patterns

Isolated actions can be useful, but patterns of actions are usually more informative. Unfortunately, patterns are often subtle, and your ability to see them is reduced by your need to react to their specific actions. You may therefore fail to see the forest for the trees.

To get an overall perspective, step away from the action so that you can think about what it all means. How does their current attitude relate to their initial position? What is the link between their proposals on price and maintenance? On which issues are they most and least willing to compromise? As you answer these questions, patterns will slowly emerge.

Look for inconsistencies

Pay particular attention to conflicts between your earlier judgments and their actions because they suggest that your original analysis was incorrect. Prospective buyers of a commercial lot might, for example, make an opening offer higher than your original estimate of their MSP. You thought that their limit was $390,000, and their first offer is $425,000.

Of course, you are delighted, but do not just take the money and run. Recognize the obvious fact that you have misread the situation. Your entire strategy is probably based on an incorrect analysis.

Revise that analysis based on all the information available to you and think of ways to get additional information. Why are they willing to pay so much? Maybe they are accumulating several properties to build a shopping center or apartment complex. Perhaps you should find out whether other properties have changed hands recently.

That sort of analysis can make an enormous difference. For example, if they really need your lot to complete a large project, you might get $600,000, perhaps even a million dollars for it.

Be skeptical

Unless you know and trust the other side, take nothing at face value. People, even otherwise honest ones, do lie during negotiations. Even those who would not flatly lie may stretch the truth or omit important elements of it.

The need for skepticism is one reason for some of our other recommendations. For example, separating observations from inferences provides some protection from the plausible liar (and there are lots of them around). Taking frequent breaks increases your chances of seeing conflicts between people's words and their actions.

Remember, in all negotiations your interests conflict to some degree, and the other side is acting on its interests, not yours—regardless of how friendly, honest, or fair they may seem. So take everything they say and do with at least a grain of salt.

Beware of apparently irrational actions

One of the most basic rules of warfare is: never underestimate your opponent. If the other side seems to act against their own interests, the natural reaction is to take advantage of their stupidity. But they may be much smarter than you think. Before committing yourself, learn why they are acting that way. Perhaps they understand the situation better than you do.

For example, after very minor accidents, insurance claims adjusters often offer $100 or so above one's direct costs for inconvenience. Some people delightedly take this free money, only to learn later that accepting it prevents them from collecting anything if unexpected injuries show up (as often occurs with back and other injuries). That "free" $100 may sometimes cost them $250,000!

The U.S. Post Office, in its campaign against postal fraud, has developed a useful slogan: "If something seems too good to be true, it probably isn't true."

If someone is being too generous, beware. Perhaps they are fools, but do not act on that assumption before checking it carefully. If they seem to be giving away too much, you may be walking into a trap.

Look for relatively reliable cues

There are no completely reliable cues. The meaning of any action depends upon its context, and people will often make mistakes or act inconsistently. Understanding them is, therefore, like putting together a puzzle. You slowly assemble the pieces, but you cannot be sure that they fit together. In fact, when you try to put them together, some of them may not fit at all.

Even though no cues are completely reliable, certain actions do provide more or less dependable hints of their objectives, power and strategy. Constantly look for these cues. When you see one, formulate and test a hypothesis.

For example, if they avoid eye contact and speak hesitantly when they make a demand, they may feel that it is not justified. Regard that possibility as a hypothesis, then test it by acting angry or hurt. If they show other signs of shame or embarrassment, you can be fairly sure that your hypothesis is correct. Probe for the causes of their feelings. Perhaps they are making a false demand to create bargaining or trading room. Or they may be under pressure from their boss to get a concession which they feel is unreasonable.

Later sections of this chapter will suggest the meanings of the most reliable cues: the pattern of offers, certain words, and nonverbal actions.

Break frequently

If you do not take breaks, you probably cannot interpret information correctly. When you are negotiating, your focus is too narrow. Having to listen to their comments and plan your responses prevents you from thinking of the larger picture. So break frequently and ask yourself: What have I learned? What additional information do I need? What does it all mean?

Some people are afraid that taking frequent breaks will make them look weak or indecisive. A few people will see you that way, but most of us respect people who think carefully before acting. Besides, the other side's annoyance or temporarily lower opinion of you is usually much less important than your need to think before acting. So take as many breaks as you need.

Breaks also help you to implement a revised strategy. It is much easier to change directions after a break than during a negotiation. You can essentially stop, set your feet, and move in a new direction. For example, Jack's break and discussion with his partners helped him to see his mistakes with George and develop a new and much better strategy. In the second session he put together a mutually satisfactory deal. However, he should have taken a break during the price bargaining. He might then have realized that he was conceding too much and bargained harder, thereby getting a higher price.

Propose, then test hypotheses

Hypothesis testing is the primary method of most modern scientists. They examine data, propose an explanatory hypothesis and test this hypothesis against new data. For example, if someone thought that a disease was caused by a specific chemical, it could be injected into healthy rats to test their reaction. This approach quickly corrects false hypotheses. If the rats do not develop the disease, the hypothesis is rejected.

This approach can help you to analyze your negotiations. When you think you know why they have done something, ask: "If my interpretation is correct, what else would they do?" Then create an appropriate situation and test their reactions. For example, if they are bluffing, they would probably yield if you gently threatened to end the negotiations. Try it and see what happens.

Many people do not test their hypotheses. They are unsure of their interpretations and afraid that a test will slow down or halt the negotiations. But the less sure you are, the more important a test is! Perhaps you are wrong, but it is much better to know than to wonder.

Tests teach you something, no matter how they turn out. If they support your hypothesis, you can act confidently. If the test proves you wrong, you know that you must analyze further. You may even know which way to turn.

Plan to acquire additional information

As you interpret your information, you will usually find gaps in it. You simply do not have all of the information you need. You should immediately write down what you need and your plans for getting it.

Again, a two-column technique is probably best.

INFORMATION NEEDED	WAYS TO GET IT
Their financial position	Credit bureau
	Other vendors
	Barbara at the local bank
Their plans	Ask them:
	Launch date
	Promotional budget
	Who is ad agency?
	Take Jim to lunch. He used
	to work for them.

A few notes like this can help you immensely. Without them, you can easily forget to acquire the information you need or attempt to get it in the wrong way or at the wrong time. For example, direct questions about their financial situation may cause them to lie or be offended, while inquiries to other parties may be both more informative and less offensive.

Constantly ask why

It is the critical question, yet it is not asked often enough. You need to know the underlying causes for their actions such as their objectives, power and strategy. You will not learn these underlying causes without repeatedly asking: "Why?"

Why did they take such an extreme position? (Perhaps they do not need the deal as much as you expected.) Why did they spend so much time on such an apparently minor point? (Probably because it is much more important to them than you thought.) Why are they so much friendlier today than they were before? (Maybe another deal has fallen apart and they really need this one.) Then, go beyond the little questions and ask the big ones: Why have they done all these things? How do they fit together? What are their real motives?

The Pattern Of Offers

Offers are the most important negotiating actions, and the pattern of these offers is an excellent cue to people's objectives. In single-issue negotiations, the Past ROM (past ratio of movement), the comparative distance that both sides have moved, is the most reliable cue. In multiple-issue negotiations you must look at the larger picture. Where and how fast are they moving?

The past ratio of movement (Past ROM)

The Past ROM ratio is meaningful only in one-issue negotiations or in multiple-issue negotiations with one supremely important issue. It tells you the ratio between the distance that both sides have moved after an equal number of concessions. For example, if you have both moved $10,000, the ratio is 1:1. If they have moved $10,000, while you have moved $5,000, the ratio is 2:1. Although the ratio can be computed as soon as both sides have made one concession, it becomes a more reliable source of information as the number of offers increases. A ratio based on only one or two offers from each side is much less dependable than one based on four or five offers.

To estimate their MSP, compute the Past ROM and divide the gap separating your current positions according to that ratio. Then go a little further to adjust for the fact that people normally leave a safety factor. If they aim for a certain number, it is probably within their limit, not at the exact limit.

The basic logic is the same as one uses to extrapolate other trends. For example, if someone has hit 19 home runs in the first half of the season, we can predict that he will probably hit about 38 home runs in the entire season. The following diagram illustrates our procedure.

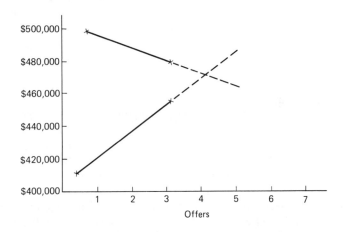

You offered $500,000 and they countered at $410,000. The initial gap is therefore $90,000, and your primary question is how that $90,000 will be divided.

After each side had made three concessions, you were at $480,000, while they were at $450,000. Since they had moved twice as far as you did ($40,000 vs. $20,000), the Past ROM was 2:1. If we continue these trends, and have them concede two thirds of the remaining gap ($30,000), you would end up at $470,000.

Since they seem to be aiming for that number, they can probably pay a somewhat higher price. Their MSP is probably higher than $470,000.

Of course, extrapolating trends is risky. The baseball player may get hurt or have a slump. The negotiator may not realize that continuing this pattern of offers will result in a deal at $470,000. Your estimate of their MSP should therefore be just a hypothesis to be tested.

The sequence of concessions

The same principles apply to multiple-issue negotiations, but you must look at the larger picture. The key questions are: where are they moving and how much are they moving? If, for example, a buyer has made three concessions on price and two on interest rate, but flatly refuses to move on the down payment, the down payment is a top priority. You can also speculate on the reasons for this priority—perhaps they are squeezed for cash.

The trades they offer and their reaction to your proposed trades can also clarify their priorities and limits. People usually offer or accept trades that give them concessions on their higher priority issues. An offer to delay a project's completion date for a change in the specifications suggests that time is less important than the specifications.

However, there may be limits to the amount that they can move. They might, for example, trade a deadline extension of one month for some specifications changes, then trade another month's extension for better financing, but refuse to extend the deadline any further, no matter what you offer to trade. That pattern clearly suggests that they could afford a two-month delay, but they cannot accept any additional delays.

Reading Their Script

You can rarely be sure that you are correctly reading their script, but certain words and actions suggest strength or weakness, acceptance or rejection, confidence or doubt. Since these cues are not completely reliable, you must interpret them cautiously and look for patterns. You cannot feel sure of your interpretation unless several cues support each other or fit the pattern of offers or other information.

The meaning of any cue depends upon the individual's personality, culture, and situation. In addition, culture is particularly important. The following points refer *only* to Americans and Canadians. Some of them may also apply to people from northern Europe. The less similar the culture, the less reliable these cues are. The same actions by various people or by the same people in different situations can have quite different meanings. You should therefore always consider a cue's context. As my associate Doug Lind says, "Take movies, not snapshots. Relate this cue to its overall context."

The cues we will discuss suggest people's thoughts or feelings, but not the underlying causes. People may, for example, seem weak or unsure of themselves because they lack self-confidence, are in an objectively weak position, or feel that their position is illogical or unfair. You must therefore probe further to learn why they feel the way they do.

Natural versus unnatural actions

Natural, relaxed, comfortable actions suggest strength or confidence, while unnatural, uncomfortable, or forced ones suggest weakness or doubts. For example, many people smile too much, laugh at inappropriate times, or are overly casual. Because it is the most general rule, always ask yourself whether actions are natural or forced.

Confidence

Genuine confidence should usually be taken at face value, but attempts to present a confident image suggest weakness or doubt. Direct statements of confidence, blustering, overselling, and so on suggest that they may be whistling in the dark to keep up their courage.

Dominance

If they naturally dominate the discussion, they probably feel powerful. If they struggle for dominance, insist upon winning minor battles, or become upset by trivial challenges, they almost certainly feel weak. They need the symbols because they doubt their real power.

Submission

Submission nearly always implies weakness or doubts. You can therefore probe by trying to dominate the discussions; if they let you get away with it, they probably feel weak.

Indifference

Genuine indifference clearly signals strength; they do not really need the deal. Selling implies the opposite; the harder they sell, the more they need it. Excessive or feigned indifference, such as failing to get down to business or frequently shifting to irrelevant subjects, hints that they may be trying to hide their weakness. Look especially for inconsistent statements such as, "I don't care if you don't participate in this investment. You are passing up a good deal, leaving more profit for us." They claim to be indifferent, but are really selling hard.

Anger

Expressing anger in a controlled way or trying to suppress it indicates confidence. Excessive reactions such as shouting, banging fists on the table, jabbing you with their fingers, and so on, suggest that they either lack self-control or feel so weak that they rely on emotions.

Friendliness

Normal, relaxed friendliness generally shows confidence. Excessive friendliness or repeated references to your friendly relationship are a reliable sign of weakness, particularly if they come from mere acquaintances. They may want to trade on your friendship or arouse your inhibitions about taking advantage of friends. Be especially skeptical about statements such as, "We have been friends for so long that our friendship is more important than this deal."

References to their importance as a vendor or customer

An occasional reference may mean nothing at all. Frequent references are a sign of weakness or insecurity. You both realize your relationship's importance, and these reminders may signify their need for reassurance.

Appeals to your sense of fairness or justice

These appeals imply weakness. They may be trying to arouse your inhibitions about using your power against them.

References to common interests

Without other information, these references are ambiguous. In mixed negotiations they could mean a genuine desire to emphasize joint problem solving. However, in essentially pure-bargaining situations, they suggest weakness. They may be trying for a cooperative climate to keep you from using your greater power against them.

Walkouts

Walkouts are hard to interpret, but too important to ignore. They can signal either strength or weakness, genuine anger or a devious ploy, depending upon the context, the manner of leaving, whether there is a visible means for reopening the negotiations, and who makes the next contact.

If neither party has to reach an agreement, walking out generally communicates indifference and power, especially if they have insisted that they will not contact you. If you do not contact them and make a concession, they will just do business with somebody else.

If you must continue to work with each other, the walkout is ambiguous. Perhaps they feel that you have to come to them, or they may feel that they cannot possibly win the negotiation. They might then let you take unilateral actions which they can ignore or disavow. For example, the Russians walked out of the UN very frequently from 1945 to 1955 when they were much weaker than the U.S., but rarely do so now that the power balance is approximately equal.

Look also at the way they walk out. If they move slowly or look over their shoulder to see your reaction, they probably do not want to leave.

The meaning of a walkout may not become clear until after the negotiations resume. If you do not contact each other, you may never learn what it meant. If you contact them and they respond eagerly, they probably felt weak earlier, but they may now be encouraged by your contacting them. If they are indifferent when you contact them, they probably felt powerful before and even stronger now. If they contact you, the walkout may have been a ploy to hide their weakness, and they may feel even weaker now. The stated reason for contacting you may not be to reopen the negotiations. They may, for example, come back to get their keys, papers, or something else. Or you may meet accidentally at the country club or a friend's house.

Not walking out

Not leaving can be as informative as walking out. It can tell you that their final offers and threats are just empty words. For example, if they do not pick up their papers after making a final offer, it is probably not final at all. If they say, "Your offer is ridiculous; we will not even discuss it," and then they discuss it, your offer may be quite attractive.

Reassurances about their honesty

If they say, "To be frank with you," or "I want to be honest with you," or "I feel that we should be as open as possible," they are probably lying. If they insist on their honesty, they are almost certainly lying. The harder they sell their honesty, the surer you can be that they are not honest at all.

Reassurances about their concern for your welfare

The more they claim to have your interests at heart, the surer you can be that they are trying to deceive or manipulate you. Statements such as, "I would not offer a deal like this to anyone else," are reliable indicators of ulterior motives.

Avoiding eye contact

Looking at their papers, hands, the wall, or any place except you implies embarrassment, shame, or insecurity. They may be lying, ashamed of their unreasonable demand, or unsure of your reaction to their proposals.

Excessive eye contact

The exactly opposite action has essentially the same meaning. If they stare fixedly into your eyes, they are probably forcing themselves to maintain eye contact. They would rather look away, but are trying not to show it.

Closed actions

Closed actions include frowning, shaking the head, folding the arms, crossing the legs, clenching fists, leaning or moving away, and buttoning one's coat. Each is a sign of rejection or a closed mind. If several of them occur simultaneously, they really do reject your position.

Open actions

Open actions include smiling, nodding the head, unfolding the arms, opening fists, spreading the arms apart, leaning or moving toward you, and unbuttoning one's coat. Each signals acceptance or an open mind. If several of them occur simultaneously, they probably accept or are at least open-minded about your position.

Holding or touching you

They may be afraid that you will go away. They may be so unsure of their position or your interest that they are trying to keep you from leaving.

Holding or touching oneself

Rubbing the hands together, stroking the face, neck, beard, or other parts of the body, and running fingers through the hair signal insecurity or weakness. The individual is essentially comforting himself the way that a parent comforts a child.

Lengthy justifications

The longer they talk about the reasons for making their offer or rejecting yours, the more skeptical you should become. To paraphrase Shakespeare: They protest too much.

Hesitation, pauses, slow speech, and lowered voice

These actions frequently occur together. Each suggests weakness or doubts, and the combination of all four almost always signifies those feelings. These cues are particularly likely to occur when they take positions they feel are unreasonable.

Statements of near agreement

Statements such as, "We are not too far apart," "We can work something out," or "Let's keep talking," imply that your last offer is within or very close to their limit. They want to try for more, but do not want to risk a deadlock.

Offers to split the difference

After a long deadlock, the meaning of these offers is ambiguous. They may just be trying to break the deadlock. At other times this offer usually suggests that they can make additional concessions.

Quick or casual offers to split (e.g., "The heck with it, let's just split the difference.") suggest that your last offer was within their range. They feel relaxed and casual because it is all your money anyway.

Offers to flip a coin for the difference

These offers are a strong signal that you have passed their limit. They can afford to gamble because it is all your money.

Approximate or tentative offers

Terms such as "approximately," "about," "in the range of," "first offer," or "initial position," suggest a readiness to make additional concessions.

Requests for agreement or comments on their offer

After making an offer, they may ask, "Do you agree?" or "What do you think of that?" or "How does that sound to you?" These questions are often bids for reassurance. They may have a low opinion of their offer and want your reassurance.

Disagreements between words and actions

Actions are generally more reliable than words because people can lie much better than they can control their actions. If they say, "No," while leaning forward, nodding their head, and smiling, they probably mean "Yes."

Therefore, whenever their words and their actions disagree, hypothesize that the actions reveal their true feelings; then test your hypothesis by probing further. For example, if you suspect that they feel insecure, you might threaten to break off the negotiations. If you think that they feel embarrassed about their offer, you could act hurt and protest that they are being unreasonable.

Inconsistent actions

If you see signs of strength and weakness or acceptance and rejection, they may be ambivalent, confused, or pretending.

Consistent actions

The more consistent their actions are, the more confidence you can have in your interpretation. For example, if they repeatedly refer to the amount of business they have done with you, avoid eye contact, lengthily justify every position, appeal to your sense of fairness, and hold onto your arm, you can be almost certain that they are unsure of themselves or their position.

The cues we have described are easy to overlook. You may be so intent on understanding their offers or preparing your replies that you miss signs of insecurity, acceptance, or embarrassment. In addition, many skilled negotiators are good enough actors to hide their true feelings.

Understanding the other side's beliefs and feelings therefore requires concentration, sensitivity, and the ability to focus on these subtle and often unconscious signals. Your task is complicated by the fact that the meaning of any cue depends upon the individual and the context. Despite these limitations, the effort spent on reading these cues is certainly justified. They can provide insights that you could not get any other way.

USE THE INFORMATION TO REVISE YOUR STRATEGY

Revising your strategy requires the same method that you used to develop your original strategy, with two important differences. First, you now have so much more information that your plans should be much more complete. Second, the actions that both sides have already taken can reduce your options; some desirable changes may be impossible. Since the method is generally the same, we recommend that you consult the "Plan your Strategy" section in chapter 2.

Four elements of your original strategy should be emphasized: the general approach, alternative approaches, questions, and concessions. One element, your initial position, cannot be revised because you have already taken it. Another one, stage setting, can be revised slightly, but large changes could undermine your credibility; for example, dramatically changing your image could raise serious doubts about who you really are.

The General Approach

The first task is to revise your general approach. Now that you have spent some time with the other party, what approach seems best? If your original approach seemed to work well, you should stick with it or revise it slightly. If you had serious problems, larger changes seem necessary. Follow that old sports maxim: Never change a winning strategy; always change a losing one.

However, your options are somewhat restricted. Extreme changes in any strategic element can create credibility problems, and the actions already taken may prevent you from selecting certain approaches. For example, if you have already exchanged a great deal of information and made substantial concessions, you probably should not shift to a curt, unyielding approach.

You must therefore choose an approach that fits both the preexisting situation and the constraints created by the prior negotiations. It may be quite different from the one you would have originally chosen with better information, but you have to adjust to the current constraints.

The negotiations between Jack and George offer a good example of revising an unsuccessful strategy. Jack's original approach had been too hard line. He got down to business too quickly, stated his position too forcefully, did not listen to George's position, and essentially tried to sell his proposal.

After talking to his partners, he dramatically changed his approach. He apologized for the problems in the first session, said that he would consider using Joan, learned why George wanted her on the project, and worked out a solution to their mutual problem.

Alternative Approaches

When you first prepared for this negotiation, you probably had to consider several approaches because your information was so limited. You essentially made contingency plans. If, for example, they had taken a hard line position, you would.... GIf they showed a lot of eagerness and flexibility, you would....

Now that you know how they are acting, most, perhaps all of these contingency plans have probably become less important, even obsolete. However, it might be useful to review those plans. Perhaps some parts of them can be incorporated into your current strategy.

In addition, you may want to dust off some of those plans just in case the other side suddenly changes its strategy.

Questions

By now most of your original questions should be answered. Check your original list, make sure that your answers are complete, and plan to get any additional information you need.

Concessions

Planning your future concessions is exceptionally important. Now that you have a fairly clear idea of their limits and priorities, concentrate on planning a series of concessions and trades that produces the best deal.

In single-issue negotiations try to maximize your share of the bargaining range. In multiple-issue negotiations try to fit together a deal that satisfies both parties' major priorities, while giving you most of the money on the table. The next few paragraphs discuss the general logic; the specific tactics are discussed in several other chapters, particularly chapter 4, "The Middle Game," and chapter 7, "The End Game."

Maximizing your share of the bargaining range

Although most people would agree that they should try to maximize their share, few of them actually try to do so. In the preparation phase they set a target that is usually a little better than their MSP. Even if they learn that the other side can give them much more, they do not seriously try for it. They settle close to the original target, without carefully considering all the money (or other things) that they are leaving on the table.

You should be more rational; since every dollar that you leave on the table is objectively as valuable as the ones you take away, plan to get as many as you can without defeating your other objectives. If, for example, you are uninterested in your future relationship, you might try to drive them right to their limit. If your future relationship is important, you might plan just to pick up the loose change (the money or other concessions that are not highly valued).

Apply the same general logic you used to set your MSP. You set it to prevent yourself from conceding too much, and you should keep it right where it is (unless your situation has changed). But revise your goal to prevent yourself from settling too soon.

First, revise your estimate of their MSP. Second, decide how confident you are that your revised estimate is correct. If you are not confident, keep probing and revising your estimate; if you are quite confident, take the next two steps. Third, decide how close to their MSP you should try to get. Fourth, plan a strategy to get there.

Fitting together a mutiple-issue deal

The same logic applies to multiple-issue negotiations, but the process is more complicated. Instead of a single bargaining range, you have to divide several of them, and you probably should not try to maximize your share of each one. Since concessions on some issues are much more valuable to you, plan to get as much as you can on your high priority issues by trading concessions on less important issues.

There is, of course, the same conflict between motives that we saw with single-issue negotiations; you may want to get the best deal for yourself and satisfy the other side. But this conflict may be less intense because the game is not zero-sum (your gains are not exactly equal to their losses).

Despite the reduced intensity, the principles are essentially the same: You need a clear idea of where you want to go and a plan to get there. You can try for any type of deal from completely in your favor to an evenly balanced deal, and your actions must fit the goal you select.

SUMMARY

Although the Feedback Loop is critically important throughout the entire negotiation, most people do not use it very well. They may not listen, observe, or probe thoroughly, or they may misinterpret the information they do acquire or continue strategies long after they are obviously unsuccessful. To correct these errors you must genuinely want to understand the other side and shift your focus from your own position to theirs.

The Feedback Loop contains four steps: acquire information, interpret it, use it to revise your strategy, then implement the revised strategy. Although the steps naturally occur in that order, there is also a circular relationship; as you interpret or use information, you may find that it is incomplete or inaccurate, forcing you to get more of it. The chapter discussed only the first three steps because implementation issues are covered extensively in other chapters.

Acquiring information is the essential first step. You have to get it before you can interpret and use it. You can get more information by applying some general principles: Make them want to communicate, take your time, take notes, appoint an observer, and separate observations from inferences. The three main methods for obtaining information are listening, observing, and probing.

Interpreting information is the next step. You have to decide what it means and how your original analysis must be changed. The important general principles are to look for patterns, look for inconsistencies, be skeptical, beware of apparently irrational actions, break frequently, propose, then test hypotheses, and constantly ask why. The chapter also listed a large number of reliable cues, but cautioned that no cues are completely reliable because their meaning depends upon the person and context. You must therefore see several consistent cues to be confident of your interpretation.

Using information to revise your strategy requires the same methods used to develop your original strategy. However, there are two major differences. First, you have so much more information that your plans should be much more complete and detailed. Second, the actions that both sides have already taken constrain you; you cannot select some strategic options because they would conflict with the past patterns. The most important actions are to revise your general approach and your anticipated concessions. You must set new targets and develop a detailed plan to reach them.

6

Positioning Yourself

We have been focusing on the the actual negotiations—the verbal exchanges—but some authorities believe that these exchanges are much less important than the negotiators' ability to position themselves. *Positioning means getting ready for actions before you take them,* and many positioning steps are taken outside the negotiations, perhaps even long before they begin.

I learned the importance of positioning in an exceptionally unpleasant way. My dissertation was on collective bargaining negotiations. Since I was training to be a psychologist, the research naturally focused on what people said and did during negotiating sessions. At the University of California, Berkeley, the reviewing committee normally included a professor from outside the department; I unfortunately had one who did not think much of the psychological approach to negotiations.

He said, "Alan, your research is not really meaningful. What counts is not what people say during a negotiation; the important thing is the positions they establish outside the negotiations. For example, if management takes a hard line, but has a weak cash position and cannot ship its inventories during a strike, the union will call their bluff because they know that management cannot afford a strike."

I did not like hearing it, but there is considerable truth to his criticism. Words are often less important than the positions both sides establish for themselves. By chance I was living in England during one of the coal miners' successful strikes. They won and actually forced a national government to resign. A few years later the coal miners, despite an extremely aggressive leader, lost a strike because they positioned themselves poorly. First, they had public sympathy in the earlier strike, public resentment in the later one. Second, they won when they struck during a cold winter with small stockpiles of coal, lost when they struck when coal was much less essential. Third and most important, they won when they had the other unions' support, lost when the railroad and other unions were willing to ship coal. Mr. Arthur Scargill, their leader, did not do his homework, and they paid for his careless positioning.

Our definition of the positioning principle is somewhat broader than my professor's. Here it means *anything* you do to build your power *before* you need or use that power. It therefore includes actions taken before the negotiations, ones taken during the negotiation, but outside of the actual sessions, and ones taken in the sessions.

By power we mean anything that can influence the other side. It therefore includes both objective and psychological power, your objective ability to reward or punish them, plus their beliefs and feelings about you and your situation. Both positive feelings such as trust, and negative ones such as fear can influence them.

Almost anything you do can affect your bargaining position. For example, if you casually let someone know that your sales are down and you really need business, a potential customer may hear of your weak position and drive a hard bargain. Or, if you have established a reputation as a sharp or even dishonest person, people may not trust you, even when you are telling the truth.

Since this subject is so broad, we will focus primarily on positioning yourself for the End Game. Positioning is important throughout the entire negotiations, but it is particularly important during the End Game because the real money changes hands, and you usually do not have enough time to improve your position.

The real money is shorthand for the painful concessions when you are close to your limit. These concessions do not necessarily concern money; the critical point is that they hurt. The early concessions may just cut away the fat built into the initial positions. As the negotiations progress, the concessions becoming increasingly painful, and the final ones are the most painful of all.

If you do not enter the End Game with a strong position, the other side may not make those final concessions. For example, if you have not saved something for a final concession, you may not be able to make a final trade to close the deal; you are therefore forced to say, in effect, "Take it or leave it," and they may prefer to leave it. Or, if you have not created the right attitudes, you may not have enough credibility to get those final concessions.

Deadline pressures increase the importance of a strong position. In earlier phases you may have time to position yourself by finding alternatives or taking other actions. When you enter the End Game, it is usually too late to change your position. You either already have a good position or suffer the consequences.

We shall recommend four ways to position yourself for the End Game. In addition, since any negotiation may end inconclusively, we will also discuss positioning yourself for the next round, such as a negotiation with someone else or an appeal to an authority. This chapter is divided into six sections:

I. Creating Credible Alternatives
II. Selecting Appropriate Attitudes

CREATING CREDIBLE ALTERNATIVES

The better your alternatives, the less you need to reach an agreement. But this objective power does not directly create psychological power (the ability to influence the other side). It comes from their beliefs, not objective reality. They must *believe* that you are willing to accept other options. You should therefore take two steps: create attractive alternatives and make them credible.

Create Attractive Alternatives

This action must always be taken outside the negotiations, usually before they begin. It takes time to find other suppliers or customers, to build up your inventories, and so on.

Attractive alternatives essentially let you set your MSP at a better point. For example, if you desperately need an immediate sale and have no other prospects, you may have to give a huge discount. If you have lots of time and two other hot prospects, you can hold out for a better price.

Not having good alternatives may also affect your entire approach. Almost any sales rep will tell you that the easiest sale to make is the one that you do not need. When you are certain of making quota and have lots of good prospects, you naturally act in a confident way that brings in business. When you really need that sale, you will often "blow it."

Unless you are one of those rare people who can act coolly and effectively in a very weak position, you need to ease the pressure on yourself by creating attractive alternatives *before the negotiations begin*. For example, a famous golfer, who had grown up as a poor boy, once made a long putt to win a major tournament by one stroke. When a reporter asked, "Have you ever felt worse pressure?", he replied, "Sure, when I was a kid playing for $5, and I didn't have it."

Only someone with his kind of nerves can expect to cope with that pressure. I would probably drop the putter. Unless you have iron nerves, try to avoid negotiating from a weak position; you will probably just give yourself away by talking too much, making large concessions, or overselling, etc. Protect yourself from your own nerves by developing good options in advance.

Make Your Alternatives Credible

Credibility depends upon both your choices themselves and the way you discuss them. With good options you will probably speak and act more confidently. You may, however, do or say something that undermines your options' credibility.

For example, avoid comments such as: "The other bidder offered faster delivery, but I'm not sure they can really provide it." or "Your products are clearly superior, but your price is higher." Politeness or honesty can cause you to make such remarks, but they weaken your bargaining position.

You would be astonished at how often people undermine their alternatives. Two rather humorous stories come to mind. Once, I had advertised for a contractor for a large house renovation. One candidate actually told me: "I really need this job because unless I pay a drunken driving ticket, I will go to jail."

Some of my banker friends have told me that business people have indirectly said: "You've got to loan me this money. If I don't get it, I will be bankrupt by next week."

Both the contractor and the bank's customers not only weakened their bargaining position; they dramatically reduced the other side's interest in doing business at all. Who wants to hire a drunk or loan money to someone heading for bankruptcy?

The basic cause for these mistakes is, of course, that they were thinking of themselves, of their own desperate needs, not of the effects their words would have on other people. Instead of pleading for help, the bank's customers should have said: "I have checked with your competition, bank X, and they offered me attractive terms. I thought I would check with you to see if you can do a little better."

In other words, build up your other alternatives. Praise their good points and indicate readiness to select them if you do not get a good deal in this negotiation. Do not oversell, because it can reduce your credibility. But make the others realize that they are not the only game in town.

SELECTING APPROPRIATE ATTITUDES

Attitudes can be affected by actions taken at any time, even long before the negotiations. For example, when Khruschev banged his shoe on the table at the UN, he was primarily positioning himself for later negotiations. His outburst scared people and made his later threats more credible.

He understood that consistency is the basis of credibility. People will not believe you are irrational or trustworthy if you have acted out of character. He therefore had to say, in effect, "I have a violent temper, and I have nothing but contempt for all this diplomatic nonsense. If you get me mad enough, I might just do something crazy, like push the button and kill us all."

Colonel Qaddafi, The Ayatollah, Hitler, and many other extremely aggressive people have applied the same principle. They have literally gotten away with murder by applying the Law of Irrationality. Qaddafi's "diplomats" even murdered a London policewoman and claimed that they had diplomatic immunity. Their legal position was nonsense, but they got away with it (the murderers were never even tried) because the British government was so afraid of a violent, irrational reaction.

Dramatists call this principle *establishing a character*. They must create a picture of a character in the audience's mind that fit later actions. Otherwise, those later actions will not seem plausible. For example, if they intend to have a man murder his wife in act three, they must show a potential for violence in act one (he kicks the dog, or has violent fantasies, or gets into a barroom brawl). Otherwise, the murder makes no sense. The viewer cannot understand it.

Another example comes from a humorous article, "How to Cheat at Tennis." The author, with his tongue very obviously in his cheek, recommended developing the reputation as the club's most honest player. Give the opponents every call. If their shot is six inches out, give them the point. Then, in the quarter finals of the club tournament, when you really need a point, steal it. Although their shot is right on the middle of the line, say, "Out." How can they question you?

They might start to do so, then realize how ridiculous it is to question the club's "most honest player." They may even apologize for their momentary lapse of judgment and begin to doubt their own eyes.

Although many attitudes affect negotiations, we shall discuss only the six most important ones: strength, indifference, irrationality, guilt and pity (combined), finality, and trustworthiness.

Strength

Regardless of your strategy, you must appear strong. Apparent weakness just invites others to try to exploit you. Strength is not hostility or rudeness; many strong people are polite and charming. It is an inner confidence and mental toughness that show that you cannot be pushed around.

To communicate strength, express your positions confidently and use firm, assertive gestures. Above all, do not *give* anything away, especially when you are under pressure. Naive people often hope that unilateral concessions will placate their adversaries, but they often have the opposite effect. By creating a weak image, they encourage others to exploit them.

Indifference

The Law of Indifference is quite simple: *the less you want a deal, the stronger you are*. Your indifference can be based on your other options (so you really do not need the deal), your dislike for this person, other pressing problems, a general lack of interest in the subject being discussed, or even your own ignorance. The indifference itself, not the causes for it, affects other people.

For example, you may not want to buy some equipment because you do not understand how superior it is. Unless the sales rep can make you understand its value, they will have to make price or other concessions to get your business.

Apparent indifference helps you to bargain, even if you really want a deal. Do not praise their product, prices, terms, or service. You do not have to criticize them; just appear indifferent. Avoid any suggestion that you really want to do business. Keep cool and distant. Make them chase you.

Hard selling violates the Law of Indifference. The harder you sell (whether you are buying, selling, or in some other role), the weaker you look. Many people weaken their position by talking too much, making excessive claims, and generally overselling. Doing so is particularly common and destructive when closing. People often get so tense at the moment of truth that they push too hard, which often creates suspicion. The other people wonder, "If it is such a good deal, why are they selling so hard?" Quiet confidence is much better. If they do not like it, so what? Other, more intelligent, people will gladly accept it.

Irrationality

The Law of Irrationality has also been called "The Madman's Advantage." Sane people are at a disadvantage because they are much more restrained than madmen. This law is derived from the previous law because irrationality creates indifference. It is, however, much more powerful than normal indifference because irrational people often disregard extremely unpleasant consequences. For example, if you and a lunatic are locked in a room and you both have hand grenades, who has the power?

He does! You are too rational to use your grenade, but you cannot tell what he will do. Airplane hijackers, Colonel Gadhafi, and The Ayatollah have used this principle brilliantly. They have repeatedly gotten away with murder because, although America and Europe are much stronger, we are afraid they will go completely berserk.

Let's take airplane hijackers, armed with explosives. They have little or no objective power: They usually cannot hurt or kill the passengers without doing the same to themselves. Yet they have won, again and again and again, because of the Madman's Advantage.

This advantage has even been supported by the courts! They have repeatedly said, in effect, " Hijackers are privileged people. They may do whatever they wish, while the authorities must respect their constitutional rights, international law, and so forth."

For example, in February 1988, U.S. District Court Judge Barrington D. Parker wrote a 47 page opinion castigating the FBI and supporting Fawaz Younis' right to hijack.[4] Although Younis was not a U.S. citizen, and his crime and his arrest had occurred outside the United States, "these constitutional principles should not be cast aside nor minimized merely by invoking . . . the fight against terrorism."

Judge Parker and lots of other people are simply too naive to realize that giving such an advantage to hijackers virtually guarantees that they will strike again and again. As long as there are judges like Parker, terrorists can hijack with impunity. They have friends at court.

What relationship does all this have to business negotiations? More than you may think. Let's forget airplane hijackers and people like Qaddafi. Let's just look at the world you live in. Does the Law of Irrationality apply there? Probably.

There are lots of "screamers" out there, and they love trying to intimidate you. There are millions of people who really do not care about the objective effects of their actions, and millions more who can fake it.

Lawyers learn, either in school or later, that irrationality is a weapon that often produces good results. Perhaps the most obnoxious examples of lawyers' feigned irrationality are New York City bankruptcy attorneys. Because they know that the deck is stacked in their favor, they often get away with totally outrageous positions. "Look, I don't care how long this takes to settle. I get paid first, and I get paid by the hour. The longer it takes, the more I get. So, you have a choice: You can settle now for 40 cents on the dollar, or settle in two years for 30. I don't care what you do."

Let's take another example. Historically, borrowers have been held responsible for their actions. If they borrowed more than they could repay, they suffered the consequences. Today, thanks to irrational courts, borrowers' debts may be forgiven, and borrowers may even be awarded damages for the lenders' failures to protect them from their own stupidity.

There have been cases where people have defaulted on loans and the courts decided that banks should not have loaned money because people were not competent to run their own businesses.

Insanity, you say? I agree, but we live in an insane world, and judges are no exception. If you ignore the Law of Irrationality, those insane people may destroy you.

In your negotiations you obviously cannot afford to be as obnoxious as New York bankruptcy attorneys, nor can you seem crazy, but you can occasionally appear to get angry. Do not just yield to your feelings. Get angry as a tactic, and do so only when it helps you. Yell! Take outrageous positions! Storm out of the negotiations! But make sure that you do so for a strategic reason, not just because you are really angry.

The "tough cop, nice cop" is a powerful variation on this theme. The tough cop is nasty and aggressive. The nice cop apologizes for his colleague and is always understanding. People often confide in or make concessions to the nice cop to avoid making the tough cop even nastier.

If they do not yield, the tough cop may blow up and walk out. If that does not produce a concession, the nice cop follows him out, stays a while, then returns to say: "Well, I have calmed him down a little, but he is still pretty mad. I am not sure, but I think that he might take a little less. Why don't you go a little further, and I will try to sell the deal to him." This tactic may seem too transparent to succeed, but it has worked many, many times.

However, irrationality works only if other people believe it. If you have always been reasonable, they will see right through your ploy. You must therefore occasionally play Khruschev. Establish your irrationality by getting visibly angry from time to time.

Guilt And Pity

You might think that these emotions have little or no influence on business negotiations, but they can be more important than you think. Some negotiators are masters at making other people feel guilty or sorry for them.

For example, many bankers who work with problem loans can tell you of defaulting customers who made them feel terrible. "Have I shown you my grandchildren's pictures? This little guy is only ten weeks old and his dad, my son, works for me. Nice boy, we're real proud of him and his wife. It was a struggle putting him through college, but we made it." "Have I told you about my husband's heart attack? Well, we're just getting on our feet again, and making those payments would just about ruin us. Can't you give us a break?" I don't know about you but, unless I really thought they were faking it, that story would probably soften me up.

You would probably dislike using such an approach but, if your your back is really against the wall, you may have to use guilt, pity, or other emotions to give you a little edge.

Finality

Your most important End Game task is to communicate credible finality. When you say, "That's it; I will not go any further," they must believe you.

Lay the foundation for that credibility well in advance. First, make your concessions progressively smaller to communicate that you are running out of bargaining room. Show them that you are approaching your limit (even if you can actually afford to go considerably further).

Second, avoid terms such as "my final offer" when you are still far apart. They can harm both the momentum and your credibility. If others believe you, they may feel that conceding equals surrendering, which can get their backs up. If they do not believe you, you have undermined your own credibility. Then, when you make another offer, you confirm their doubts about you. Besides, what do you call that next offer: "my most final offer"? And the one after that? Later, when you make your real final offer, they will not believe it. They might then stonewall or push you to make impossible concessions.

Occasionally, you must go further than simply communicating finality; you must threaten to punish them, and sometimes you must carry out those threats. The punishment can be as mild as a lost sale or as violent as a war, but they must believe that you are able and willing to hurt them if they go too far. Credible threats are so important that no major nation has ever had a pacifist leader or disbanded its army. In fact, Switzerland and Sweden, who have been neutral and at peace for more than a century, have large military budgets and military conscription. They know that a credible deterrent is essential for peace.

Union leaders make the same point: "Every once in a while, you have to hit the bricks (go on strike). Otherwise, when you threaten to strike, management won't believe you."

Threats should normally be made tactfully and indirectly because direct threats can make the Law of Irrationality work against you. People may become so angry or concerned about saving face that they act stupidly. Nonverbal threats are particularly effective. Increasing a military budget, building up an inventory, hiring an attorney, and taking a strike vote send clear messages without directly insulting the other party.

You should therefore ask yourself, "What punishments am I willing and able to inflict?" Then make sure that they realize how far you will go. Avoid bluster and empty threats because they reduce your credibility. Just make sure they believe that, if necessary, you will reluctantly punish them.

Trustworthiness

Since some distrust is almost inevitable, you must work hard to build trust. Unless you have built trust continuously, you will not have it when you need it. Nearly everything you do affects trust, including actions taken in entirely unrelated places. If you have a general reputation for sharp business practices, or you have stretched the truth with other people or started this negotiation with an attacking first offer, people probably will not trust you, even when you are being fair and honest.

You must therefore make a strategic decision well in advance. If you will really need their trust at a critical time, you must act in a consistently trustworthy manner.

The same principle applies to all attitudes. They must be consistent with your own reputation and other actions. You can create an image of indifference, irrationality, or trustworthiness, but you cannot create all of them. You should therefore decide which attitudes fit your objectives and what preconceptions the other side has about you; then select an appropriate attitude and make sure all your actions fit that attitude.

SETTING UP TRADES

Trades should generally be set up (positioned) in advance. Without proper positioning, your trades may not work. Two major principles apply here: Create and maintain lots of bargaining room and make value-adding trades.

Create and Maintain Lots of Bargaining Room

Most people believe that mutual concessions are the essence of negotiations. Refusing to compromise signals that you are not negotiating in good faith. You therefore need lots of room for concessions. If your first offer is too close to your MSP, or if you reach your limit too soon, you cannot make those essential concessions. The other party may therefore break off the negotiations, even if your offer is within their limits.

Our general principle is the basis for several more specific ones (which may overlap with earlier recommendations).

Make ungenerous first offers

The more bargaining room you create with that first offer, the more you can afford to concede later. You can therefore appear to bargain in good faith without conceding anything important.

Save something for a final concession

Saving face is particularly important in the End Game. Painful concessions and high tension can cause extreme reactions to any "insult." You should therefore prepare for a final, face-saving concession. It may be significant, a bargaining chip, or even just a token, what some people call a "fig leaf" (to cover one's nakedness), but they need it to feel good. So hold something back and then make them feel better by beating it out of you.

Sometimes that fig leaf can be so tiny that it is hardly visible. The 1986 trade of the Soviet spy, Zakharov, for Daniloff, the American journalist,[5] is a nearly perfect example. Daniloff, a respected journalist, was arrested in Moscow on spurious charges; Zakharov had been apprehended in the United States while spying. President Reagan repeatedly insisted that he would not trade a spy for a journalist, but he then made that trade. To provide the tiniest of fig leaves, the Russians agreed that two dissidents could also leave Russia, and Zakharov would delay his departure from the United States for one day and go through an absurd courtroom ritual. He pleaded "no contest" to serious charges, and was then released to fly home to Russia. If the President of the United States needs such silly symbols, how important are face-saving concessions to the people you encounter?

Lay a foundation for splitting the difference

Deals are usually reached near the middle of the hard bargaining range, the distance between the points at which both parties dig in their heels. To get additional, perhaps painful concessions, you need enough bargaining room to reciprocate. In fact, they may offer to split the difference. If you cannot afford a split, they may feel you are acting in bad faith.

You should therefore try to enter the hard bargaining range in the best possible position. Move slowly and avoid unnecessarily large concessions, even at the start. Large concessions may seem irrelevant when you are far from your limit, but they can weaken your position later. In fact, every dollar you concede early can cost you fifty cents later because you have to split the difference from a poorer position.

Keep the Future ROM as low as possible

We have already shown how the Past ROM (ratio of movement) can help you estimate the other side's limits. Now let's look at the positioning implications of the Future ROM. It compares the distance that both parties must move to reach your MSP. To compute it, subtract your MSP from their most recent offer, subtract your most recent offer from your MSP, and divide the first number by the second. The following diagram illustrates these calculations, and shows that they have more room than you do.

Your offer	Your MSP	Their offer
$9,000	$10,000	$12,000

$1,000	$2,000

The Future ROM is therefore 2:1

$$12,000 - 10,000 = 2,000$$

$$10,000 - 9,000 = 1,000$$

$$2,000/1,000 = 2:1$$

They have to move twice as far as you do to reach your MSP. That ratio suggests that you may be heading for trouble.

The same general logic can be applied to nonquantitative issues, but without exact ratios. The important point is to control the relative distance that both sides have to move.

Ratios below 1:1 are particularly desirable. You can then either demonstrate your good faith by moving faster than the other side, or end up well within your limit by moving at the same speed or perhaps even more slowly.

Many people violate this principle, especially when the other side takes an extreme position. They say, in effect, "Since they are being so unreasonable, I had better make a generous offer to keep the negotiations going." In addition to encouraging them to make outrageous demands, this pattern of offers creates a very unfavorable Future ROM.

To illustrate, let's say your MSP as a buyer is $100,000, and they offer $140,000. If you make a reasonable offer of $95,000, you have only $5,000 to trade for concessions of $40,000; the Future ROM is 8:1. Since they will probably not move eight times as fast as you do, a deal is unlikely.

A $60,000 offer might anger them, but it would protect you and tell them what you think of their offer. You can make that message clearer and suggest a way out of the impasse by saying, "My offer is no more unreasonable than yours." That comment implies that you agree that your offer is unreasonable and that you will become reasonable when they do the same.

Even if their offer is reasonable, keep the Future ROM as low as possible. If, for example, they had opened with a bid of $110,000, you should counter with $90,000 or less to keep the Future ROM at or below 1:1. Your future concessions should also be a little less than theirs so that you end up below your limit of $100,000.

Let's look at a sample series of offers.

- They start with $110,000; you counter with $90,000.
- They come down $3,000; you come up $3,000.
- They concede another $2,000; you do the same.
- They drop $1,000; you match their concession.

In summary, you both started $10,000 from your MSP. Since you matched their concessions totaling $6,000, you are both now $4,000 from your MSP ($104,000 versus $96,000). That pattern may seem reasonable, but you have already made a serious mistake. What is it?

You are aiming toward your own MSP. If you both continue to make equal concessions, you will end up at your limit, $100,000. The seller will get all the money on the table. You should be aiming for a lower number.

The results could be even worse if you had started at $90,000 and then made somewhat larger concessions than they did. If you had responded to their concessions totaling $6,000 by moving $8,000, they would now be at $104,000, while you would be at $98,000. The ratio would be 2:1 ($4,000/$2,000). That ratio does not sound too dangerous, but watch how it changes against you if you make additional matching concessions (and the "split the difference" emphasis of the End Game often forces people to do so).

If you both move another $1,000, they are at $103,000, and you are at $99,000. The ratio is now 3:1 ($3,000/$1,000).

Move another $500 each, and it becomes 5:1 ($2,500/$500).

If you trade one more $500 concession, the ratio becomes infinity. You are at your MSP and have nothing left for a final concession, while they are $2,000 above your limit. Since you can no longer negotiate, you must insist they take it or leave it. To save face they may walk away, even if your last offer of $100,000 is within their limit.

Many, many people get into this position. You can avoid it by keeping that Future ROM as low as possible.

Make Value-Adding Trades

This principle applies only to multiple-issue negotiations; you cannot add value in single-issue, pure bargaining negotiations. For example, if price is the only issue, you are playing a zero-sum game; price concessions cost one side exactly as much as the other side gains.

Many negotiations appear to have several issues, but there is really only one. For instance, you might negotiate price, shipping costs, and the fee for a particular amount of after sales service. Since all three issues concern price, you are essentially negotiating the total price for the package.

With several issues, difference in priorities create opportunities for value-adding trades. Both parties should make concessions that are less valuable to them than what they get in return. For example, if price is more important to you than it is to me, while delivery is more important to me than it is to you, we both gain by trading price for delivery.

You cannot make value-adding trades without positioning yourself in advance. You must determine both sides' priorities, create trading value for your concessions, and time your trades.

Determine both sides' priorities

Without knowing these priorities, you obviously cannot add value by trading. You should therefore clearly define your own priorities and learn theirs. You may want to communicate your priorities openly, or create a slightly or completely false picture of them, but you must know your own priorities and try to learn the differences between your priorities and theirs.

Create trading value for your concessions

Trading value (how much they will give you to get something in return) depends upon two factors: the value to them of what they receive, and their perception of its cost to you. If they think that a concession costs you very little, they may not trade you much for it—even if it is quite valuable to them.

Let's illustrate with an attempt to sell your house. The prospective buyers like your drapes and feel that they are worth about $2,500. You then say, "We already have drapes in our new house. Besides these are not the right color and size anyway. So you can have them for $2,000." They would probably offer much less because the drapes have little value to you. You should therefore build up the value to you of anything you intend to trade. For example, you could say instead that your drapes fit the windows in your new house and match your furniture.

Time your trades

In the early stages trade in principle. "Would you accept a slower delivery for a discount on the price?" That sort of offer helps you determine their priorities while communicating yours. If they refuse, delivery probably means more to them than price. If they respond positively, price is probably more valued.

The next question is: How much more do they value it? As the negotiations progress, you answer that question by becoming more specific. "Will you accept a two month delay for a five percent discount?"

In the End Game, execute the most difficult trades. Deadline pressures and the fear of losing the deal help you to make trades that were previously unacceptable.

At the very last moments of the End Game trade your bargaining chips. These relatively small concessions have two purposes: to create momentum at impasses and to close the final gap in the last few minutes. Bargaining chips are essentially a cheap way to make those essential final concessions. They make the other side feel like winners without costing you too much.

However, you cannot trade them at the end if you have not created them earlier or if you have used them too soon. To create a bargaining chip, just create trading value for any relatively minor concession such as the drapes in the sale of a house. Then use the bargaining chip when such a minor concession makes sense.

For example, if you and the buyer were $10,000 apart on the price, do not offer to trade the drapes for acceptance of your price. The gap is too great to be bridged by such a small concession and once you have offered a bargaining chip, it loses much of its trading power. Wait until you are $2,000 apart; then offer that trade. They might accept it.

MANAGING TIME PRESSURES

Time pressures can greatly affect a negotiation. For example, because we are so impatient, Americans have lost negotiations to the Russians, Vietnamese, Japanese, and other more patient people. The Japanese are masters at manipulating westerners' impatience. They stall and stall and stall until the other side gives up. We observed that strategy in a workshop outside Tokyo. In one room a Japanese team negotiated against an American- European (western) team. In the other room two western teams negotiated.

The all western negotiators reached a deal about 9:30 P.M. In the other room, progress was agonizingly slow and the westerners became quite impatient. At 1:45 A.M. the instructor said, "You are still so far apart that you obviously cannot reach a deal quickly. Since we have to be awake tomorrow to review the negotiations, I'm calling an end to the exercise."

The westerners were pleased by his decision; in fact, some of them grumbled that it should have been made hours earlier. The Japanese were furious (but polite about it). Their entire strategy had been built around negotiating all night. They felt confident that, sooner or later, the effete westerners would collapse. They were probably right.

Deadlines create another sort of time pressure, one that often forces people to make concessions which they would not otherwise make. Deadlines have also caused many people to make serious mistakes.

Since they have such large effects, you should obviously manage time pressures. Your approach should depend upon three factors: whether you are problem solving or bargaining (because pressure fits bargaining and inhibits problem solving); the amount of objective time pressure both sides face; and both parties' reactions to time pressures.

Close the Gap

An extremely common error is to enter the End Game too far apart to reach a deal through any sequence of controlled, deliberate moves. The gap is so great that it can be closed only if one or both sides essentially collapse, which prevents thorough analysis of alternatives and careful, controlled movement.

The 1987 American-Canadian free trade negotiations offer a splendid example of this process and its dangers. Both sides refused to make essential concessions. A few days before the deadline they were so far apart that most observers expected the negotiations to fail; the Canadians even walked out shortly before the deadline. They threw together an agreement in the last few hours, but it was obviously a carelessly drawn and confusing deal, one that will keep the lawyers and lobbyists busy for years. In fact, at this moment (about four months after the deadline) nobody can confidently state what the agreement means!

If you enter the End Game too far apart, the only three outcomes are a deadlock, dangerously uncontrolled movement, or an extension of the deadline (which is often impossible). Protect yourself from these unattractive choices by starting to move early, and continuing to move slowly so that you enter the End Game with a gap that can be bridged in a controlled, deliberate way.

You may have to begin positioning yourself from the first few minutes of the negotiation. If you have lots of time and the other party is flexible, you can afford to start far apart. Conversely, if you have relatively little time and the other side tends to move slowly, the gap between the first two offers must be smaller. There must be a rational relationship between the size of the gap and the time you have to close it. Think of negotiations as a trip. It obviously takes longer to go from New York to San Francisco than from New York to Chicago.

Manage Objective Time Pressures

If one side is under greater pressure, the other side has a distinct advantage. If you need a quick deal, while they have lots of time, you must try to minimize their advantage. Other time pressures can help or harm you. For example, managers, when negotiating with unions, must often keep their line responsibilities, while the union leaders face no other demands. The managers may be interrupted frequently, and they know their in-baskets are filling up. They therefore want to settle things, while the union people are happy to negotiate indefinitely. Guess who wins?

The same unbalanced pressure occurs if you have another meeting or must rush to the airport while they have lots of time. You feel more pressure, even though you both face the same deadline.

The lesson, of course, is to avoid getting into those positions. Schedule important negotiations for low pressure times. Allow enough time to negotiate effectively. Temporarily transfer some tasks to other people. Negotiations are hard enough without handicapping yourself with time pressures.

Adjust to Personal Reactions

Most people respond poorly to time pressure; they get flustered or act foolishly to escape the tension. Some indecisive people need time pressures to stop procrastinating. And a few people work best under pressure.

Consider these reactions when planning your strategy. If you are negotiating with procrastinators, create visible and tight deadlines to force them to make decisions. If they get flustered, perhaps you should stall to intensify deadline pressures. If you get flustered, while they love pressure, avoid deadlines and minimize other pressures. Create the kind of situation that favors you.

POSITIONING YOURSELF FOR THE NEXT ROUND

Occasionally, you can predict that the current negotiation will be followed by some other round, such as another negotiation with these people, a negotiation with their boss, an appeal to authority, or a strike, war, or other forceful action. As soon as you expect another round, start positioning yourself for it.

Positioning Yourself for Another Round with These People

You should consider four general principles. First, the attitudes and positions from your current negotiation will inevitably affect the next round. If, for example, you have been aggressive or taken extreme positions or stretched the truth, they will be skeptical, perhaps even hostile in the next round.

You must therefore consider the longer term effects of your actions. If your actions in this negotiation will damage your position for the next round, take corrective action as soon as possible.

Second, there is no substitute for time. The deal they will reject today, they might accept tomorrow. After deadlocking with you and considering their alternatives, they may decide to change their MSP or priorities. You should therefore give them time to think before starting the next round. That round might even become irrelevant; they might decide to accept your last offer or one with only minor changes.

Third, keep the door wide open for more negotiations. Make it easy to start again without their losing face. For example, do not insist that they call you. Do not demand a better offer before talking to them. Instead, communicate very clearly that you hope to meet with them *without any conditions.* "I'm sorry we could not reach a deal today, and I certainly hope we can get together and talk things over in the future."

Fourth, *make sure that you can reward them for reopening the negotiations.* Because of pride and politics, they usually cannot accept the deal you have already offered; they need some additional concessions. They have to prove to themselves and their organizations that they have gotten something from that second round of negotiations.

Therefore, as soon as you can anticipate another round, plan to save some trading room for it. In fact, apply all the principles for setting up trades. Many people violate these principles; they go all the way to their MSP, hoping for a deal. Then they fail in the next round because they have nothing left to trade.

Of course, sometimes you will go to your limit before realizing that there will be another round. Before starting that next round, create some bargaining room or bargaining chips. If necessary, ask your boss for additional latitude.

The concessions need not always be large, but they must be visible. The other side must be able to convince itself and its bosses that it has won something during the new round. Bargaining chips are much cheaper than major concessions, and they are often enough to close the deal. The other party may just need a little face saving concession. Create it by redefining an issue or finding some inexpensive new concession. For example, perhaps you can give them a little better delivery or extra service. The actual concession does not have to be costly, but you must usually give them something.

Positioning Yourself for Negotiations with Their Boss

The preceding principles are even more important when you must negotiate with their boss. Bosses are frequently touchy about their dignity and image. Many of them will not risk losing face by calling you or accepting any preconditions to another round of negotiation, and nearly all of them *must* get concessions to protect their image. They have to show that they can get better deals than their subordinates.

You should therefore call them, say how delighted you are to meet with them, offer to come to their office, and make sure you have some real trading room. They may settle for a face-saving bargaining chip, but they often need to get significant, substantive concessions. In fact, for political and face-saving reasons, they may prefer a deadlock to a deal that is only slightly better than their subordinates have negotiated.

Positioning Yourself for Appeals to Authority

If a higher authority will resolve a conflict, you have to balance two conflicting needs: appearing reasonable, but preserving the maximum amount of trading room.

Authorities such as your mutual boss, judges, and arbitrators naturally favor the side that appears most reasonable. You must therefore prepare to demonstrate the logic and correctness of your position. The negotiating restrictions on debating no longer apply. Gather evidence, prepare to argue your position eloquently and to punch holes in the other side's arguments because they are no longer the people you have to convince.

In addition, save as much trading room as possible. As soon as you see that an authority will decide, stop making concessions. Authorities frequently just split the difference between the last two positions. Even if they do not split it exactly, authorities often try to end up someplace near the middle.

There is, however, an exception to that rule. To prevent this sort of positioning and to encourage concessions, some arbitrators and other authorities follow an all-or-nothing rule. For example, baseball's major leagues use this rule for salary arbitrations. If the player demands $1,500,000, and the team offers $1,000,000, the arbitrator selects one or the other, not any figure in between. If your authority is likely to decide on an all-or-nothing basis, you obviously should make your final position as reasonable and credible as possible.

SUMMARY

The positioning principle is quite simple: You must establish your position *before* you need it. Four ways to establish a strong negotiating position are to create credible alternatives, select appropriate attitudes, set up trades, and manage time pressures.

The same principle applies to many other dimensions. For instance, you should get your management's approval in advance so that you know how far you can go.

We also considered the problem of positioning yourself for the next round, whether that round is another negotiation or an appeal to authority.

To position yourself effectively, you must be ruthlessly objective. First, step back and evaluate your position: What are my alternatives? How much do I like these alternatives? Will the other side believe that I like them? How do those people really feel about me? What effect will those feelings have on the negotiation? Do I have enough bargaining room and trading power? Will they genuinely value my bargaining chips?

Then decide whether your position is viable; if not, you must find ways to improve it. You may even have to postpone the negotiations to get enough time to improve a weak position.

These evaluations and plans can be unpleasant. It is a lot easier to try to talk your way to a good deal. But ignoring the positioning principle can lead to disasters. A good analogy is that a strong negotiating position is like life insurance: If you wait until you need it, it is too late to get it.

7

The End Game

The End Game is the most stressful part of most negotiations. The concessions are often painful, and deadlines intensify the stress. Both parties know that there is a lot at stake, and they often do not have enough time to think carefully or to correct their mistakes.

The resulting tension causes many serious mistakes. In fact, the critical personal quality during the End Game is good nerves. Without them serious blunders are extremely common. People respond to their emotions, not to the situational demands.

Some people become aggressive and intransigent, so determined to win that they ignore their need for a deal within their limits. They may even walk away from a satisfactory deal to avoid losing some silly symbolic conflict. "I don't care whether it's a good deal. It they don't give in on this point, I'm walking. It's a matter of principle."

Others just run away from the tension and ignore obvious chances for additional concessions. For example, the other side may have indicated that they will go further, perhaps much further. "We thought that 'X' is fair to both of us, but if necessary, we can make adjustments." Instead of taking advantage of this obvious opportunity for a better deal, some people just settle, leaving lots of money on the table. "OK, that sounds reasonable."

To minimize the effects of these stresses, you must get ready for the End Game. You need three kinds of preparation.

1. *Psychological*: You must be psychologically ready for the stress and demands. Your nerves must be under control, and you cannot afford to be tired, intoxicated (not even a little bit), or fuzzy-headed. You need every bit of your mental and physical energy.

Get to bed early the night before. Watch the alcohol. Wake up early enough so that you can come to the meeting without worrying about traffic, late trains, and other delays. Get everything else off your agenda. Focus all your attention on this negotiation.

2. *Informational:* By now you should have a fairly clear picture of their objectives, power, strategy, and so on. If you do not have this information before entering the End Game, you cannot play it well. You do not have time to get that information; you need it *now.*

And you need to know what it means. Review your notes. Write down your estimates of their limits and priorities. Make written, explicit predictions of their tactics during the End Game. Writing them down forces you to think more clearly and explicitly. Plan counters for each expected tactic. The Feedback Loop Questionnaire in Appendix 2 can help you to plan your strategy.

If you can, discuss everything with someone else. Just explaining your analysis and plans will clarify them in your mind, and you might also get some good questions and suggestions.

3. *Positional:* The same principle applies to your bargaining position. You do not have time to create a good position; you need it *now.* If you do not have it already, try to create it as quickly as possible.

What should you do if you realize that you are not well prepared? The answer is simple conceptually, but it can be hard to execute: Get out of the End Game.

Extend the deadline in order to take whatever steps are needed to prepare yourself for the next End Game. "Get your head together." Or learn more about their objectives and strategy. Or improve your bargaining position.

They may object or even refuse to extend the deadline. They may even escalate the costs of not meeting it and put great pressure on you. It takes nerve to stand up to that pressure, but you cannot afford to yield to it. If you enter the End Game unprepared, you are probably going to make costly mistakes. In other words, *if you are not ready for the End Game, do not play it.*

Once you are prepared, you can shift your attention to the End Game's four primary tasks:

   I. *Test the limits.* Learn how far you can push the other side.
  II. *Communicate Finality.* Make them believe you have reached your limit, that you will not go further.
 III. *Use deadline pressure.* Make that pressure and tension work for you, not against you.
  IV. *Let them save face.* Let them feel they have won by your manner, words, and perhaps a final "sweetener."

TEST THE LIMITS

Throughout the entire negotiation, you have tried to learn their limits. If you have used the Feedback Loop well, you should have a fairly accurate estimate of how far they will go. Now make a final test of their limits. Use all the Feedback Loop skills to acquire, interpret, and use information, but concentrate more intently because things happen so fast.

There is a circular relationship between probing for their limit and attempting to push them to it. You cannot just probe until you make an estimate of their limit, then push them until you reach it. You could leave money on the table or deadlock if your estimate is wrong. You should therefore continuously move back and forth between trying to determine their limit and trying to drive them to it.

In fact, attempts to drive them to their limits should be partly probes. Their reactions will help you to decide whether your earlier estimate was correct. If their reactions suggest they have more or less room than you expected, you should revise both your estimate and your strategy.

After Passing It, Ignore Your Own MSP

People often push hard until they get to their own limit or a little past it, then ignore obvious opportunities for additional concessions. They essentially take the money and run.

When asked why, they usually say something like this: "I had already passed my MSP, so I didn't see any reason to go for more." Each additional dollar obviously has the same objective value as the ones they have already gotten, but it has much less psychological value. They simply do not care very much about the money (or other things) they leave on the table. We call it the "loose change."

This readiness to settle for less than the best possible deal conflicts with the traditional conception of the profit-maximizing, economic individual, but it does fit more modern conceptions. Herbert Simon, my colleague at the Carnegie-Mellon graduate business school, won the Nobel Memorial Prize in economics for his analysis of how people and organizations make decisions. He coined the term "satisfice" to contrast with the traditional terms "maximize" and "optimize."

> Most human decision making... is concerned with the discovery and selection of satisfactory alternatives; only in exceptional cases is it concerned with the discovery and selection of optimum alternatives. (James G. March and Herbert Simon, with the collaboration of Harold Guetzkow, *Organizations,* New York: John Wiley, 1958)

People satisfice rather than optimize because it is easier; it takes time and painful effort to get the best deal. They say, in effect, "I have enough." Professor Simon compares it to hunting for a needle in a haystack. They do not hunt for the sharpest needle; they settle for any needle that is sharp enough for sewing.

Satisficing is particularly likely to occur while negotiating because trying to get more usually has psychological, relational, or other costs. It is generally easier and cheaper to settle after reaching your own MSP. As many people have put it: "Who cares about a few extra dollars? I got what I wanted. Why should I push for a few dollars that I do not need?"

In most organizations, the answer to the who cares question can be answered with two words: top management. They almost invariably want greater profitability, and they are usually frustrated by the readiness of people at lower levels to say, in effect, "Enough is enough." In fact, saying it, then settling for less than you can get is a nearly perfect way to guarantee that you will *never* even be considered for top management! The people with whom you negotiate may like your fairness and reasonableness, but the people who determine your future may regard you as too soft or "not hungry enough."

The natural human tendency to satisfice, to accept less than you can get, has two implications for you. First, you should fight against it in yourself. Do not just settle at or near your MSP; go for more. Second, if the other party is within their limits, they probably do not care that much about getting a better deal. They may therefore yield quite easily. A small effort, a few minutes of discomfort, could make you hundreds, or thousands, or occasionally, even millions of dollars.

Remember, your MSP is not your goal; it is the worst deal you can accept. Once you have gotten to it, ignore it and go for the rest of the money on the table. You will often be pleasantly surprised about the ease of getting lots of concessions you never expected.

Push Until They Push Back

Because the pressure is on, gentler forms of probing may be ineffective, and you may have to push harder than you did earlier. The critical point is to push for concessions and watch their reactions. If they do not communicate any finality (any readiness to walk away), they are probably not at their limits yet. You should therefore keep pushing, seeing how far they will go.

In diplomacy this approach is called *brinkmanship*. One country pushes another closer and closer to the brink of war, watching intently for their reactions. Of course, in most business negotiations you do not want to push that hard or get close to the brink. You should therefore decide how strong their finality signals have to be before you will back off. The following diagram and explanation show how resistance and finality signals increase as you approach their limit.

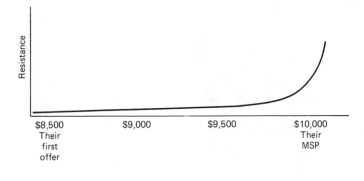

When you are far from their limit, concessions are easy to get. The other party does not seriously resist moving from $8,500, their first offer, to $9,000 because they never expected to buy for only $8,500. The next move, to $9,400, is a little smaller; they are starting to slow down, but they are still far enough from their limit to move comfortably. The next move to $9,700 is smaller; their resistance is increasing.

The next move to $9,800 is much smaller than previous ones, and you can see that the concessions are starting to hurt. They complain, show signs of tension, speak in a firmer tone. They will go higher, but they had hoped they would not have to do so.

The fifth move to $9,875 comes slowly and reluctantly. You are into the hard bargaining range where the real money (the painful concessions) changes hands. Now the signs of tension are much more visible.

The next two concessions to $9,925 and $9,960 are even smaller and harder to get, and you can see strong signs of stress and a readiness to leave. You are clearly at or approaching their absolute limit.

The next concession to $9,985 is only $25, and they have stood up and very firmly stated that they are running out of room.

The last concession to $10,000 is made after the negotiations have apparently ended; you have said good-bye and walked with them to the elevator. It is so obviously their limit that you accept it.

As you can see, their resistance to conceding increases as you approach the limit, and the resistance increases faster. It is much harder to get that last $15, than it was to get the first concession of $500.

So how far should you push them? It depends entirely on your objectives. The more you value money (or other concessions) the harder you should push. The more that you value the relationship, the sooner you should settle (but beware of buyer's remorse, discussed in the next section).

Every increase in resistance, every push beyond the point that they seriously start resisting, can cause stress on the relationship. However, settling before they start to resist can cost you money without improving the relationship. These general principles can be converted into specific action rules.

1. If you want to get every penny on the table, push until they walk away, then accept their last offer.
2. If you value the relationship and want to continue it, you should probably settle when the concessions start to hurt (about $9,800 in our previous example).

At a Minimum, Pick Up the Loose Change

Many people do not push at all. They settle even though the other side shows no finality or discomfort; they may even ignore obvious signs that the others are ready to make additional concessions.

They therefore leave the "loose change" on the table. That term refers to the money (or other concessions) that the other side does not care about. In this example, the dividing line between loose change ends and the real money is around $9,700. Accepting any less than that would cost you money, without making the other side significantly more satisfied with the deal.

In fact, settling so cheaply could cause buyer's remorse. A quick easy agreement could arouse their suspicions or their greed. They might think they have purchased something defective, or that you are in such a weak position they should have offered you even less.

So push until they push back. Try to get all their loose change and perhaps even some of their real money.

Ask For a Discount For Cash

When you are buying, you can often get a discount for cash, if you time your request well. These requests are essentially a method for testing the limits, perhaps even pushing past the old limits, because paying cash provides additional value to some vendors.

The technique is simple; after you have agreed on everything else, ask for a cash discount. "Cash" may also mean a check; the critical point is that you are paying immediately. Don't ask before the other terms are settled because the seller may just raise the price to allow for it.

Cash discounts are normal business practice in a few industries such as lumber and plumbing supplies, but you generally will not get them without asking for them. Many other businesses would gladly give you 2-5 percent to get your money today. Billing you costs money and time, and there is always the risk that you will not pay.

Some businesses will also give you 2 to 5 percent for paying cash rather than charging your purchases on your credit card. They may pay the credit card companies 5 to 7 percent and must spend additional time and money billing them.

If you feel uncomfortable asking for a cash discount, just ask yourself: "Why should the merchant get a higher net price from me than from a credit customer? Why should I pay for other people's credit?"

Some businesses and many professionals have an even better reason for preferring cash; they do not report it on their income tax! To them $100 in cash is worth up to $150 in reported income. Cash discounts may therefore be much more than 2 to 5 percent.

Test Your Assumptions

Because people assume that they know the other side's limits, they often settle at or before those assumed limits. But if your assumptions are wrong, you may leave a great deal of money on the table. If you can do so without damaging a valued relationship, test your assumptions by trying to push them *further* than you think they can go. You will often learn that they can give you much more than you had thought.

Numerous stories have been told about the legendary J. P. Morgan. As they have been told and retold over the years, they have naturally been changed. I therefore cannot swear that the numbers are right, but the principle probably is.

J. P. was famous for his impatience, and it was particularly strong while he was creating U.S. Steel. In addition to making him a great deal of money, U.S. Steel would become his monument, his claim to immortality, the very first billion dollar corporation. So many pieces had to be fitted together—this little steel company, that iron company, that shipping corporation—that Morgan naturally wanted to settle things before the entire deal fell apart.

Two brothers owned most of a steel company, and, as they walked to Morgan's office, they argued about the price they should request.

"We should definitely ask for $9,000,000."

"No, no, he is too shrewd to pay that much. Let's ask for eight."

When they met J. P., he astonished them by saying: "Gentlemen, I am too busy to haggle with you. I won't give you a penny more than $15,000,000."

Virtually any of us would have been overwhelmed by this windfall and gratefully grabbed it, but one of the brothers had the cool nerve to say, "We could not even think of it. Our bottom price is $20,000,000."

Morgan responded as hoped: "Let's split the difference."

They replied, "Done."

The brothers made an extra $2,500,000 in less than one minute. You will probably never earn so much so quickly, but testing your assumptions can produce much better deals than you ever thought you could get.

You do not know how far they can go until you test their limits. So avoid acting on your assumptions until you have challenged and confirmed them. You may be pleasantly surprised.

Look for Signs of Tacit Acceptance

If you look sharply, you will often see signs that they can accept your last offer. They may try for more, but their signals say, "We can live with what we have already gotten." For example, they may not reject your offers as firmly as they did earlier. They could just look relaxed and comfortable. They may even say, "It looks as if we can work something out along those lines." Occasionally, the signals will be even more obvious: They might lean forward, nod their heads, smile, perhaps even reach for their pens or their check books.

Even if they cannot accept your entire offer, they may signal that they can live with parts of it. For example, they might ignore your offer on one issue and talk extensively about other issues. In negotiations not saying "no" often means "yes." The fact that they did not reject your offer suggests they can accept it. Some signals can be considerably clearer: They essentially say, "We can accept your last proposal if you will make an additional concession on issue X."

Whenever you see signs like that, note them carefully so you will remember that you are within their range on that issue. Then, since they are already satisfied, do not make additional concessions on it.

Do Not Offer More Than They Have Explicitly Accepted

If they have explicitly accepted your offer on an issue, additional concessions usually have little trading value. They will therefore not make much of a concession in return for your generosity.

For instance, as a vendor you are negotiating price and delivery, and they have accepted your last offer on delivery. Faster delivery has a cost to you, but little or no value to them. In fact, a faster delivery might actually be a nuisance to them; they might need it on a certain date, but not be ready for it before then. A concession on delivery would therefore not cause them to give you much (or perhaps anything at all) on price.

People are most inclined to make such offers when they run out of bargaining chips in the End Game. Because they need something to trade, they offer trades that would actually decrease the overall value of the deal to both parties! We call such trades *value-subtracting*. One side concedes something that is more valuable to it than it is to the party receiving it.

Such trades are obviously undesirable, but the need for trading power can cause them to be made. This pattern shows the importance of preparation and timing. It would be better to save those bargaining chips, and then trade them to close the deal.

Make Gentle Threats

If they are not yielding at all, you need to know whether they have truly reached their limit (perhaps through poor positioning), or if they are just testing *your* limit.

Threaten to break off the negotiations, but do it gently. A direct threat could make them angry or defiant. They might then refuse to move, even if you make an offer within their limits. A gentle threat may sound like a contradiction, but it is really not contradictory at all. The threat is clearly there, but it is delivered in a gentle manner. For example, instead of saying, "That is my final offer, take it or leave it," you can say sadly, "I'm sorry we haven't been able to agree on this deal, but I hope we can do business next time."

Mikhail Gorbachev, the Soviet leader, makes absolutely brilliant gentle threats. For example, at a news conference on November 30, 1987, he said: "The Soviet Union is doing all that the United States is doing to defend against nuclear attack, but will not build a space-based system...I guess that we are engaged in research, basic research, which relates to these aspects which are covered by the SDI [Star Wars] in the United States."

However, he claimed: "We will not build an SDI. We will not employ SDI. We call upon The United States to act likewise. If the Americans fail to heed that call, we will find a response."

In simple English he stated what Ronald Reagan had maintained all along: The USSR has been working on its own SDI, and it will build one if it regards it as necessary. However, Gorbachev is too good at public relations to make the crude threats of a Nikita Khruschev ("We will bury you.").

The media applaud Gorbachev as a man of peace, while castigating Ronald Reagan as a war-monger, even though their substantive actions are the same. Why? First, because of their antiAmerican bias. Second, because Gorbachev's words are less bellicose, even though his actions are essentially identical.

He uses the carrot and stick much more effectively than President Reagan, while communicating to American decision makers that he can take extremely aggressive actions. "Andrei Gromyko, speaking for the gerontocrats of the Politburo, nominated the relatively youthful Gorbachev as the man who had a 'nice smile'but 'iron teeth.'"[6]

If, during a business negotiation, you need to make a gentle threat, it may be best to do so nonverbally. Just show that you are getting ready to leave. Your signals can be quite direct, such as standing up and turning toward the door, or much more subtle, such as putting away your pen and starting to arrange your papers.

If they do not stop you, you have to decide why. There are three possibilities. They did not understand the signal that you were ready to leave. They did not believe that signal. Or they were at their limit. If you think they missed or did not believe your threat, you can make a more forceful one. You can shake hands and start walking away, or very clearly state that you will leave unless they make some concession.

If you think, but are not sure they are at their limit, you can make another concession and see how they react. Offers to split the difference are particularly effective here because both sides will concede. Neither side loses face by surrendering.

If you are confident that they are at their limit, and their last offer is within your range, accept it as graciously as you can. This option shows another benefit of gentle threats. You can accept graciously without losing face because you have not committed yourself to walking out.

Watch For Signs That You Have Gone Too Far

Because the tension is so high, you must listen and observe very, very carefully. That tension can cause overreactions: people often get angry, storm out, or take extreme positions. You should therefore balance pushing with delicacy and sensitivity. Put on the pressure, but back off—quickly—if they seem ready to blow up.

If Necessary, Accept Their Last Offer

If their last offer is within your range, and they seem unwilling to go any further, accept it. A surprising number of people ignore that obvious principle. They get so involved in the competition, so intent on beating the other side, that they forget that *the. purpose of negotiations is to reach mutually satisfactory deals.*

Of course you want to win, but winning—especially if the contest is over a symbol or an unnecessary concession—is much less important than avoiding a defeat. Losing a satisfactory deal is a defeat for both parties.

You set your MSP before negotiating because you were more rational then. That firm limit was set to help you to resist the natural tendency to go a little further, then further still until you reached a bad deal. But the MSP should also help you to resist the tendency to fight for every penny on the table, and perhaps a few that are not even there. Since it is within your range, their last offer is, by definition, objectively satisfactory. Take it while you can. It might not still be there tomorrow.

COMMUNICATE FINALITY

Your most important End Game task is to communicate credible finality. Failing to test the limits properly can cost you some loose change; not making them believe your own limits can cost you the deal, a strike, a lawsuit, or even a war.

By far the best discussion of this subject is in Walton and McKersie's *A Behavioral Theory of Labor Negotiations.* [7] They show how skilled negotiators gradually escalate finality to make sure that the other side gets the message.

Unless you communicate credible finality, the other side may try to push you further than you can go and then take extreme actions to back up its demands. For example, one reason for World War II was that the German high command did not believe that England and France would fight for Poland; they had not fought for the Saarland, Austria, or the Czech Sudetenland. Poland was not militarily defensible; it sits on a broad, flat plain, a nearly ideal invasion highway, while the Sudetenland is mountainous and heavily fortified, exactly the sort of place that aroused the German high command's greatest fear: a two-front war of the sort Germany lost in 1918. That fear was so great that the German generals planned a coup to depose Hitler rather than risk a two-front war.

After France and England collapsed at Munich, the generals never seriously opposed Hitler again. So Germany invaded Poland; England and France belatedly got tough; and tens of millions of people died needlessly. Greater firmness at Munich might have prevented that awful tragedy.

A more recent example occurred early in Ronald Reagan's first term. The Air Traffic Controllers (ATC) went on strike, and the President told them that if they did not return to work quickly, they would be fired and never work for the U.S. government again. They simply did not believe him because they had struck illegally twice before in the previous few years, and the government had backed down both times. So they stayed out on strike; the president fired them, and nearly everyone has suffered. They lost excellent jobs; air travelers have spent countless hours waiting for ATC problems to be sorted out; the economy has lost billions of dollars. And some authorities even believe that hundreds of people have died in unnecessary airplane accidents. Why did Ronald Reagan take such a hard line?

Because, after four years of a wimpish president, he had to establish his own and the presidency's credibility. The unions, Russians, terrorists, and many other people and institutions had to realize that they could not push too far. It was a terribly expensive message, but one that needed to be sent. It is not an accident that, from then to the end of President Reagan's term, there were no significant strikes against the federal government, while there have been countless illegal strikes against city and state governments.

Many people simply refuse to understand that point. Even today they insist that the former strikers should be rehired (and that the government should nearly always back down). They want to return to the "good old days," when the law and the government's word meant nothing at all, when anyone with a grievance—however absurd it might be—could act outrageously, confident that the media would insist that the government must be reasonable and flexible.

Don't fall into that trap. Do not take unnecessarily hard lines or convert minor disputes into "macho" contests, but do remember that the first principle for communicating finality is to position yourself properly. Create situations and a reputation that make your finality believable. Let people know, directly and indirectly, that when you say, "This is my final offer," you mean it.

Escalate Finality Gradually

Abrupt finality, such as an unexpected, but very firm final offer, is usually counterproductive. First, they may not believe it because it does not fit the atmosphere or the pattern of offers. For example, most people will not believe that an offer containing a large concession is really final; a large jump suggests that you can go much further.

Second, abrupt finality does not give the other side time to adjust; it forces them to shift immediately from trading concessions to surrendering or fighting. Extremely abrupt finality can cause a nasty confrontation. One side suddenly says, "final offer." The other side tries to bargain or argue. Then the first group walks out in a huff, leaving the others scratching their heads, wondering what has happened.

It is much better to escalate finality gradually by making your concessions progressively smaller and by slowly becoming firmer and more visibly willing to walk away. Give them advance warnings with expressions such as, "I'm running out of room," or "I'm almost at my limit." Make the warnings clearer as you go further: "I don't know how I can go any further," or "I'm afraid that we may not have a deal."

Then, when you say, "That's it! I cannot go one inch further," they will probably believe you. They will also have had enough time to adjust to the changing game.

Your nonverbal messages should support your words. Gradually make your voice and manner firmer, slowly arrange your papers, then stand and put on your coat, and start walking toward the door. Make it easy for them to stop you, but do make sure they believe that you are getting ready to leave.

Use the Testing-the-Limits Tactics

Threats, whether gentle or forceful, and other testing-the-limits tactics can help you communicate finality. Although the tactics are the same, their purposes are different.

You test the limits to see how far you can push them, but communicate finality to stop them from pushing you.

Be Gentle, But Credible

Avoid communicating such extreme finality that they lose face. Remember, finality essentially changes the game to "take it or leave it." Since you will not move, they must either move all the way to your position or the negotiations will break down. All of the points made earlier about gentle threats apply here.

Commit Yourself

Perhaps the most credible finality comes from a visible commitment to reject less than your position. If they believe that you just cannot afford to take less, that compromising would result in severe embarrassment, a lawsuit, loss of your job, or other punishment, they may not seriously try to push you.

President Kennedy's radio and TV speech during the Cuban missile crisis was a dramatic example of such a commitment. He publicly stated that he would regard any missile coming from Cuba as coming from the USSR, and that he would retaliate against the Soviets. He went so far that the Soviets knew he simply could not afford to back down. It would have destroyed his credibility and made him a lame duck for the rest of his term. The Russians yielded, partly because they had less at stake.

Of course, you cannot make such a dramatic commitment, but you can use many commitment tactics. You can, for example, make a public commitment to your boss or client, or you can stake your reputation. The more you stake, the more credible your commitment, and the more likely they are to believe that you cannot afford to back down.

A commitment strategy is obviously risky. If they call your bluff, you can really get hurt. You should therefore commit yourself only when you really cannot afford to make additional concessions, or when you are extremely confident that your position is within their limits.

Even then there is considerable risk. You may be wrong about their limits, or they may be so frustrated that they reject an objectively satisfactory deal. Therefore, before making a commitment, look for an escape route, a way to get out of the commitment if they refuse to give in. Of course, that escape route should be hidden to protect the commitment's credibility.

For example, you might acquire a document that lets you modify your position, if absolutely necessary. Keep it secret to maintain the credibility of your commitment, but show it if you have to retreat.

Time Your Move Carefully

Timing is critically important. Communicating finality either too soon or too late can defeat your purpose.

Acting too soon

If you act when you are too far apart, a deadlock is highly probable. You may have misread their limit and failed to reach it. In that case, they would rather walk away than accept your final offer. Even if your offer is within their range, you may be so far apart that they refuse to move all the way to your position. They may regard doing so as a surrender and prefer no deal to humiliation.

Let's say, for example, that a vendor's bid was $1,000,000, and your counteroffer was $900,000. After a few moves, they are at $975,000 and you are at $925,000. If you flatly refuse to go any higher, they may make one or two concessions, then stonewall or break off the negotiations.

It would have been better to make a lower first offer and to start slowing down sooner, to have made smaller concessions instead of mirroring theirs (moving at the same speed as they do). If you had been at $900,000 when they were at $975,000, you could have made several more concessions before stopping at $925,000.

Acting too late

If you act too late, you create two different risks. They are clearest and most extreme if you have reached your absolute limit, but similar, if smaller risks are created by any delay.

First, you may leave considerable money on the table. Since you are near or at your limit, they have gotten most or all of the bargaining range (unless the range is tiny or negative).

Second, you would have no room to maneuver. You might even be unable to make a final face saving concession. The negotiations therefore can break down, even if your "final offer" was within their range.

You should therefore communicate finality or near finality while you can still afford one or a few small concessions. Then you can let them save face by very reluctantly yielding to their final demands.

USE DEADLINE PRESSURE

Because the final concessions are so painful, they are often held back until just before the deadline. Until they feel that deadline pressure, many negotiators simply will not move, and they may even sincerely believe they will never make certain concessions. Only when they fully realize the consequences of not reaching an agreement—when they feel that a strike or lawsuit or failure to complete a project on time is likely—will they agree to those painful, but essential final compromises. In fact, research indicates that most deals are closed just at or shortly after the deadline.

When President Carter, President Sadat of Egypt, and Prime Minister Begin of Israel met secretly at Camp David to try to negotiate an end to the Egyptian-Israeli War,[8] neither Egypt nor Israel made the important concessions until shortly before the deadline. In fact, a few hours before the deadline, they were preparing one of those bland, diplomatic announcements: "We had a full and frank exchange of views and...."

Then, they suddenly realized that, in a few hours, they would have to tell the world that they had tried, but failed. Only then did they make the painful concessions that they had so strenuously resisted earlier.

Deadline pressures have had the same sort of effects in countless business negotiations. In fact, without that pressure some people would never make up their minds. They would dither, refer problems to committees, plan further research, and so on. Anything is better than that terrible risk of making a mistake.

To get people to move, you may have to create deadlines, even artificial ones. "We can guarantee this price only until February 14; after that it will be 3 percent higher." "Our capital expenditures committee meets September 27, and they must have three days to study any agreement; therefore, if we have not agreed by September 24, we will have to wait for their next meeting, which will probably be in early December." You may dislike creating this sort of pressure, but it is often essential. Some people need that deadline pressure to make those painful concessions.

Learn and Use Their Deadlines

Sometimes the other side faces deadlines that put extreme pressure on them, but mean absolutely nothing to you. If so, you can put pressure on them, without feeling any on yourself.

For example, most sales reps work on quota, and the quota year is clearly defined. Only sales made by November 30, for instance, count toward that year's quota. The difference between making and not making quota can be enormous—a raise, bonus, trip to Acapulco, and, perhaps even more important, the distinction of being one of the winners. Almost all sales reps will tell you the hardest sale of the year, and the one for which the will make the most concessions, is the one that makes quota for them, particularly if the quota year is almost over. Even if they have already made quota, the end of the quota year can be important to them. The percentage over quota often affects bonuses, salary increases, and so on.

Your strategy is obvious. Plan to have the End Game occur at or near the end of their quota year. You really do not care whether the deal is settled on November 30 or December 15, but they care very much. They may therefore make concessions that they would not even consider a few days later, when the new quota year begins.

The same principle can apply to other deadlines, including quite informal ones. For example, if the other side's boss is going on vacation, he may have told them: "I do not want to worry about this problem while I'm playing golf. Get it settled by Friday." Friday, Monday, Tuesday—they are all the same to you, but the other side can almost see the boss's frown and hear him saying, "Oh, no, you mean I still have to worry about this. What is the matter with you, anyway?"

Manage the Deadline's Credibility

Deadlines have little effect if people do not believe them, and many deadlines are essentially ignored. For example, any publisher, including mine, will tell you that authors are terrible about deadlines. The deadlines are important to the publisher because they know all the work that has to be done to bring out a book, the importance of providing that book to the sales force by a certain date, and so forth. Authors are cavalier about deadlines because missing them costs us little or nothing. If we are late, however, the publisher has to work overtime, juggle schedules, plead with editors and printers, and so on.

Publishers have to learn to make their deadlines more credible, and you should probably do the same. If possible, manage both their timing and their credibility. If deadline pressure is against your interests, try to reduce the deadline's credibility and vice versa.

Reducing their credibility is quite often easy. Just say that you do not take them seriously, that they have been set arbitrarily or for administrative convenience. Of course, if the other side asserts that the deadlines are binding, the problem becomes more difficult. But even then you can weaken the deadline's impact by insisting that you will negotiate as long as necessary.

If deadline pressures favor you, magnify the deadline's importance. If necessary and possible, add teeth, punishments for not agreeing before the deadline. The need for deadline pressure is so common that one or both sides often add those teeth. Workers threaten to strike, countries threaten war, businesses threaten lawsuits if their demands are not met by a certain time.

The most credible teeth are events that you cannot control. For example, since a threatened strike, war, or lawsuit can usually be easily delayed, the other side may not take it seriously. But a deadline created by people you cannot easily influence such as a judge, higher executive, or board of directors is much more credible. For instance, if the boss has insisted that she be given a project plan before the Tuesday morning meeting of the budget committee, everyone knows they had better agree on it by then. If such a strong deadline would help you (if, for example, the other side likes to procrastinate), ask the boss to set it.

Lawsuits demonstrate the importance of deadlines. Many out of court settlements occur just before the trial is scheduled because both sides' expenses increase dramatically once the trial begins. Before then, neither side will compromise. You might therefore be forced to go to the trouble and expense of filing suit and waiting for the trial date to get the other side to negotiate seriously.

Manage the Final Momentum

As the deadline approaches and a deal is in sight, the momentum often builds quickly. The momentum can even take over, weakening people's judgment and caution. People may make concessions without carefully considering their implications because making a deal becomes the primary goal.

We discussed rapid momentum in chapter 4, "The Middle Game," and all those principles apply here. In fact, they are especially important because deadline pressures often accelerate the momentum and interfere with people's judgment.

If you can manage the final momentum, you may be able to get most of the dollars that are still on the table. The other side may relax and ignore the ratio of movement, especially if they are already within or very close to their range. They may just want to close the deal, to "grab the money and run."

Your bargaining position is an important factor, of course. If you have positioned yourself well, you can afford to move rapidly during the final moments. Therefore, if at all possible, plan to enter the End Game with lots of bargaining room and bargaining chips.

The other important factor is the ratio of movement during this final momentum. There are three possibilities. You may move faster than they do, at the same rate, or more slowly. Unless you have positioned yourself so well that you can afford to move more than they do, you must strive for the second or third pattern.

More generally, watch that ratio of movement, see where it is taking you, and move only as much as necessary to keep things going. Resist the temptation to escape from the tension by moving quickly. Try to ignore the time and other pressures. Keep cool, and make sure that you know exactly what you are doing. Do not move so rapidly that you give away any more than necessary.

Break Before Closing the Deal

Even though you may dislike inhibiting the momentum, break before the final agreement. A few minutes of careful thought then can save you years of problems. Check to make sure that the proposed agreement covers every important issue and that both sides have the same understanding of the agreement. If not, take as long as is necessary to settle things *now.* You can negotiate a compromise much more easily now than you can later.

The American-Soviet agreement on West Berlin offers a perfect example of the need to review an agreement before signing it. The American negotiators foolishly assumed that we had automatic, unrestricted access to West Berlin, but the agreement said nothing about it. We therefore had to spend billions of dollars on the Berlin Air Lift, and we still have frequent problems on the highways and railroads—more than forty years later!

Omitting an important clause is not the only reason to think carefully during those final moments. You must also make sure you understand the implications of every one of their requests, and the End Game's pressures and that final momentum can reduce your skepticism. Some devious negotiators will take advantage of this tendency by casually sliding something right past you. You may not even realize its importance until much later.

For example, in the late 1950's, when the inflation rate was only about one percent a year and the economy was in a recession, some unions made an absolutely brilliant move. Wage increases were generally quite low. A few unions therefore said to management, "Look, it is going to be very hard to sell this small increase to the workers. They are afraid the cost of living might get out of hand. We all know that inflation is running only about one percent a year now, but our boys aren't that sophisticated. Why don't we put in a cost of living adjustment, and it won't even be effective until the inflation rate passes, say five percent. There is no real danger to you, but it will make our people happier and help us to sell the deal to them."

A few managements accepted that adjustment without thoroughly analyzing its implications. Now they would give almost anything to get it out of their contracts. The automatic cost of living wage increases since then have often exceeded the negotiated ones.

Two points are important here. One, never accept anything unless you have a chance to study it. Even if you have to take a lengthy break or reject this offer out of hand, even if you have to bring the momentum to a screeching halt, do not accept it carelessly. Two, if you want to try to slip something past the other side, wait until the final momentum. Then they will probably be less cautious and analytic than at any other time.

LET THEM SAVE FACE

Preserving their face is always important, but it is particularly critical during the End Game when tension often causes people to overreact to even the slightest insults. A mutually beneficial deal can be lost for the silliest of reasons. For example, billion dollar merger negotiations have broken down over the title, reporting relationship, or even the kind of car that the president of the acquired company would have.

In addition, people often remember those last few minutes better than other parts of the negotiations. The earlier sessions often become a bit blurry, but they can vividly recall those final minutes. If they believe that they were beaten or tricked, you may have problems implementing this agreement or negotiating the next one.

Make Them Feel That They Have Won

Underlying many negotiations rituals is the need for everyone to appear to win. Most negotiations contain some win-lose elements and nobody likes to lose. In fact, many people would rather lose money than admit they have lost a negotiation. They will fight for the symbols of victory and walk away if they cannot get them.

If possible, *let them feel that they have won.* Even if you have gotten an exceptionally good deal for yourself, you might complain, "You really beat me this time, but I'll get you next time." If they give a transparent rationalization for a concession, do not gloat or punch holes in it; nod your head, agree with their reasoning, take the concession, and perhaps even try for another one.

Make a Final Concession

The mutual concession ritual virtually demands that both parties give a little at the end. In fact, some people would rather walk away from a profitable deal than make all the final concessions. If you have positioned yourself properly, you have bargaining chips or something else left for that final concession. Use it at the very last moments, *even if you do not have to do so.*

In his novel, *Texas,*[9] James Michener called this approach "leaving a little something on the table." You and they both know that you could have gotten a little more, but you let them have it. Your apparent motivations for conceding should depend upon their style. Certain people want to feel they have beaten that last concession out of you. Let them believe that by yielding grudgingly. Others would appreciate a gracious gift; give it to them, and say it is a token of your respect.

Offer to Split the Difference

Splitting is generally seen as a fair way to close the final gap because both parties move. Offers to split are therefore much more likely to be accepted than offers that are substantively identical, but expressed differently. For example, if you are $1,000 apart, you may get a better response to an offer to split it than to a concession of $500.

Obviously, you cannot offer a split unless you have positioned yourself properly. You must have enough bargaining room to split within your limit. The ideal position would allow you to split and end up well within your range and very close to your perception of their limit.

Watch Your Language and Your Manners

Because of the tension and sensitivity to insults, you must be very tactful. Never openly say, "take it or leave it," even when your position is so final that they really have no other choice. Make requests rather than demands. Do not imply that moving toward your position means surrendering.

Avoid personal remarks and attacks, no matter how angry you are. You may be sorely tempted to attack them, but it can cost you dearly. Instead, ease the tensions with an occasional joke or smile. Avoid gloating, especially when you really want to do so.

In other words, make those final moments as comfortable and natural as possible. Obscure the power-oriented competition with its implication of winning and losing. You are not trying to beat them up; you are working with them to settle the last few details of a mutually rewarding deal.

If You Win, Act Graciously

When you win, the natural thing to do is to gloat, especially if the negotiations have been tense or adversarial, but that is exactly the wrong thing to do. You usually need their cooperation and good will to implement the agreement, and you will probably have to deal with them again.

General Grant's graciousness at Appomatox is a splendid example of how a winner should act. The Northern armies had clearly won the Civil War. Since it had been so long and bloody, Grant could have been forgiven for trying to humiliate General Lee, the commander of the Confederate Army. But he knew that the North and South would have to work together to rebuild the country. When Lee arrived, the northern band played "Dixie" (the Confederacy's national anthem) and Grant offered unexpectedly generous terms, especially on symbolic issues such as the officers' keeping their personal weapons.

Most lawyers act graciously when they win. For example, they often shake hands with the losers and congratulate them on the way they handled the case. "Your cross-examination of Bob Jones was really brilliant, and I was worried when the judge ruled in your favor on disallowing Sheila Johnson's testimony." Some attorneys have even made public statements praising their opponents. For example, the attorney who successfully defended Bernard Goetz, who shot muggers in the subway, was quoted as saying that the prosecutor presented his case "brilliantly."

Why do they go out of their way to be gracious? Because they know that, sooner or later, they will meet again. They may even be on the same or cooperating sides next time, and they need a foundation for future cooperation. Above all, they do not want the losing attorneys to be so angry about losing that they are smarting for revenge, willing to do whatever it takes to win the next time. "I don't care that my client is paying me only $10,000. I'll put in another $30,000 worth of time to make sure I beat him this time."

SUMMARY

The End Game can be intensely stressful because the concessions are often painful, and the deadline creates time pressure. This stress creates so many problems that good nerves are essential. Otherwise you might respond to the tension, not the requirements of the situation. You may fight too hard or run away, and either action can damage your interests.

To ease the pressure on your nerves, prepare thoroughly for the End Game. You should be psychologically ready for its demands, understand the other side's objectives, power, and strategy, and have a good bargaining position. If you are not well prepared, you should probably try to extend the deadline.

Your first task is to test their limits. How far can you push them? To do so you should ignore your own MSP, push until they push back, look for signs of tacit acceptance, and use gentle threats and other tactics. While testing them, intently watch their reactions; if you seem to have gone too far, back off quickly. If they seem to be at their limit, and their last offer is within your range, take it, even if you have to swallow your pride. The purpose of negotiating is to reach mutually satisfactory deals, not to win symbolic victories.

Your most important task is to communicate credible finality. If they do not believe you when you say that you have reached your limit, they may try to push you further than you can go, causing a catastrophy such as a lawsuit, strike, or war. To make your finality credible you should escalate it slowly, use many of the tactics for testing the limits, commit yourself, and carefully time your statement of finality.

Deadline pressure must often be used because people resist making those final, painful concessions. In fact, most deals are reached at or shortly after the deadline.

Learn the other side's deadlines and use them, if possible. Manage the deadline's credibility: If the pressure helps you, increase the deadline's importance and vice versa. Manage the final momentum, the tendency to move too quickly when a deal suddenly seems within reach. You should definitely break before closing the deal;

make sure that it covers all your objectives and that you understand all its implications.

Your final task is to let them save face. This task is particularly important because the End Game's tensions often cause overreactions. Save their face by letting them feel that they have won, making a final concession, offering to split the difference, and watching your language and manners. And do not forget the importance of face after the negotiations are over. If you have won, ease their pain by acting graciously. You never know when you will need their good will to implement the agreement or when you will negotiate again.

The End Game is stressful, but if you keep cool, it can be enjoyable and very profitable.

8

Reviewing Your Negotiations

Because the End Game is so tense, you naturally want to ease that tension. When the negotiations are over, especially if they ended unsuccessfully, you may want to forget about them by playing golf, working on something else, or just putting your feet up. But that is *exactly* the wrong thing to do.

Instead you should immediately and carefully review the entire negotiation and the agreement. Most people dislike analyzing the past. They say, in effect, "It's over and done with. Let's get on to something else." That feeling is understandable, but harmful. It can cause implementation problems, interfere with your next negotiation with these people, and prevent you from improving yourself.

Professional negotiators know how important that review is. Most of them review their negotiations the way top bridge players review their hands and good football coaches review the game films. Every demand and concession is viewed through a microscope; words, gestures, even silence are weighed for significance. Other experts may be asked to comment. They may even use a computer to compare this one to others. They know the value of reviews, and you should know it too.

You obviously cannot afford to spend so much time reviewing, but any organized review can help you with the three tasks that this chapter discusses.

I. Implement the agreement

I. Plan future negotiations with these people

III. Develop your own skills

IMPLEMENT THE AGREEMENT

After signing the contract there are almost always details that have to be worked out. Who will do what? When will it be done? How can the work be evaluated and approved? If these and similar details have not been carefully agreed upon, further negotiations may be needed.

That is, implementing the agreement is often quite difficult, and many implementation problems are caused by conflicting perceptions. Disagreements about jobs clearly illustrate these problems. The job that you agreed to take is rarely the one you actually do, and both you and your boss may be frustrated by the other's insistence that the job be defined in a certain way.

> " I thought my primary job was to plan the overall strategy."
>
> "No, you're supposed to make sure that the strategy gets implemented. Barbara plans the strategy."
>
> "Barbara? I thought she was going to report to me."
>
> "No, both of you report to me, and she is actually a little more senior than you are."
>
> "I can't believe it!"

When someone acts according to their own perception, the other side may believe that they are violating the agreement. They may then file lawsuits, appeal to higher organizational levels, or use other means to force acceptance of their interpretation. They essentially negotiate the meaning of the agreement they have already reached, and these negotiations are often longer and more difficult than the earlier ones. That is, it is often harder to agree upon what a "contract" really means than it was to negotiate the original contract!

Why? Because both sides often righteously insist that they are correct, and sincerely believe the other side has acted in bad faith. With that attitude, compromise can be almost impossible. Rationality flies out the window; trivial issues become important symbols; trust and good will disappear. Neither side will let the other "cheat" them, even though nearly all disagreements are honest misunderstandings.

These problems are particularly common for negotiations within an organization because very few contracts are written down. Countless people have participated in a scene like this.

> " Where is it?"
>
> "What?"
>
> "That report you agreed to write on the quality control problem."
>
> "I never agreed to write any report."
>
> "Of course, you did, during the meeting in Ed's office."
>
> "You're kidding."
>
> (angrily) "No, I'm not."

A few simple steps can ameliorate these problems, but nothing can prevent them completely. As long as people are human, they will see things differently. You will be certain that they committed to do something, and they will be equally certain that they never made such a commitment.

Immediately Review and Clarify the Agreement

Before leaving the bargaining table, go over every point in the agreement. Check your interpretation against theirs and resolve the conflicts now. Resolving them is immeasurably easier now because you both remember the way you talked about each issue, and have that natural inertia that comes from making a deal. You probably feel good about the deal and about each other. Later, those positive feelings may be replaced by doubts; the inertia disappears or even reverses, and you cannot remember your discussions as clearly.

Your recollections of the negotiations are critically important because people's understanding of the agreement is naturally colored by the discussions. Most of us naturally hear what we want to hear and interpret our own remarks in ways that favor our position. While you both clearly remember the discussions, you can resolve the inevitable disagreements by discussing what each party said and how you interpreted these remarks.

You can also review the bidding and relate the concessions to the discussions. You might, for example, show that a certain trade meant that you were conceding this item, but not that one. A few minutes of discussion will usually settle most disagreements. Even if you do not settle everything, immediate discussions will help you both realize that you have an honest misunderstanding, that nobody is trying to cheat or act in bad faith. A discussion at the bargaining table might go something like this.

"Don't you remember that I said '....'? Then you said '....'"

"Yes, but I meant...."

"You did? I thought you meant...."

"Why?"

"Because you...."

"I can see how you could interpet it that way, but it is not what I meant. That is why I made the concession on..."

"OK, now I understand. Well, it looks like we've got a problem. How can we solve it?"

Note that this sort of conversation often ends with both greater understanding and a sense that *we* have a problem that we have to work out together.

If you do not learn of your disagreements until later, they are much harder to settle. Both sides may see the disagreement, not as an innocent misunderstanding, but as a deliberate attempt to cheat. They may therefore become stubborn and even abusive; minor disagreements become major symbols and neither will let the other get away with cheating.

Prepare a Written Memo of Understanding

After deciding how the agreement will be interpreted, write a memo of understanding and have both parties sign or initial it. These memos are particularly necessary if there will be no formal contract, or if other people will write the contract or implement the agreement. Despite the obvious value of these memos, people often refuse to write them, especially for agreements within an organization. It seems too formal, too cold. Or they do not want to appear dictatorial. Then they find some important tasks are either not done or done incorrectly.

If possible, write it before separating; a difference of opinion that could take several letters to resolve can often be settled in minutes if you write the memo together.

If time pressures prevent your working together, agree on who will draft and send it within a day or two. The cover letter should state that the memo represents only his or her perceptions, and it should encourage the other party to correct any misunderstandings. That message allows differences of opinion to be resolved smoothly, while a more authoritative tone can create unnecessary rigidity and unpleasantness.

Write Clear Agreements

An ambiguous agreement can create countless problems. The people who negotiated it may understand it, but the ones who must implement it will usually interpret it differently, with each side's interpretation naturally favoring them. The negotiators may not be able to explain the agreement (because it is implemented someplace else or the negotiators have changed jobs, or nobody asks). Implementation problems then become almost inevitable, and they can severely damage the overall relationship.

Both sides may feel that the other side is not keeping their word, thereby causing distrust and reducing cooperation. The agreement should therefore be so clear that it means the same thing to everyone. The only way to ensure this clarity is to use very simple language. Delete all flowery phrases, general philosophy, passive voice, and ambiguous words, and *write down exactly what everyone will do and when they will do it.*

Then discuss it with the other side to make sure that you both interpret it the same way. Rewrite any ambiguous parts so they mean the same thing to both sides. You may dislike "wasting" this time, but a clear agreement can save you much more time and money than it costs to write.

Of course, if you have a long-term, trusting relationship, detailed agreements become less necessary. Over time you have developed customs and understandings about how tasks will be performed; you also can resolve disagreements without the acrimony and skepticism we discussed earlier. However, even with this solid foundation, a written agreement such as a memo or letter can be useful. Countless relationships have been damaged by misunderstandings.

Keep the Lawyers Firmly in Their Place

Many lawyers are outstanding negotiators; others just think they are, and they can disrupt the negotiations and ruin the agreement. They can become so obsessed with legal minutia that the agreement becomes incomprehensible; the critical question of who does what gets lost in a mass of legal verbiage. No one can implement the agreement because only the lawyers know what it means!

To reduce this problem, insist that the lawyers act *only* as legal advisors, not as chief negotiators, spokespeople, or general business advisors (unless you have one of those rare lawyers with good business judgment, common sense, and the ability to write clearly). Do not let them say much during the negotiations, and insist that they direct their remarks to you, not to the other side. Do not let the lawyers take over the negotiation or get involved in endless debates about meaningless language issues.

Insist that they write an agreement that laymen can understand and implement. Then carefully review the agreement with the other side to make sure that you both interpret it the same way.

Some people have told me that their lawyers refuse to accept their control. The answer to this problem is very simple: Fire them (at least for this kind of work). They work for you, not vice versa. If they are too arrogant to accept the counselor's role, replace them with someone who will accept it.

Agree on a Means for Resolving Future Disagreements

No contract, no matter how well it is written, can cover all the contingencies of any but the simplest agreement. There will always be gray areas that have to be resolved on a continuing basis. You should therefore agree in advance about how they will be resolved.

Some means are quite formal such as grievance procedures or arbitration. Some are both formal and legalistic, such as a clause that "disagreements shall be resolved according to the laws of the State of New York." Formal actions should usually be taken only after other steps have been unsuccessful, and those steps should be specified in advance.

You might, for example, agree to meet at regular intervals to resolve disagreements. Or you can simply establish the principle that the primary negotiators will call each other whenever necessary. You might also agree that the people who negotiated the contract will be present at any meeting that attempts to resolve disagreements; the negotiators can often relate a disagreement to their original intent, which the agreement may obscure.

The important point is to agree in advance to try to resolve disagreements in a friendly, informal way, then continuously work to build a relationship that allows that approach to succeed.

PLAN FUTURE NEGOTIATIONS WITH THESE PEOPLE

If you are likely to negotiate again with these people or their organization, make your general plans now, while this negotiation is still clear in your mind. Some people object to that recommendation: "Why waste time? We will not negotiate with them for at least six months."

This objection is backwards. The longer the wait, the more important it is to plan now. If you wait until just before your next negotiation, you will certainly forget important information. For example, you may forget that they make outrageous first offers to see how you react, or that they do not answer questions directly and complete-ly, or that you should try for a relaxed, informal approach.

Planning future negotiations is a long-term application of the Feedback Loop principle, and it involves the same three steps: acquiring information (what happened?), interpreting it (what does it mean?), and using it (what should you do in the future?).

We therefore suggest that you use the Feedback Loop Questionnaire in Appendix 2. Do not go into too many details; just use its questions to organize your analysis and plans.

What Happened?

Before deciding why the negotiations went the way they did, you must clearly determine what actually happened. A common error is to omit or minimize this essential step by jumping to conclusions and planning your next negotiation. Fight that tendency by trying to recall, as objectively as possible, the actual sequence of events. What did they say and do? How did you respond? etc.

Your own emotions can also cause distortions. If you won, you may naturally remember the actions that contributed to your victory. If you lost, your frustration or dissappointment can easily color your recollections. But negotiations are rarely a complete victory or defeat, nor should they be so one-sided. Regardless of whether you won or lost, some actions had the effects you wanted, while others did not work at all. Focus on what happened, how both sides reacted, and minimize both your interpretations and your emotions.

If you negotiated as a team, have your entire team report their recollections, but leave the interpretation until later. Premature interpretations can cause you to overlook important facts.

For example, if you took a hard line and got a good deal, you may conclude that you should always take a hard line with these people. However, an objective review might reveal that they were in an unusually weak position because they did not have another vendor. They yielded grudgingly because they had no choice. They resent your hard line strategy, and they clearly intend to request competitors' bids before the next purchase. A hard line strategy could therefore be disastrous.

The same logic that we applied earlier about separating observations and inferences applies here, but, because you are focusing on a much larger picture, it is even more important. If you do not carefully analyze what happened, you can easily draw incorrect conclusions.

Reviewing your notes and making additional recollections will stimulate your memory and help you to see patterns you may not have suspected. You will get the clearest and most complete picture if you minimize interpretation until after you have a complete picture. Premature interpretations can cause you to ignore or misread information that does not fit them.

Try to review the agreement, the way they seemed to feel about it, both parties' initial positions, the pattern of concessions, and the way they talked and acted about each issue.

What Does It Mean?

After getting a clear picture of what happened, decide *why* it happened. Review the data, look for patterns, and ask yourself leading questions. The most important question, of course, is: How much money or other things did you leave on the table? You may have gotten a better deal than you anticipated, but how much more could you have gotten?

Then ask yourself how you could have gotten a better deal. Each possible tactic should be evaluated on two criteria: What concessions would it have produced? How would it affect the overall negotiation and your relationship?

To answer those questions, you must ask some additional questions about the other side. You have reviewed the bits and pieces: their offers, words, gestures, and so on. Now put it all together and ask the big questions: What kind of people are they? What kind of strategy were they using? Why were they using it?

Then break the negotiations down into individual steps. Ask how well you performed each step and what you could have done better. For example, during your preparation were you missing any important information? Did you make any incorrect assumptions? Did you define the issues correctly? Should you have set different objectives? During the Beginning Game did you create the right atmosphere? Communicate your position effectively? Really learn their position?

Then step back and look at the overall negotiations and ask some general questions: What did you do well? Poorly? How can you get a faster or more accurate understanding of their position? How can you communicate more effectively? Going back and forth from general to specific to general will help you to see how things fit together, the way the specific steps influence the general approach, and vice versa.

What Should You Do in the Future?

After answering these questions, write down your general plans for future negotiations. Use the same strategic dimensions we have repeatedly discussed: your general approach, alternative approaches, initial position, and so on. Within these dimensions set general guidelines for future negotiations: Decide whether you should take a harder or softer line, emphasize power, facts, or friendliness, be more or less detailed, start with a more or less generous first offer, and so on.

The few minutes you spend planning can be an enormous help when you prepare for your next negotiation. Instead of having to try to recall what happened and remembering it only vaguely, you just look at your notes and convert your general plans into specific ones for the subjects you will discuss. Therefore, in addition to planning a better strategy, you will actually spend much less time on it.

DEVELOP YOUR OWN SKILLS

After planning future negotiations with these people, you should consider the more general subject of your negotiating skills: How can you negotiate more effectively with *everybody?* The analysis of this last negotiation should have revealed some of your strengths and weaknesses, and analyses of other negotiations should certainly show some patterns. You probably make the same mistakes and demonstrate the same strengths in most negotiations.

Identify and plan ways to take advantage of your strengths and overcome your weaknesses. Two other parts of this book will help you with these tasks. Chapter 9, "The Effects of Personal Styles," will help you to see how your personal style affects your negotiations. Read it carefully, but cautiously. It provides general guidelines for certain basic styles, but you are an individual who does not fit exactly into any category.

Appendix 4: "The Self-Analysis Questionnaire," is much more specific. It requires you to describe or rate yourself on a number of negotiating dimensions and tasks, and then suggests how you can perform them more effectively. For example, you describe your own negotiating style and discuss its implications. You evaluate your ability to control the momentum and suggest ways to improve.

In addition to helping you to organize and plan your own development, this questionnaire can help you to get comments and suggestions from other people. In fact, we originally developed it for our workshop participants. Virtually every authority on training encourages people to discuss a training program's lessons with their boss, but these discussions will not be very useful unless they are structured properly. Without a clear structure, the discussion could go something like this.

> "Boss, the instructor suggested that we discuss our negotiating skills, strengths, and weaknesses with our boss. So here I am. What should I do to negotiate better?"
>
> Most bosses' first reaction would probably be confusion or even annoyance: I don't need this hassle, especially not today. Then they would probably make some vague suggestions such as read this book, take that course, or practice whenever you can. The question is just too vague and general for them to handle.

If you carefully complete this questionnaire and then discuss it with your boss (or anyone else), the conversation might be more along these lines.

> "I've been trying to improve my negotiating skill. I've read a book and completed a questionnaire, and I'd appreciate your reactions to it."
>
> "OK, let's take a look at it.... (looks through it). I agree with this point.... I disagree here, but it is not important.... Ah, here's something I've been meaning to discuss with you."

The reaction is much more positive and helpful because the topic becomes much more specific, and the other person can react to something concrete. In addition, the fact that you have analyzed yourself suggests that you are sincerely trying to improve, not just get reassurance.

We therefore encourage you to complete this questionnaire carefully and discuss it with your boss, friends, spouse, and co-workers. Doing so will help you to develop your skills, not just for the short term, but continuously.

The word "continuously" deserves additional comment. Negotiations are so complex, and the demands are so contradictory that nobody ever masters them completely. Each negotiation is different because it involves different people, different goals, demands, and so on. No style can always be right. Even the best hired guns make many costly mistakes. You should therefore regard developing your skill as a continuous task, one you must keep working on indefinitely. That may seem a bit depressing; we all prefer tasks that end at a specific time, preferably tomorrow morning, but life is not like that. Some tasks, especially those related to personal development, just go on and on.

But look at the positive side. If you keep working at it, while most other people do not do so (and they won't), you will slowly get an edge and, as time passes, that edge will get bigger and bigger. You won't win them all, because nobody wins every time, but you will win most of them.

9

The Effects of Personal Styles

Personal styles obviously affect negotiations. For example, a forceful, aggressive person might try to overpower people. That approach would produce some very good deals, but it could also result in many deadlocks. Lots of people would walk away or become rigid and stubborn.

A warm, friendly person would make many deals that the aggressive person would lose, while developing long-term, trusting relationships. In addition, that trust and the friendly person's natural sensitivity could cause the kind of open communication and understanding that results in a mutually satisfying, win-win deal. However, that same person might also be too trusting, even gullible, and some people, especially aggressive, competitive ones, might regard that friendliness as a sign of weakness and try to exploit it.

These two examples illustrate a point we made much earlier: There is no such thing as an ideal negotiating style. Each kind of situation requires a different approach. Always negotiating in the same way virtually guarantees some good results and some horrendous ones. You must therefore understand your own and other people's styles and adjust your approach.*

There are many different ways to describe people's styles, and all of them are both useful and incomplete. People are just too complicated to be described accurately and completely. We shall emphasize the way people relate to each other because relationship styles have so much impact on negotiations. However, this emphasis

*The system for describing personal styles was derived from my book and computer-based training course, *Selling: The Psychological Approach* (Minneapolis; Control Data Educational Publishing Company, 1978).

causes us to overlook many qualities such as intelligence and self-confidence which are so important that you must understand and adjust to them.

There are three basic ways to relate to other people: We can move toward them, away from them, or against them.

- Dominant people relate to *power;* they move *against* others with force and aggressiveness.
- Dependent people relate to *warmth;* they move *toward* others with warmth, trust, and friendliness.
- Detached people relate to *impersonal facts;* they move *away* from others with caution, aloofness, and indifference.

Please note that we are describing personal characteristics or dimensions, not discrete types. One can be high, medium, or low on any one of them. In addition, nearly everyone changes styles from time to time. One may even act in all three ways with the same person during the same meeting. However, most people have a preferred style that emphasizes one or two of these dimensions.

Which is the best style? It depends upon the situation. The personal qualities that help you in one kind of situation, harm you in another. For example, dominance is valuable, perhaps even essential, in highly adversarial, pure bargaining negotiations, but it alienates many people. Dependence helps to build strong, trusting relationships, but it can cause excessive concessions, and be seen as weakness or irrationality by dominant or detached people. Detachment helps one to prepare thoroughly, to master the numbers, and to avoid the destructive effects of emotions, but it also causes insensitivity and can make other people dislike one's coldness.

In addition, the value of each quality changes as the negotiations progress. Detachment is especially valuable during the preparation phases, particularly if the issues or numbers are complex. Dependence helps you to build trust and openness during the Beginning Game, to get moving during the Middle Game, and to pick up and respond effectively to cues about relationships. Dominance creates sensitivity to power issues, and it is invaluable when testing the limits and communicating finality during the End Game.

Therefore, if we had to say which style is best, we would say, balanced. There are times that an extreme style is desirable, but balanced people can relate to a wider range of people and situations, and they can act more flexibly and effectively. More extreme people are often controlled by their needs for power, warmth, and distance, which reduce their flexibility. Regardless of what the circumstances require, they may act in ways that make themselves most comfortable.

In fact, most of us emphasize personal comfort, not effectiveness. We do what makes us most comfortable and rationalize that we expect our natural style to get the best results. "I have found that you have to take control; let them know who is boss." "I think a personal relationship is most important; you have to build trust." "You're both wrong. You'll get the best results if you stick to the facts and keep personalities out of it."

All three of them are rationalizing because there is no *one* best approach. In fact, one reason that negotiations are so difficult is that you are often required to shift from a comfortable pattern to an uncomfortable one. The more sensitive and adaptable you are, the more effectively you will negotiate.

This chapter will explain how to make those adjustments. It contains four sections:

I. The Extreme Styles
II. Combinations of Styles
III. Negotiations Between People with Different Styles
IV. The Ideal Negotiator

THE EXTREME STYLES

The three extreme styles are essentially caricatures. Pure types are extremely rare and, when you encounter more balanced people, you must modify your assessments and approach. Eight aspects of each extreme style will be presented:

1. General characteristics
2. Fears
3. Hidden question
4. Attitude toward negotiations
5. Negotiating strengths
6. Negotiating weaknesses
7. Best way to approach them
8. If you are extremely...

Extremely Dominant People

Because dominant people crave power and success, which often bring fame and notoriety, there are many prominent examples: John Wayne, General Patton, football coach Vince Lombardi ("Winning isn't the most important thing; it is everything."), N.Y. Yankees' owner George Steinbrenner (one of his limited partners once said, "Nobody is more limited than his limited partners.").

General characteristics

Extremely dominant people nearly always want to take control. They are very competitive and must win at everything. Business, golf, even cocktail parties are contests. They need to make more money, have a lower handicap, and score more points at parties.

Status-consciousness is a natural part of their competitiveness. When they meet a stranger, they want to know: "Am I better than he is? Do I make more money, own a larger house, play better golf?"

They tend to be ambitious, tough, aggressive, manipulative, overbearing, closed-minded, and antiintellectual.

They are usually insensitive and very poor listeners, partly because they do not really care about what most other people think. They will listen to the few people they respect, but the heck with everyone else. This indifference comes from their feelings of superiority and the corollary attitude that only powerful, successful people have anything worthwhile to say. Since they value their own time much more than other people's ideas, they often interrupt "lesser mortals."

Since everything is a contest, they cannot afford to think about abstract subjects or other people's feelings. It would distract their attention from the only goal that matters—winning.

Their insensitivity relates primarily to other people's opinions and feelings. They are often extremely sensitive to the things that they really care about: money, power, and other people's MSP. In fact, some of them possess an instinct for the jugular, an almost uncanny sense of where other people are weak and how hard they can be pushed.

Since winning is so important, some extremely dominant people may cut corners. They would rather not lie or cheat because it taints their victory, but a tainted victory is infinitely better than a defeat. Because they will do anything to win, they assume others will do the same. They therefore distrust other people.

James Bond's character, Goldfinger,[10] illustrates this emphasis upon winning at any price. When they played golf, James knew that it was not enough just to beat Goldfinger; he had to beat him by *cheating!*

They tend to be impatient and inattentive to details. They often regard details as beneath them, something for lesser beings to consider, and they regard their time as so valuable that they resent wasting it, even on essential social rituals, understanding other people, and other valuable tasks.

Dominant people are independent and individualistic. Taking orders, accepting advice, or following procedures are kinds of defeats. They insist on doing things their way and may break rules to do so. One of the Robber Barons (ruthless nineteenth century tycoons) once said, "The hell with the law. Don't I have the power?"

Fears

They are afraid of losing, of weakness in themselves, and of being dependent on other people. In fact, psychiatrists have coined a term for them, *counter-dependent.*

Some dominant people are so counter-dependent, so afraid of any sign of personal weakness that they cannot ask for help or even admit that they have made a mistake. A few of them literally kill themselves by playing five sets of tennis or working excessive hours a short time after a heart attack.

Hidden question

Nearly all of us have hidden questions about other people. In essence, we ask: "Are you my kind of person?" We may test people repeatedly until we get an answer.

The hidden question of most dominant people is: *Are you good enough to do business with me?* (Because I do business only with people like me, the best.)

It can be phrased in many ways. "What is your title?" "Did you make quota last year?" "Where do you live?" "What kind of car do you drive?"

Extremely dominant people often play games. They test your toughness by keeping you waiting, interrupting you, taking outrageous positions, or just generally acting rudely. If you let them get away with it, they often decide that you are too weak to work with them.

I was tested that way once, and I failed. I had recently moved to Belgium as a visiting professor. In Europe, professors are almost always treated with extreme deference.

While interviewing me for a position as a part-time consultant, the prospective client said, "You've got the right background, Schoonmaker (not Mr., Dr., or Professor, the only polite forms of address between strangers). But the problem with you is that you've got no scruples. You'll work for anyone, and we have some very sensitive information here."

If I had become indignant, he almost certainly would have apologized. Instead, because I was young and eager for the business, I said, "I can see how you would be worried about confidentiality."

I lost two ways. I never got any business from him, and now, twenty years later, I'm still angry!

Attitude toward negotiations

Many dominant people love negotiations. They are seen as a game, another type of competition, a challenge, and an opportunity to win. Because all's fair in love and war, the goal is usually to defeat the opponent as completely and visibly as possible.

Because they understand and relate to power, they especially like and excel at power-based, pure bargaining. They find its inherent conflicts stimulating and exciting.

As we shall see in a moment, their attitude produces both strengths and weaknesses.

Negotiating strengths

Their greatest strength is their sheer enjoyment of the process. Other types of people avoid negotiations or rush through them, while they are more than willing to play the game.

They excel in adversarial negotiations, such as bitter labor versus management bargaining, price negotiations, or emotionally charged litigations. In any situation where power is the deciding factor, they have the advantage.

They are also comfortable with conflict and its associated emotions. They often excel at using the Law of Irrationality. They have few, if any, qualms about using extreme demands, aggression, and anger as tools to intimidate or sway an opponent. Stalling, balking, and devious tactics to squeeze a last concession are natural actions for them, while many other people simply refuse to act that way.

As we noted earlier, they often have a great instinct for the jugular. They sense where other people are weak and just how far they can be pushed. They will push right to the limit, getting virtually every penny on the table.

They may also position themselves well. They build their power well in advance, while less power-oriented people often neglect positioning. They also create lots of bargaining and trading room by making ambitious, even outrageous offers.

In the End Game they can be formidable because most of its demands match their strengths. They have probably built a strong position and have a fairly clear idea of the other side's strengths, weaknesses, and limits. The End Game's tension bothers most people, but they thrive on it. They may therefore make those final few minutes very profitable. They may "hang tough" and are often good at bluffing, at going right to the brink of a deadlock. Since other types of people are usually more flexible, dominant people often get some last minute concessions.

Negotiating weaknesses

The preceding description may have implied that these people are natural negotiators, but they excel only at competitive, adversarial negotiations. They are terrible at satisfying other people's needs, working together to solve joint problems, and building long-term, trusting relationships.

Extremely dominant people lack the essential sensitivity and balance. They often overemphasize pure bargaining, even when they should be problem solving. They have to win, even if a victory costs them more than it is worth. For example, they may fight hard to win symbolic conflicts or push the other side to their absolute limit, thereby damaging or even destroying the relationship. They may even try to push past the other side's limit, thereby losing both the deal and the relationship.

Their need to dominate often prevents them from creating trust and cooperation. Their competitiveness and suspiciousness inhibit the open communication needed to solve joint problems.

The essential win-win nature of problem solving is alien to them; they respond to it the way the Boston Celtics would react to the suggestion that they make a game more interesting by giving the Los Angeles Lakers a few easy baskets.

It just goes against their grain to make good will concessions or to accept less than they can get. Compromises are often seen, not as a means toward reaching a mutually satisfying deal or as a way to build good will, but as a sign of weakness. They may not make some essential compromises or do so in such a grudging way that the other side resents it.

Their concept of giving is to toss a crumb. They may feign cooperation to deceive and catch their opponent, but sooner or later, most people can see through such ploys.

Their extreme competitiveness often creates unnecessary and destructive stubbornness. They can essentially make the Law of Irrationality work against them: Other people can become so upset that they refuse to make concessions they had originally intended, and they may even walk away from a profitable deal.

They also tend to think in terms of only one strategy, and they may continue with it long after it should have been discarded or modified. Changing strategies could be seen as admitting that the original strategy was a mistake, and they tend to have a simplistic approach to negotiations. If pushing hard doesn't get the right results, push even harder. If the other side does not agree with their position, they repeat it, but speak more forcefully.

They say, in effect, "Since you are not able to understand my manifestly correct position, I will repeat it using words that someone of your limited intelligence can understand."

Their insensitivity creates numerous problems. In fact, a major reason for their failure at mixed negotiations is that they often do not know what the other side really wants. They cannot fit together a mutually satisfactory deal because they are too insensitive, too talkative, too weak at listening to understand the other side's signals.

Their impatience and lack of attention to detail can be serious problems. They may, for example, rush into an agreement without fully understanding its implications. Or they may sign an agreement that is so vague and general that the people who have to implement it cannot interpret it accurately.

The End Game, when they often excel, can also be the time they make their greatest mistakes. They can get so caught up with winning, with testing those limits, that they push a little too far. Either the negotiations break down, or the other side feels so defeated, that they smart for revenge or decide not to do any future business. They win the battle, but lose the war.

Best way to approach them

Your most effective approach is smooth dominance. You must prove that you are tough and competent without appearing to challenge them. Do not let them push you around, but don't try to push them too far. Show that you are a winner who deserves their respect, but also show respect for them.

Relate directly and respectfully to their success and toughness, but show that you are also tough and successful. Never grovel or beg, and use strong, assertive words and gestures.

Do not smile too much or spend a lot of time on small talk. They perceive those actions as signs of weakness or lack of seriousness. Get right down to business and move briskly. Talk rapidly, in short sentences, and avoid details. Relate as one "big picture" person to another.

Establish a powerful position *before* the negotiations because they will probably test you and your position.

Leave yourself lots of bargaining and trading room by making an ungenerous first offer. Then move from your initial position by trading small concessions. Do not move too quickly or too easily, because they want to beat concessions out of you.

Never give them anything in the hope they will appreciate your gift and reciprocate. They will probably just see it as a sign of weakness and become even more demanding.

In other words, walk in there ready to fight, but do so in a good humored, sporting way. It is all just part of the game.

If you are extremely dominant

Lighten up. Don't push so hard. And concentrate on understanding the other side.

These two themes interact with each other because that obsession with winning may prevent you from understanding, or even trying to understand them. All of our specific recommendations relate to one or both themes. Build on your natural strengths, but adjust to the negative effects of your personal style.

Don't make everything into a contest or battle, and be a little selective about which battles you do win; focus on the important ones, and let other people win once in a while.

Work on listening better. Remember, learning the other side's position is the single most important negotiating skill.

Listen with your eyes as well as your ears, and try to understand more than just their negotiating positions. Look for signs that you are pushing too hard, that other people are becoming unnecessarily stubborn or are even thinking of walking out. Try to understand how they feel, and what they want from you besides a good deal.

Be more flexible. Make your offers a little more reasonable, your concessions a little larger, and your compromises less grudging. Make them want to concede instead of creating unnecessary rigidity. Don't make the Law of Irrationality work against you.

Get away from that overemphasis on pure bargaining. Look for problem solving and trading opportunities. How can you structure a deal that satisfies *both* parties?

Continuously remind yourself of the importance of letting them save face; then make a concession or take whatever action will make them feel better.

In other words, *try for a greater emphasis upon win-win.*

Extremely Dependent People

Elizabeth Taylor, Mickey Rooney, and many other people who marry repeatedly illustrate extreme dependence. They are so desperate for love and acceptance that they can never get enough of it; they change mates again and again, hoping that someone, somewhere, will fill that aching void.

Jimmy Carter had many extremely dependent characteristics. Instead of leading forcefully, he was deliberately self-effacing (carrying his own luggage, walking at his inauguration, being called "Jimmy"), and he constantly pleaded for understanding and affection from us, our allies, even the Soviets. He also illustrated some of dependency's positive effects. After years of war, Nixon, and Watergate, we needed a decent, honorable president who inspired trust and openness.

General characteristics

Extremely dependent people crave love, acceptance, understanding, and approval from others. That is, they really are *dependent* upon others' feelings about them.

They are warm, friendly, and sincerely interested in other people. They are happy being part of a group and enjoy most social gatherings. They are gracious and welcoming, with a natural ability to make others feel welcome and comfortable.

Because they sincerely like other people, they are good listeners who are genuinely sensitive to other people's needs and feelings.

They communicate openly and honestly and expect the same from others. Because they know that they can be trusted, they tend to trust other people, even when they should be more cautious or skeptical. (Used car salespeople love this kind of customer.)

They are cooperative, flexible, and compliant. They go along with other people's ideas because they trust others and want to be liked.

They also tend to be givers. They want to help people, especially those who reward them with gratitude and affection.

All these characteristics make dependent people popular. Many people naturally like and trust them. However, some people, especially dominant ones, can easily manipulate and exploit them. They go along with suggestions, even when they should be more skeptical, perhaps even when they suspect they are being exploited.

Fears

Dependent people are afraid of being alone, of rejection, and of all forms of conflict (including competition). They are also frightened by hostility, especially their own. They want to believe they feel warmly toward everyone and vice versa.

These fears can create serious problems during certain kinds of negotiations. They nearly always try to create a friendly atmosphere, even when an indifferent or even adversarial one might be more appropriate. Or they may appeal to the other side's generosity, even when dealing with a devious, manipulative crook. Or they may take an impersonal conflict as a personal affront.

Hidden question

Do you really care about me? They want to deal only with people who sincerely care about them, so their key concern is your sincerity.

Part of the reason for this question is their past experiences of being exploited. Knowing that they are vulnerable to exploitation, they may be suspicious about others' sincerity. They wonder, are they really trying to help me, or do they just want to get me to do what they want?

Some of them therefore play their little games. These games are different from those of dominant people, but they have the same general objective: to answer that hidden question, to learn if you really are their kind of person.

For example, dependent customers often object that sales reps ignore them except when they want to make a sale. "How come I never see you except when it's time to buy something?" They may smile while asking, but it is often an extremely serious question.

Attitude toward negotiations

Dependent people generally dislike negotiations, especially their competitive elements. They may also fear that bargaining will cause other people to reject them. They therefore tend to avoid negotiations, rush through them, or make unnecessary concessions just to escape the tension.

If they do negotiate, they generally overemphasize joint problem solving. Even in situations that clearly call for bargaining (such as price negotiations with strangers or ones in which the other side is taking a hard line), they may try to work cooperatively. They may even rationalize, "Well, one of us has to be reasonable. Since they are being so unreasonable, I'll have to move and hope they will do the same."

In addition to causing them to lose many negotiations, that attitude actually encourages some people to take advantage of them. They are essentially rewarding the others for making outrageous demands, stonewalling, or lying.

Because they abhor conflict, they are comfortable only when joint problem solving, but virtually all negotiations contain a significant amount of conflict. In some negotiations, especially ones with a great deal of conflict, this discomfort can be an extremely serious liability.

Negotiating strengths

Their pattern of strengths and weaknesses is almost exactly the opposite of dominant people's. One is strong where the other is weak and vice versa. Dominant people are natural bargainers; dependent people are natural problem solvers. Dominant people exaggerate conflict, while dependent people minimize it or deny its existence.

Dominant people will tend to win many negotiations, but they will also miss many deals. Dependent people will make deals that nobody else could make, turn around bad relationships, and establish a foundation for future cooperation, but they will frequently leave lots of money on the table.

Dependent people excel at joint problem solving negotiations for many reasons. First and most important, they genuinely want to work out a fair, mutually successful agreement. This desire for fairness is especially valuable during negotiations within an organization; they will strive for an agreement that is best for the company as a whole, while protecting everyone's interests. They will not try to develop a personal empire, nor will they play dirty politics.

They also know how to diffuse tensions, to bring together people who do not want to cooperate, to break deadlocks and get on with the business at hand, qualities that nearly every organization can use.

Because they communicate openly and honestly, they encourage many other people to do the same. Both sides can therefore build on that essential foundation of trust and information.

Since they genuinely want to understand others and are good listeners, they often learn the other side's goals, motives, and constraints. Then, their natural fairness allows them to work out a mutually satisfactory agreement.

Their natural flexibility can result in creative explorations and problem solving. Instead of considering only one or two ways to put together a deal, they may experiment and explore, thereby coming up with a creative and superior solution.

They build solid, trusting, long-term relationships. Many people like to work with them, and some of them will even accept an apparently inferior deal because they know that dependent people can be trusted to implement the agreement honestly, give that extra service, make sure that they are treated fairly.

They are usually exceptionally good team members. Instead of insisting on doing things their own way or using the team to advance their own selfish interests, they cooperate with their teammates and follow instructions.

These strengths make them valuable members of most organizations, especially highly competitive ones. They add relatively rare, but virtually indispensable qualities.

Negotiating weaknesses

Their strengths as problem solvers are matched by their weaknesses at bargaining. In fact, these weaknesses often are generally greater liabilities than those of extremely dominant people. Not all negotiations contain significant problem solving opportunities, but conflict is an essential element in virtually all negotiations. Without conflict, there is, in fact, no need to negotiate.

Many dependent people simply cannot accept that reality. In fact, the greatest negotiating weakness of dependent people is naiveté about conflict. They are so frightened of conflict that they may even wish it away, ignoring the obvious fact that it is as inescapable as death and taxes.

Their naiveté affects many aspects of negotiations. For example, they may openly share information and expect that others will reciprocate, but many, many people withhold information, bluff, or even lie during negotiations.

Jimmy Carter clearly demonstrated this naiveté. He ignored history and many of his own advisors, believed the Soviets' most outrageous lies, and made many unnecessary concessions. Then, when they invaded Afghanistan, he publicly lamented that he had never understood what kind of people they were.

Extremely dependent people may essentially invite exploitation by approaching nearly all negotiations as problem solving sessions. They may even feel guilty about competing or trying to protect their own interests. Therefore, in many situations that call for bargaining, they give away too much, letting the others win handsomely, rather than fight for their share.

Despite their perceptiveness about people's needs and feelings, they are not at all sensitive to power and other people's limits. In fact, they tend to be gullible, to believe people when they pretend to be strong or insist that they cannot make concessions.

A final weakness derives from their inherent fairness. When they feel that it has not been reciprocated, they can become extraordinarily rigid. They let people push and exploit them again and again; then, because they feel betrayed and exploited, they absolutely refuse to move one more inch, even if some concessions are clearly justified.

For example, deadlines for video productions can be extremely rigid. Studios, actors, and directors are booked months in advance, and it costs over $10,000 for each scheduled day whether you are shooting, waiting for the star to show up, or rewriting the script. The final scripts must therefore be approved well in advance because the actors must memorize their lines, sets and special effects must be designed, the director must decide how to shoot each scene, and so on. Any lateness creates numerous problems for other people.

A dear friend is a highly talented writer. Although she is responsible for the final script, she must rely upon the people who provide input or approve the scripts, and they often take advantage of her. They submit things late, do not even read their assignments before script conferences, and generally make her life miserable. She may have to work 20 hours a day for a week or more to compensate for their irresponsibility.

Because she is exceptionally fair and reasonable, she lets them get away with it until they go too far; then she "flips out." "I won't change one word! Not one comma! I don't care if the script makes sense or not!"

Less extreme, but similar reactions occur fairly frequently. Very few people are as rigid and stubborn as a dependent person who feels exploited. If you do not return their sincerity and fairness, they may become so angry that they refuse to make justified concessions or may even walk away from an acceptable deal.

Best way to approach them

Focus on the relationship. They do business with people they like and trust. Establish rapport and build trust, and make sure you deserve that trust.

Recognize that they instinctively avoid conflict, and the entire idea of negotiating may be distasteful to them. They would rather determine what is fair to both sides and accept it without dickering.

Stress fairness throughout the negotiations, and do so sincerely. Do not take an outrageous position and insist that it is fair. Take a reasonable, but ambitious position and show *why* it is fair. They will probably try to please you if they believe it is fair to both of you.

Remember that their concern for fairness and mutual satisfaction presents both opportunity and risk for you. The opportunity is that they may want to help you to meet your objectives, if they feel that you are being fair. Conversely, if they feel you are being devious, or playing games, or trying to exploit them, they can become stubborn, inflexible, or even spiteful. Therefore, when dealing with extremely dependent people, especially ones with whom you want a good long-term relationship, you should usually resist that natural tendency to take advantage of them; it can backfire on you.

If you are extremely dependent

Toughen up. Be less trusting and generous. Accept the fact that conflicts during negotiations are inevitable, and that most conflicts do not imply personal rejection or hostility. They are just part of the game. Try not to feel hurt or rejected.

Build on your natural strengths, but adjust to the negative effects of your personal style. Do take advantage of your natural ability to please people and build relationships, but do not become so accommodating that others treat you as a doormat.

Stand up for what is rightfully yours, and let people know well in advance what you think you deserve. Then, after you learn to demand what is rightfully yours, try for some of the money and other concessions that are rightfully nobody's, that money on the table (or at least the loose change).

When the situation calls for it, bargain, even if it makes you uncomfortable. Don't overdo it, but look out for your interests. Take more ambitious opening positions. Make smaller concessions. Trade concessions instead of giving them away. Use that natural flexibility to move toward creative win-win solutions, but avoid making concessions just to get an agreement or in the hope of creating good will.

Be a little more skeptical. Accept the unpleasant fact that lots of people are not completely open while negotiating, and some people will flatly lie. Do not violate your cherished values, but don't be much more open and honest than they are. Remember, information is power until you give it away; then it can return to haunt you.

Tune in to power, people's limits, and their priorities. You are already sensitive to their feelings and attitudes toward relationship issues. Use that natural sensitivity to decide what people really want and how much they will concede. Then try to get a little closer to their limits instead of leaving so much money on the table.

Insist on reciprocity. The best negotiation is one in which both parties are being frank and flexible. If they are willing to act that way, by all means go along. But don't play that game all by yourself. Be only as open, trusting, and flexible as they are. If they refuse to reciprocate, get tougher because the worst negotiation is one where you are frank and flexible, and they are devious and rigid.

Apply the MSP concept. Set a firm MSP based on your economics, then commit to it with someone important such as your boss. Doing so will help you to resist those pressures to go too far.

Above all, realize that you can bargain, even bargain hard, without making people dislike you. In fact, most people will respect you more if you become a little tougher.

Extremely Detached People

Because detached people shun publicity, we know relatively little about their personalities. We have all met highly detached accountants and engineers, but *People* magazine does not write about them (and they would be horrified if it did).

Two excellent examples are fictional characters, and one of them is from another planet, Spock of "Star Trek" ("I have no emotions."). The other is Joe Friday of "Dragnet." He would listen with that bored, cynical look on his face while witnesses talked about feelings and told personal stories; he then would say, "Just give me the facts."

General characteristics

They are more comfortable with things, ideas, or numbers than they are with people. They do not understand emotions and try to avoid them. They suppress their own emotions and ignore other people's. They are usually insensitive to other people's feelings, and they tend to be shy, aloof, impersonal, sometimes even uncommunicative.

Because they are so indifferent to emotions, most people regard them as cold and uncaring, a criticism that is often justified.

They usually like order and predictability. Their desks, homes, offices and checkbooks are neatly arranged, and they often have tightly controlled routines and schedules. This need for order is a major reason for avoiding people, because they are not as orderly and predictable as numbers or machines.

They are independent, but in a different manner from dominant people. They have even less need for people, but do not want to flaunt authority. They readily accept the impersonal authority of rules and procedures (at least those that make sense to them), but avoid people who attempt to control them directly.

They tend to be quiet, and many of them are low reactors. They do not say much, nor do they communicate their thoughts and feelings by their voice, gestures, and facial expressions. One computer systems analyst showed so little emotion that we called him "OCR." He reacted like an optical character reader—"Data received and stored. This is a recording."

Many people find their lack of reactions so disturbing that they talk too much or take extreme positions in a vain attempt to force a reaction. I learned that lesson the hard way. While I was still a professor, I gave a talk to a group of Swiss bankers. Previous audiences had reacted well, laughing, smiling, nodding their heads, but this group just sat there, frozen faced, arms and legs crossed, revealing nothing.

I started to perspire. My voice got louder, my delivery faster, my gestures more extreme. I ad-libbed, told exaggerated stories, threw in every joke I could think of.

Nothing! They sat there like a bunch of statues.

As I was packing up my things, wondering whether to slit my wrists or jump off a bridge, someone came up and said, "Professor Schoonmaker, you were so funny we could hardly keep from laughing." I stared at him, absolutely flabbergasted. "Then why didn't you laugh?" He replied, "Swiss bankers would never laugh at a professor's lecture, it just isn't done."

Detached people are usually open-minded, especially about impersonal issues. They like facts and logic, and they value objectivity. If someone challenges their position, they do not respond angrily. They analyze the facts objectively and will change their position if the data disagree with it.

They like to work alone and tend toward fields that require objective, impersonal analysis, such as chemistry, physics, engineering, mechanics, accounting, statistics, and computer science. They enjoy this type of work and are most comfortable with the kinds of people who enter these fields.

Fears

Extremely detached people are afraid of intimacy, dependency, and unpredictability. When people get too close to them, they may become extremely uncomfortable, so upset that they simply have to get away. Their fears of dependency and unpredictablity are closely linked. If they are dependent upon someone, they cannot tell what will happen, which can really scare them.

Some extremely detached people cannot tolerate any kind of disorder, even on trivial issues. For example, a friend's ex-husband would become furious if she put his long and short sleeved shirts in the same part of his closet. Other detached people may alphabetize their spice racks or put their wine lists onto their personal computers.

Hidden question

Are you a logical, rational problem solver? Or are you one of those people who relies on emotions? Both kinds of emotions, the dominant person's tough ones, and the dependent person's tender ones are undesirable. They would much rather deal computer to computer than person to person.

Attitude toward negotiations

They generally dislike negotiating, and this antipathy can be quite intense. They dislike nearly everything about negotiations: the rituals, the illogical positions, the concern for atmosphere, the emotional factors, and so on. If they could do so, they would simply refuse to negotiate. If they have no choice, they would like to negotiate by mail or telex—anything to avoid all those emotions and illogical actions.

They tend to overemphasize joint problem solving, but for different reasons from dependent people. They are realistic about conflict, but want to resolve it, not by appealing to good will, but by using facts, objectivity, and rational analysis. Instead of bargaining, they would prefer to shop around, find the best price and value, then just pay it. If they have to deal with a particular person or organization, they would rather avoid give and take negotiations by finding an objective standard such as an impersonal appraisal or a market value.

They intensely dislike pure bargaining because it seems irrational to them. They simply despise the entire idea of asking for much more than they expect to get, distorting their position, playing the mutual concession game, and so forth. They find the entire process repugnant.

Negotiating strengths

Their natural objectivity and analytical ability are sources of both strengths and weaknesses. They can gain an advantage by remaining cool and analytic, even when others become emotional or irrational. However, as we will see in a moment, detached people often ignore essential, but irrational aspects of negotiations.

They prepare thoroughly. In fact, it is their favorite negotiating step because it is the neatest. They can focus on the facts without having to think about what other people think, how they are acting, and so on.

Their preparation regarding the issues can be exceptionally thorough, but they may ignore the human elements. In addition to studying the other side's proposal, they may do extensive research about other alternatives. For example, as buyers or sellers they may carefully study the market, learn how products compare and what they cost, and the terms offered by different vendors.

This thoroughness builds their power in several ways. First, during the negotiation they have important facts right at their fingertips. Second, they almost automatically position themselves well; while researching the market, they learn about other alternatives. Third, this research and their alternatives increase their natural indifference. They can walk away from this deal and make a different one.

During the negotiations they clarify issues thoroughly and almost never act impetuously. They understand the implications of any position or concession before acting. Controlling the momentum is therefore rarely a problem, but they often have trouble creating it.

They do not give away valuable information. On the contrary, they often get much more information than they give. Their low reaction style causes many people to talk too much, even about sensitive subjects, trying to force some reaction out of them.

They are also willing to walk away rather than accept a bad deal, perhaps even rather than respond to an unrealistic position. In fact, some of them are masters at applying the Law of Indifference. They use it, not as a ploy, but because they genuinely are indifferent to negotiating when the other side has taken an unreasonable position; they would rather talk to someone else or drop the entire subject.

Negotiating weaknesses

Their greatest weakness is clearly their dislike for negotiations. They may respond to their discomfort, not the demands of the negotiating process. In fact, some of them are extremely ignorant and indifferent to these demands. They simply cannot be bothered with them.

They may therefore avoid some negotiating sessions, or ignore the need to create the right atmosphere, or try to convert bargaining sessions to analytic problem solving meetings, or violate essential rituals.

This last point must be expanded. Despite detached people's dislike for them, most people like rituals such as shaking hands, making small talk, and discussing the agenda. They regard the mutual concession ritual (You move a little; I move a little; and so on) as the essence of negotiations. Violating it is often seen as a sign of bad faith.

Many detached people violate it regularly, perhaps without even realizing that they are doing so. Instead of building "fat" into their proposal, then trading it away, they start near or even at their MSP. The other side often resents their rigidity and bad faith, and they may even break off the negotiations rather than make all the concessions.

Detached people also tend to be insensitive to the other side's motives and concerns. They may miss signals, including quite obvious ones, because they really do not care what the other side wants. They care only about objective facts and figures.

They are particularly insensitive to emotions, politics, and other irrational subjects. For example, they may not see any need to make concessions to build good will, create momentum, or help the other side with its management or constituents. Countless people have said that negotiations with their own people are often more difficult than those with other organizations, and one frequently needs help from the people across the table.

For example, if a detached person makes a proposal with no fat in it and refuses to move, the other side's political position may be weakened. Their bosses may criticize them for gaining nothing from the negotiation.

Union negotiators often need a similar sort of help. Political factors may force them to make undesirable demands. For example, the unskilled workers may demand a reduction in the wage differentials between skilled and unskilled workers, which the union leader knows will alienate the long-term, highly skilled workers that both the union and the company need. To placate the unskilled workers, the union leader may make the demand very forcefully, even threatening to strike for it. If the management negotiator does not pick up the signals that say, "Don't take me seriously," the reduction may be granted, thereby hurting both sides.

The same sort of problem occurs in negotiations between corporations. The buyer's vice-president of engineering might insist on such unrealistic specifications that a piece of equipment cannot be priced realistically. Since the buyer's purchasing people cannot ignore a vice president, they have to demand these specifications. The vendor's negotiator must understand the situation and strenuously resist this demand. Then they can settle on more realistic specifications and prices.

That thorough preparation which can be so valuable also has a negative side. Some detached people prepare so thoroughly that they become rigid and closed minded. They will not even consider alternatives that they have not thoroughly researched. They may move forward, executing those plans, ignoring obvious signals, irritating the other side, and preventing consideration of more creative and mutually beneficial arrangements.

They may also be too rigid for another reason. Sometimes they believe that what is right or just or most cost-effective cannot be compromised. They may place so much emphasis upon certain facts, principles, or procedures that they cannot make the compromises, especially the essentially tactical ones. The momentum may never start, or it can break down, or the detached person may even walk away from an otherwise satisfactory agreement rather than accept an illogical position on a relatively minor issue.

Their thoroughness may directly inhibit momentum. So much time can be spent clarifying issues, including quite unimportant ones, that there is not enough time to make trades, explore creative alternatives, etc. The whole process can become bogged down in the details.

Their final weakness is their predictability. The other side can usually determine their limits, priorities, power, and strategy fairly easily. Skilled negotiators can often take advantage of that predictability.

Best way to approach them

Virtually the only way to deal with them is with facts, figures, and logic. Keep personalities and emotions out of the discussion. Do not try to intimidate or warm them up. Attempting either one can just turn them off.

Prepare thoroughly, and make sure you have all the facts needed to support your position. They can be swayed by cost savings and economies, but only if they are substantiated by convincing proof.

Propose detailed, well organized positions, and make them reasonable! Outrageous or even slightly ambitious proposals can end the negotiations before they start. Detached people typically make and expect offers close to the final deal, and they may walk away rather than respond to a proposal that they regard as unreasonable.

While preparing, make sure that you allow enough time to negotiate slowly and carefully. They will thoroughly study your proposals and the evidence supporting them. Then, if you have convincingly shown that costs or the market or other objective facts are different from their expectations, they will probably move—slowly.

Above all, adjust to the fact that negotiations are not a game to them. They dislike the game aspects of negotiations so much that they will frequently refuse to play.

If you are extremely detached

Loosen up. Accept the obvious fact that negotiations are often illogical, that there are gaming elements, that emotions and other irrational factors frequently and inescapably affect many negotiations.

Build on your natural strengths, but adjust to the problems your personal style creates.

Accept the fact that most people like rituals, so go through them. It doesn't cost that much time or energy to shake hands, make small talk, and so on.

Try to tune in to the other people. Broaden your focus beyond the facts and figures and try to understand what they want, why they are acting this way.

If they are likely to bargain, suppress your natural tendency to make reasonable offers, then stay at or near them. Position yourself by making a first offer that gives you enough trading room to swap some concessions.

Try to put together deals that satisfy both sides, and this satisfaction should include the other side's personal and political motives. You may not care about those motives, but they do.

Continue to plan thoroughly, but try to build some flexibility into your plans. "If they do this, we'll do that. But, if they object to this position, we will...."

During the negotiation show a lot more flexibility. Set your plans aside temporarily and focus on what both sides want to accomplish. Then openly consider a variety of acceptable solutions, resisting the tendency to stick to one best solution. Not all people are logical, and some solutions can seem illogical and still work. Negotiations, by definition, include ambiguous areas. Therefore, seek a solution that is perhaps less than ideal, but still satisfies both parties' major objectives.

If possible, consider completely new ways to put the deal together. Since you naturally dislike rushing into areas you have not analyzed, get their ideas about other ways to structure the deal, then break to analyze their proposal. You might be surprised; their approach might be better than yours, or some combination of the two might be better still.

Above all, accept the fact that negotiations are between people, not computers, and work on that personal dimension.

COMBINATIONS OF STYLES

Now that we have discussed the three extremes, let's consider combinations of styles.

Dominant - Dependent

President Lyndon Johnson was a good example of a dominant-dependent style. He was extraordinarily power hungry and manipulative, yet he constantly complained that people did not like him.

These people have strong drives for power and acceptance, and they may be sensitive to both power and people. At their best, they have a drive to succeed and an ability to work well with other people. They therefore tend to perform well in many managerial and sales positions.

That missing detachment can create some real problems. They may not prepare carefully, see the big picture, or understand the long-term implications of any strategy. The name of the game is now. Get this contract. Establish that working relationship. Ignore the dangers and ambiguities. Damn the torpedoes; full speed ahead!

For example, Lyndon Johnson rushed into a massive escalation of the Vietnamese War, while increasing domestic spending for his Great Society. Any economist could have told him that massive inflation was almost inevitable (and many of them did so), but he simply did not listen. He was going to win that war ("Nail that coonskin to the wall"), and everybody was going to love him because we would all be so prosperous.

This type of person is also unlikely to succeed in fields requiring considerable analytic strength. For example, putting such a person in charge of highly skilled scientists in an R&D unit would probably be a disaster. They would regard the boss as a lightweight, a politician.

For many negotiations it is a superb combination. That drive to win, ability to relate to people, and sensitivity to power and people will win many negotiations. Once again, Lyndon Johnson is a good example. He was terrible on television and some of his policies were disastrous mistakes, but he was an incredibly effective negotiator as a senator and president. He knew just how to use carrots and sticks, where the real power was, and how to get things done. He therefore could push bills through a congress that flatly rejected similar bills from John Kennedy.

The dangers are, of course, that these people's lack of vision and inability to prepare may cause deals that do not fit into a coherent strategy, plus the high probability that the deal itself may be so carelessly drawn that people cannot implement it effectively.

Dominant - Detached

Harold Geneen, former chairman of ITT, had an extremely strong need for power; he would do almost anything to win, even support a bloody revolution in Chile. But he was also an extraordinarily thorough planner with an unbelievable mastery of details. Again and again he would astonish people by pointing out the inconsistencies between an apparently trivial action and the overall plan.

Many high level executive positions have similar, but less extreme patterns. At the very top, people are often regarded as essentially irrelevant: employees, customers, even other executives are disregarded. For example, President Roosevelt essentially ignored his vice-presidents; when Harry Truman became president, he was astonished to learn that the United States had built an atomic bomb.

Top executives live in a rarified world, almost completely divorced from the mundane concerns of most other people. Conceptual skills are the ones that count, and they must be combined with that drive to move the organization in the right direction. As my friend, Jay Meagher put it, "Up there all anybody talks about is planning and control."

It also fits the demands of many managerial jobs in high tech and other analytic organizations. Engineers, scientists, accountants, and so on prefer to be led by people who understand their technical specialties, keep their distance, but provide direction.

As a negotiating style it is much less desirable, except in a few situations. It can work when both parties are this kind of person; the issues are complex; and the negotiations require combining bargaining and problem solving.

In most other situations, this style can have very negative effects. The drive to win while remaining aloof strikes many people as very cold and manipulative. Add pushiness, insensitivity, and indifference and you have a pattern that can prevent any genuinely human communication. People may respond the way all of us react to a computer's insistent demands. "Our records show that you have not paid your outstanding balance of $0.03. If that amount is not paid immediately, our attorneys will file suit." None of us wants to negotiate against a domineering computer.

Dominance and detachment also create two mutually supportive types of rigidity. Dominance causes people to push harder when they encounter resistance, and detachment causes people to prepare thoroughly, then execute their strategy, even if it does not work.

Robert McNamara repeatedly stated that if we increased troops, or dropped so many tons of bombs, or took some other action the Vietnamese would negotiate, or surrender, or take some other positive action.

They never did what he expected them to do, and he never changed his strategy, with disastrous results for everyone.

Dependent - Detached

This combination is extremely rare. It is rather difficult to go toward people and away from them at the same time. Albert Einstein may have been this sort of person. Certainly, he was indifferent to power and status, and his work and habits showed extreme detachment: His mind was in a different world from ours. However, some anecdotes suggest that he was also an exceptionally warm person, at least at times. For example, he would tactfully and patiently coach promising young scientists.

Since it is such a rare combination, we can only speculate on where it would fit in business or other organizations. It could be a good pattern for the head of a group of exceptionally well- trained, independent professionals. For example, it might fit at Bell Labs, IBM research, or a science department at a top university, where outstanding people essentially "do their own thing." This kind of person would have the warmth and patience to be supportive, and the analytic ability to understand the issues.

It may not be an appropriate pattern for negotiations which contain substantial conflicts. More dominant people could take advantage of the combination of rationality and the desire to please.

It would, however, be an ideal combination for negotiations with complex issues, relatively little conflict of interests, and a mutual desire to have a pleasant, long-term relationship. For example, it would be an excellent approach for members of a task force assigned to a complex problem that was important to two parts of the same organization or organizations with a close, long-term relationship. The detachment would help them to solve the problem, while the dependence would facilitate their working relationships.

Balanced

Giving examples of famous balanced people presents the same sort of problems that political cartoonists face when they want to draw caricatures of a face with no prominent features. Cartoonists need a nose like Richard Nixon's, or a jaw like Brian Mulrooney's, or a grin like Jimmy Carter's. Since the essence of balance is nothing in extreme, we are far from certain that our examples are correct.

John Kennedy and Abraham Lincoln are possibilities. They certainly had strong power drives; one does not become president without them. They both seemed to care about people, and they knew how to appeal to people's emotions. And they seemed to be visionaries, able to step away from short-term issues and look objectively at the larger picture.

The critical distinction of balanced people is flexibility. Instead of being controlled by their own need for power, warmth, or distance, they can shift from one style to another: friendly today, analytic tomorrow, pushy when necessary. They can therefore act effectively in more situations than other people.

This flexibility can, however, confuse and irritate some people. They wonder: "Who is he? What is he really like? What does he really want?" The more extreme the other people are, and the more flexibly the individual acts, the greater this problem can become.

Despite this negative, we have to repeat that—other things being equal—balanced is the best style. Sometimes you need a less balanced person; in a few cases, such as when you are negotiating against a real power player, you even need an extreme person. But the balanced person can work effectively in the broadest range of situations.

NEGOTIATIONS BETWEEN PEOPLE WITH DIFFERENT STYLES

Birds of a feather do not just flock together; they also negotiate well with each other. Dominant people get the best results from other dominants, and people with different styles should usually become more dominant when negotiating with them.

People with different styles often have serious problems negotiating with each other; they neither understand nor satisfy each other's needs. Understanding these problems can help you to adjust your style or select someone else to negotiate with certain people. Do not send Bill to negotiate with Susan because their styles clash. Send Tom if you really want the best possible deal this time, or Barbara if you are more concerned with the long-term relationship.

Dominant with Dominant

When dominant people meet each other, it is often war. Both feel, "Either you or I will win, and it is not going to be you." Their negotiations often contain very visible power clashes with direct threats, theatrics, and brinkmanship—a scenario most people would find nerve racking, if not abhorrent.

Because both sides are so intent upon winning, many of these negotiations end in deadlock. One or both of them might prefer losing a profitable deal to yielding to the other side, perhaps even on a trivial or symbolic issue.

Even if a deal is reached, one or both of them may feel cheated or defeated. Implementation problems often occur because agreements tend to be carelessly drawn, and the negotiators may try to win back what they lost during the negotiation. They may therefore fail to fulfill their commitments, insist on renegotiation, or appeal to a higher authority.

The long-term relationships are, of course, contentious. Trust is rarely established, and both sides may keep a mental black book recording all the insults, lies, and defeats that they intend to repay, with interest.

Surprisingly, despite extreme unpleasantness, they often respect each other. They respect worthy adversaries, and despise wimps. After all, what fun is competition if there is no challenge? They are like two boxers who batter each other for ten rounds, then hug each other after the final bell.

If you are primarily dominant, the earlier suggestions about dealing with dominant people and adjusting to your own dominance apply here—in spades! Both sides should lighten up, soften the conflict, and protect each other's pride. Try to make it less win-lose, more a mutual victory between two strong, competent parties. You should also be more careful about writing the agreement. Spell out clearly who will do what. Otherwise, implementation problems, perhaps even demands to renegotiate or appeals to a higher authority, are quite probable.

If the other person is clearly dominant, your negotiator simply must have considerable dominance. If possible, choose someone whose dominance is tempered by tact and sensitivity, but who has that essential core of dominance. Sending a dependent person is like sending a lamb into a lion's den. A detached person has a better chance to survive, but probably will not be tough enough to fight back effectively. In fact, they may both become so frustrated that they cannot reach a deal.

Dependent with Dependent

They usually relate well to each other, and have pleasant, productive negotiations. They satisfy each other's relationship needs, communicate openly, understand each other, and strive for a mutually fair agreement. They may even end up with an exceptionally creative conclusion because both sides are flexible and willing to explore a wide variety of alternatives.

However, selecting a dependent negotiator may reduce the stronger organization's profits. Its negotiator may not take advantage of its power and settle for a poorer deal than it could have gotten with a tougher approach.

This negative is trivial compared to the positive benefits. Therefore, you should normally send a dependent to negotiate with another dependent person, unless you have compelling reasons to send someone else (such as wanting to take advantage of a strong position).

If you are dependent and are negotiating with another dependent person, you might want to be just a little tougher than usual. Do not deceive the other person or push too hard, but do try to pick up some of that loose change, that money in the middle of the table that neither of you cares much about. Your bosses might care a lot more than you do.

Detached With Detached

Their relationships with other detached people are comfortable, but distant. They enjoy each other's minds, and neither makes emotional demands upon the other.

Negotiations between two detached people are typically rational, unemotional, and tedious. Every detail, implication, and remote possibility must be explored. Decisions are rarely made quickly; in fact, negotiations that their bosses hope will take one day may require several meetings over a period of weeks. But the negotiators usually do not mind because the process is not stressful; in fact, it is as close to an enjoyable negotiation as they are likely to encounter.

Although their bosses and other people may be frustrated by the delays, that time is often well spent. When working together detached individuals' natural rigidity often softens, and several possible solutions may be considered, including quite creative ones. The final agreement may be much better for both sides than either could have achieved on its own.

In addition, the agreement itself is usually carefully drawn, with little left to chance. Implementation is therefore likely to be quick, smooth, and economical, which may more than compensate for the "wasted" negotiating time.

Therefore, unless you need a quicker agreement, or you want to take advantage of a strong position, you should usually send a detached person to negotiate with another detached individual.

If you are both detached, you might personally try to move things along a little faster, but do not push it. A creative agreement that can be implemented quickly and smoothly is usually worth that extra time.

Dominant with Dependent

Now that we have seen how people with the same style interact, let's shift to interactions between different styles.

There are natural conflicts between people with different styles, regardless of who they are or where they interact. Both sides naturally think that their style is right, that the other's style is a sign of weakness, irrationality, coldness, or some other negative quality.

Since negotiations always contain conflict, these personal conflicts are often magnified. Skillful negotiators find ways to diminish conflict, or to use it to their own advantage. We will therefore describe these conflicts and recommend ways for both sides to modify their normal approach.

The conflict

When dominant and dependent people must negotiate with each other, they have markedly different reactions. The dominant person may smile and think, "Ah, lunch is served." The dependent person may feel dismayed and frightened, "Oh my gosh, how am I going to cope with Attila the Hun?"

When encountering a dependent person, dominant people often act even more aggressively than usual. They despise the other's weakness and feel they can get away with almost anything. They may flaunt their power, make personal insults, scream, keep the other person waiting, make extraordinary demands, stonewall, and threaten to break off the negotiations. For example, during some negotiations, Hitler allegedly became (or faked being) so enraged that he threw himself on the floor and chewed on the carpet, thereby terrifying his more rational opponents.

Many dependent people let them get away with outrageous actions, at least for a little while. They naturally accept a submissive role, and do not know how to handle direct conflicts, personal attacks, and irrationality. They may therefore "eat crow," make unnecessary compromises, even beg the other side to be reasonable and generous. These reactions often have exactly the opposite effect. The dominant person, seeing that the hard line approach is working, becomes even more contemptuous, and takes an even harder line.

Obviously, the dominant person wins most of these negotiations (unless the dependent one becomes so angry that the negotiations break down). The victory may be too easy to be really gratifying, but it can be very profitable.

However, that profit is usually very short term. Many dependent people will simply avoid future negotiations. They will go someplace else, even if doing so is objectively costly. They would rather pay a little more or settle for a little poorer service than put up with such unpleasantness.

If they are forced to negotiate again, they may change their entire strategy. Away with reason, trust, and flexibility. "You want to fight, you son of a gun? OK, let's fight, and I will fight dirty."

This shift in attitude can even occur during the same negotiation. After reacting reasonably to the insults, attacks, and outrageous positions, the dependent person may become even nastier and more rigid than the opponent. Their resentment becomes so great that they forget that they are there to reach an agreement and lash out in extremely destructive ways. They may flatly refuse to compromise or even deliberately sabotage the negotiation or the agreement's implementation.

Recommendations to the dominant person

When dealing with dependent people, remember and respect their need to be liked. That need is neither better nor worse than your need to win; it simply exists.

Instead of showing your contempt for that need, respect it and realize it creates a splendid opportunity for both of you. Your needs are complementary, not conflicting. You can satisfy their need for warmth while also satisfying your own need to win.

Soften your entire approach and make it more personal. Take the time to establish a warm atmosphere; communicate more openly than usual, and treat them as equals to gain their trust. Many dependent people admire the dominants and envy the confidence you exude; if you offer them your friendship, it will usually be accepted. Because they are eager to please, it is easy for a friend to get a favor, even in a negotiation.

Remember also that they want to find a fair compromise and that they almost invariably emphasize joint problem solving. If you soften your approach, they may not even notice that you are essentially pure bargaining.

Depersonalize and soften conflicts. For example, instead of insisting that they must yield to you, tell them you have an insoluble problem. "I wish I could go farther. In fact, I called my boss and tried as hard as I could to get authority to do so, but he said that management's policies absolutely prevent my moving." Many dependent people would accept that position, perhaps even sympathize with it. "We have the same kind of bureaucratic rigidity in our organization. How can we work it out?"

Appeal to their sense of fairness, and base those appeals on a reasonable foundation. You cannot sincerely ask them to be fair if you are being manifestly unfair and unreasonable.

Above all, make sure you do not push them too far. Watch for signs that you are approaching their objective or psychological limits. If you sense that you are pushing too hard, back off in the most gracious possible way. Don't turn a potentially valuable, flexible friend into a rigid, vindictive enemy.

Recommendations for the dependent person

Nowhere must you be more cautious and suspicious. You are the natural prey of a dominant negotiator. Most of your tendencies to trust, to be open and honest, and to be fair and flexible merely invite exploitation, even contempt. This exploitation and contempt may be shrewdly camouflaged, but they are probably there, working against your interests.

You must therefore be cautious, skeptical, even devious. A direct confrontation will probably end with your defeat because they know how to handle power, threats, and so forth better than you do. So use their personal style against them. Let them have the appearance of victory, while you get what you really need.

Plan a careful strategy and use the Feedback Loop to revise it. Try to learn when the dominant person is bluffing, distorting the facts, or trying to bully you. Do not take it personally. It is merely the way they play the game.

Suppress your natural instincts and take extreme positions. You must create lots of bargaining room. Then slowly swap concessions, crying all the way, to make them believe they are pushing you right to your limits.

Make indirect proposals and suggestions that do not directly contradict their proposals. Use their terminology and format for proposals to give them a symbolic victory. "Show weakness" in precisely the places you want them to push. That is, let them push you right to where you want to go.

If you are really lucky, you might even manipulate them into "stealing" your ideas. For example, the Soviet proposal that led to the 1987 nuclear reduction treaty was essentially a proposal that the United States had made several years earlier. They got the credit for taking a dramatic step forward, but we got the kind of treaty we wanted.

Use your natural flexibility and problem-solving ability to find alternatives, then let the other side choose among them. Take advantage of their obsessive competitiveness by letting them feel that they are defeating you, without your making unnecessary sacrifices. At the end of the negotiation, pretend to be defeated, even dejected. Later, you can "cry all the way to the bank."

In other words, let them have the symbols of victory, while you get the substance.

Dominant with Detached

This is not a match made in heaven. Dominant and detached people naturally dislike each other.

The conflict

Dominant people see the detached ones as bean counters, trivial clerks, regardless of their title or authority. The detached people see them as emotional, illogical bullies.

Dominant people are actually more frustrated by detachment than by dependency. They may feel contempt for wimps, but at least they get a reaction from them. They get virtually nothing from detached people. They have a strong need to be noticed, while detached people ignore almost everyone. To get that attention, they may become even more aggressive, which causes further withdrawal, perhaps even a request to negotiate with someone else. Eventually, the dominant person may just give up ("he's hopeless").

Detached people feel equally negative. They value rationality, have little interest in power, and cherish their privacy. They dislike dominant people's superficiality, lack of planning, and inattention to detail. They fiercely resent the pushiness, insistence on personal reactions, and attempts to intimidate.

The net result is that negotiations between them often get nowhere. Since neither side can understand the other, they may never even get started toward a deal. It is not just a personal relationship problem, one that can be solved through better communication. They have fundamentally different values and approaches to negotiations.

For example, their first offers are grossly misinterpreted. The detached person's first offer is close to the MSP, but the dominant person naturally decides that there is lots of bargaining room and tries to get most of it. The dominant's first offer may seem so unreasonable that the detached person breaks off the negotiations because a deal seems impossible.

They may also have doubts about the other's competence and authority. Dominant people may assume that a "bean counter" cannot possibly be a decision maker, while the detached person doubts that someone so irrational could really be influential.

Their negotiating styles do not clash; they just miss each other. They base their approaches on premises that the other ignores. The dominant person naturally uses power tactics, but to no avail. The detached person is not easily intimidated, because only facts have intrinsic power. Yet these facts mean little to dominant people because they tune in only to power, money, and so on.

Their negotiations are therefore akin to the irresistible force meeting an immovable object.

Recommendations for the dominant person

Detached people present an extremely difficult and frustrating problem, one which requires you to adopt an entirely different negotiating strategy. You may have contempt for dependent wimps, but at least you could understand them; you both need reactions from people, albeit different kinds of reactions. Detached people are "a breed apart." They really do not care about other people's reactions, and their entire way of thinking is alien to you.

Your first and most important task is to accept this fact. Until you do so, you have little chance of influencing them. They simply do not care about the things you value so highly, nor will they be intimidated, coerced, or bullied. They will not fight back, nor will they beg for mercy. They will simply walk away.

That reaction frustrates you, and you naturally want to grab them and force them to fight, but the more you try to force them, the further they will withdraw. You must therefore deal with them on their terms.

Set that whole power trip aside; it is simply irrelevant. Focus only on the facts because facts are all that they care about.

Recommendations for the detached person

First and most important, resist your natural aversion to dominant people. Of course, you dislike, perhaps even feel afraid of them. But you have to deal with them.

Why? Because there are lots of them, and they tend to occupy important positions. If you think about it, their success is not really surprising. They have such a strong need to succeed that they naturally end up in influential positions.

Since dominant people tend to attain power, many negotiations are power-oriented. The people in charge of any activity naturally ensure that it satisfies their needs. For example, most R&D departments are managed in a low key, logical, orderly way.

Do not expect that facts, which have so much power over you, will necessarily influence other kinds of people. They may simply ignore undesirable facts. To dominant people the only facts that matter are the ones that affect power. They simply do not care about the technical details that are so important to you.

Therefore, build your power by acquiring and using the right kind of facts. Your natural thoroughness is a major asset here. Gather the facts that support your case, not on logical grounds, but on power. For example, when selling something, do not justify your price by providing facts about your costs. A dominant buyer does not care about your costs and profits (or losses). Provide the facts that the buyer cares about, the competition. "We are 3 percent cheaper than the competition, and our delivery is more reliable."

Your power is based on the competition, and the better your price (or other factor), the stronger you are. Of course, your power depends ultimately on the other side's motives and situation, and most detached people are not at all sensitive to those subjects. For example, if your prices are higher, but you can deliver much faster than the competition, you are in a weak position with price-oriented buyers, but a very strong position with ones that need prompt delivery. Of course, the shrewd buyers will not tell you that delivery is their key priority.

You must therefore work on your critical general weakness: insensitivity. With dominant people you must find out what they really want and what they will do if they do not make a deal with you. Those are the critical power questions, and you must tune in to them.

Tuning in is important because dominant people do not respond to questions the way you do. If you are asked a question, you normally answer honestly. If they are asked the same question, they may give whatever answer supports their position. You must therefore focus on subjects that you normally ignore, such as their tone of voice, gestures, postures, and facial expressions. Try to learn their real situation, not the one they want you to believe.

Detached with Dependent

This combination can cause a rather unusual relationship. Nothing dramatic happens, but both parties are often profoundly uncomfortable.

The conflict

The word "conflict" is a bit inappropriate here, since there usually is no overt conflict. Instead, there is an awkward, little dance. The dependent person keeps trying to get closer, while the detached one keeps dancing away. The closer they get, the better the dependent one feels, and the more the detached one needs to escape.

Their needs are completely contradictory: Closeness and distance are absolutely antithetical. Detached people need space, and they feel contempt, fear, hostility, and anger toward dependent people. They regard them as illogical and emotional, the two most deadly sins in their book. They resent dependent people's demands upon them and are frightened by their attempts to get close.

Dependent people need closeness, and detachment makes them feel rejected. Detached people's need for distance and emphasis upon impersonal facts is seen, not as an expression of their inner needs, but as a personal rejection.

These feelings affect nearly every aspect of negotiations. The dependent person wants to socialize, while the detached person is cold and indifferent. The detached person presents a lengthy proposal and explains it in great detail, which the dependent person regards as boring and irrelevant. The dependent person appeals for fairness, and the detached one says, in effect, "Spare me the speeches. What are the facts?"

Recommendations for the detached person

First and most important, try to accept the other person's need for closeness as legitimate. Of course, it bothers you, but the need for closeness is just as legitimate as your need for space.

Loosen up and try to relate more personally. You will never be, nor do you want to be "chummy," but you can afford to spend a few minutes in small talk, and you can probably find a few common interests.

Ask more open-ended questions and listen to the answers. Some of those answers will be vague, general, or irrelevant, but you will also learn facts that you would never get from more specific questions. You will also learn how they see the situation, which, despite your prejudices, might be even more important.

Accept digressions and personal stories as legitimate, even desirable. They may make you uncomfortable, but they also provide information that you could not get from direct questions.

Minimize details. You love them, but they may irritate dependent people. Agree first on general principles, including ones that seem meaningless to you (such as, "We will try to work out all problems in an informal, cooperative way."); they need that sort of agreement. You can discuss the specific details later, perhaps with technocrats to whom you can relate more comfortably.

Do use your logic, but soften it and make it more personal. Remember, dependent people want to agree, so give them lots of reasons to do so. But present those reasons in a way that they can relate to, not as if a computer had made a decision that they must implement.

In simplest terms, suppress for the moment your need for distance and relate to their need for closeness. It will not be pleasant, but it is the best, perhaps the only, way to deal with them.

Recommendations for the dependent person

First and most important, set aside your feelings of being personally rejected. There is nothing personal about it; detached people want to be distant from everybody.

You must therefore relate to them on their terms, using facts, not feelings. You may believe that you and dominant individuals are extremely different, but people are important to both of you. You both care about how they think, feel, and react. It is therefore difficult for either of you to accept that detached people simply do not care about people, feelings, status, closeness, and so on.

Detached people are different, as different as humans can be, and you must relate to them and negotiate with them as they are, not as you would like them to be. Most of our recommendations to dominants apply to you with only a little modification.

Focus on facts, facts, facts. Remember that their objectivity can help you. They will accept your positions if you have the facts to support them.

Prepare thoroughly, and emphasize facts. Ignore or minimize the relationship issues that you would usually emphasize. Get those essential facts about costs, benefits, and alternatives. Go even further: get documents and other evidence supporting those facts. They will take nothing on faith; they believe in evidence.

Suppress your need for a more personal relationship and create a rational, analytic atmosphere. Even if it bores you, analyze all the issues thoroughly and objectively before either side makes an offer. Provide factual, logical justification and evidence supporting all your offers, even though they may be extremely reasonable. Do not expect them to take even the most reasonable offers on faith. These people believe only in evidence.

Whenever you offer a trade or ask for a concession, provide logical, factual support for it. Why should they agree?

Avoid all emotions, especially appeals to fairness. Emotions simply do not matter to them.

By now you may be saying, "Those recommendations make sense, but I just cannot implement them." Do your best with them, while following a few, much easier rules. Shorten the handshake. Forego the coffee and small talk. Keep your distance, and be especially sure not to touch them. Minimize jokes and digressions. In other words, remember that your natural desire to make people comfortable means that you must act in a rather unnatural way.

THE IDEAL NEGOTIATOR

Earlier chapters have ended with a summary, but it seems unnecessary here. The theoretical personality types are quite simple, and we have related them to a wide variety of situations. We shall therefore end this chapter with a brief answer to a perennial question: What are the characteristics of an ideal negotiator?

Our answer is quite simple: There is no such thing.

Of course, some qualities help in nearly all negotiations. Intelligent people are better than dummies. Flexible people are better than rigid ones. People who prepare do better than those who "wing it." But once we get past a few cliches, we see that the very qualities that are indispensable in one negotiation can be disastrous in another one. Each negotiation makes its own demands, requires a different approach, and needs a different kind of negotiator.

Therefore, if I had to describe the relationship pattern of an ideal negotiator, I would say:

The ideal negotiator has an extremely rare combination of essentially incompatible drives and skills.

He or she has the dominant person's drive to win, toughness, and ability to use power, the dependent person's sensitivity, warmth, and ability to build long-term trusting relationships, and the detached person's objectivity, analytic strength, and ability to master complex information.

Do you know anyone like that? Neither do I. So we all have to do the best we can with what we have. We have to look honestly at ourselves, and the situations and people we encounter, build on our strengths, and try to overcome or compensate for our weaknesses.

It is certainly not easy to do that. We have to be really tough on ourselves, accept unpleasant truths, make painful adjustments. But it is worth the effort!

10

Negotiations Between Teams

Negotiations are a complicated process, and working as a team adds a whole new set of complexities. This chapter will help you understand and adapt to these complexities. First, it will help you to decide whether to negotiate as an individual or as a team; then it will tell you how to organize and control your team. It consists of four sections.

    I. Should You Negotiate as a Team?
   II. Organizing Your Team
  III. Controlling Your Team
   IV. Summary

SHOULD YOU NEGOTIATE AS A TEAM?

That question should always be asked, and it is often hard to answer. You gain a lot, but you can also lose as much or more. You must therefore make a judgment call about which way to go. This section will analyze the very substantial advantages and disadvantages of negotiating as a team rather than as an individual.

Advantages of Negotiating as a Team

Teams have a number of advantages over individuals, but their value depends upon the situation.

More information and ideas

A team has more information and ideas than just one person. Two or more heads are usually better than one. How much better they are depends upon the range of information and talent within the team and the issues to be negotiated.

For example, if a negotiation will focus upon a narrow set of issues, experts in other subjects can be superfluous, perhaps even disruptive. Conversely, if a wide range of subjects will be considered, and some of these subjects require specialized expertise, the team should include the appropriate specialists.

Technical experts are not the only people who can provide useful information and ideas. In fact, a layman can often contribute insights the experts would miss. The experts are so well trained, such complete masters of their specialty, that they may miss points that might be obvious to a layman, perhaps even to a child.

A senior director at a major consulting company put it this way:

> The ideal consulting team would consist of a senior director and two six-year-olds. The director would provide the judgment, and the six-year-olds would provide the new information. They would bring new pairs of eyes to the situation, see things that I would miss, and report them with their customary frankness.
>
> For example, they might say, "Nobody smiles, and everybody looks so grouchy." Presto, you see that you have a morale problem. Or they might say, "They sure seem to have a lot of people doing the same thing," and you realize that the company is overstaffed.

A Nobel Prize winning physicist approached this subject somewhat differently. He said, in effect: In the next few years physicists will do wonderful things, make amazing discoveries, but I won't be one of them. I'm too old (he was about 45 then); I know too much. As soon as a new idea comes into my head, I immediately know why it won't work.

History certainly supports his position. Many great scientific discoveries were made by young people. For example, Newton and Einstein, the two greatest physicists, had completed their major contributions long before they reached 30.

Superior analysis

Teams usually analyze situations better than individuals. In addition to having more information and ideas, they also have superior analytic processes. Individuals tend to analyze intuitively. They get a general feel for the other side's objectives and strategy, but do not really challenge their own assumptions.

A team's analysis is more explicit and objective. People have to explain their positions, justify their assumptions, and consider each other's perspectives. Anyone who has worked on a committee has experienced this process. Just trying to explain your position to someone else helps to clarify it. In fact, we have all tried to explain a position to a willing listener and suddenly realized that our position just did not make sense. Putting it into words forced us to see that it did not hang together.

In chapter 2, "Getting Ready to Negotiate," we suggested discussing your plans with someone else. Such discussions will generally be even more valuable with members of your own team because they will be more knowledgeable and motivated than outsiders.

The same principle applies to the negotiating and reviewing phases of the process. After the negotiation is over, a team's review will almost always be better than an individual's.

The superiority of a team's analysis is particularly significant during the negotiations phase. Teams use the Feedback Loop much better than individuals do. Members must explicitly state their positions and the information on which they are based. Other people challenge their facts or interpretations, causing everyone to understand the situation more clearly. A team meeting might go something like this.

"I think that their top priority is price."
"Why?"
"Because you can see how they talk about it."
"What do you mean?"
"Well, it seems really important to them."
"Then why have they made two price concessions, but refused to move on the length of the contract?"
"Gee, I hadn't thought of that…Maybe price is not that important after all."

Specialized roles

In many negotiations, particularly those that combine bargaining and problem solving, there are direct and important conflicts between responsibilities. For example, the open communications needed to solve joint problems can weaken your pure bargaining position. The atmosphere that builds your power can create mistrust. If people take specialized roles, some of these conflicts can be reduced. A tough person can take a hard line on certain issues, and a more friendly person can work on joint problems. Your specialists can work with their specialists on technical issues.

Complex issues often require other divisions of responsibilities. Trying to master complex numbers can prevent an individual from thinking strategically. But in a team the responsibilities for numbers and strategy can be divided; John crunches the numbers, while Suzanne looks at the overall strategy.

Relief of intraorganizational tensions

Virtually all organizations have internal tensions. Personnel, planning, and other staff units may resent the way other departments ignore their need for information. The field and headquarters may act almost as if they were competitors or even adversaries. Different regions or plants may compete intensely for money, people, and other resources.

Including people from various units on a team can relieve these tensions. They feel they can protect their interests and make sure the negotiators do not make unrealistic decisions. In addition, they and the people they represent will feel more "ownership" of the agreement and will probably implement it more willingly.

For example, people from operations units frequently believe that salespeople make promises that they must fulfill, often at great cost to themselves. In addition, the mere fact that they have not influenced the negotiations usually creates tensions. Including operations and sales on the team reduces these problems.

A major reason for the Japanese's economic success is their inclusion of just about everyone in decisions. For an important negotiation, an American team of two or three people might face a Japanese team with ten or more members. Most of them will not say a word during the negotiations. Some of them might not even attend the negotiating sessions. But they will all have their chance to speak in the team's private meetings.

The Americans often consider this a waste of time. Why are all these people sitting here, not saying anything? But maybe the Japanese know what they are doing. The Americans have to go back home and sell the deal to credit, operations, distribution, and so on, and each of them may object to the deal and request changes in it. The Japanese don't have to sell anything, and all the people who have to implement the deal have already "bought into it" through their representatives on the negotiating team. Guess who has more implementation problems?

Increased confidence

There is a natural psychological advantage to being part of a team, particularly one that is larger, higher ranking, or more talented than the other team. This advantage is most noticeable in two-on-one negotiations. The person working alone nearly always feels at a psychological disadvantage.

Harold Geneen, former Chairman of ITT, was a superb games-player, who would do almost anything for an edge, even with his own executives. One of his little games was to travel with an entourage, the modern-day equivalent of a medieval court. He would literally try to overwhelm people with the sheer size and information of his group, and it often worked!

Many other executives have followed the same principle. They discover your group's size and status and then make sure that their group is bigger and more prestigious. It is childish, of course, but it still gives them an edge—at least in power-oriented negotiations.

Disadvantages of Negotiating as a Team

Negotiating as a team is not always a good idea. There are some very substantial disadvantages, and their effects depend upon the situation.

Leaks

The larger the team, the greater the danger that some information will be leaked. People talk to their spouses, colleagues, and friends. Some of these people will then repeat what they have heard. In addition, people can be careless when they are talking; you have probably overheard conversations about sensitive negotiations in restaurants, elevators, airports, and so on. Millions of dollars have been lost through careless and malicious leaks.

The 1986-1987 insider trading scandals on Wall Street showed how common and dangerous those leaks can be. More than 15 people went to jail for reporting or using insider information, and the investigations have shown that not all of this information was maliciously communicated. Bob told Harry, who told Sue, who told John, who then sold it to Ivan Boesky or a similar operator.

The fear of leaks is so great in some large negotiations (for example, those involving mergers of major corporations) that the negotiating teams are kept very small, and they may go to great lengths to conceal their names and objectives. In fact, the reports of some merger negotiations sound like bad spy movies.

The president of a huge multinational flies to Dallas under one assumed name, and checks into a hotel under a different assumed name, paying cash, of course. There, in room 426 at 8:15 P.M., he answers a knock on the door, and meets the treasurer of another multinational, dressed in a trench coat with his hat pulled down over his eyes.

They negotiate all night and finally ask their high-priced lawyers to type up the agreement. They do so, using two fingers; the lawyers do not know how to type, but it is safer to type the agreement themselves than to let a secretary do so.

Their obsession with secrecy may seem excessive, but it is probably necessary. If even a rumor got out that company A was considering buying part of company B, the stock prices could move rapidly, destroying the deal.

Fragmented strategy

If a team contains people with quite different interests and perceptions, their negotiating strategy may not fit together. It may be a negotiated compromise that is not nearly as coherent or effective as the strategy that any one of its members would develop independently.

Let's say that you and Joe are partners. If either of you negotiated individually for your organization, you would have a different strategy, and that strategy would probably make sense. It would be based on a set of consistent assumptions, would fit your own or Joe's personal style, and so on.

As partners, you might work out a common strategy, but it might not make sense. It could be a little of this and a little of that and a little of something else. Each idea may be good, but the overall strategy would not fit together or work smoothly. Therefore, either strategy might be better than a combination of both.

A cynic once came up with an aphorism that fits this situation: "A camel is a horse designed by a committee." The legs are too long; the body is too short; the whole thing is ugly; but everybody got a chance to contribute.

Unauthorized concessions

If the team is not tightly controlled, there is a real danger that a member may make an unauthorized and unwanted concession. For example, someone may respond to a proposal by accepting some items.

These unauthorized concessions clearly weaken the team's position, and they can also create severe tensions within the team. The other side can use that acceptance or concession against you: "Look, even your own people think this is a good idea." They may also claim, or even believe you are not negotiating in good faith if the team rejects that unauthorized concession. Worst of all, you may have to live with that concession, even if it destroys your bottom line.

Senior executives are, by far, the worst offenders. Countless people have told us horror stories about home office executives who have flown in, known almost nothing about a situation, given away the store without checking with the local people (who are often too junior to stop or correct them), then patted themselves on the back for their brilliant negotiating. As the locals are driving the executive to the airport, worrying about how they are going to live with the mess the executive has created, they get the final twist of the knife. "I don't know why you had so much trouble settling this deal. You can see how easy it was for me. I guess it's just a matter of experience. If you ever have a similar problem, just give me a call. I'll be glad to help."

Slower response

The larger the team, the slower the response. It takes more time for a group to analyze the other side's proposal and to decide upon its response. The greater the differences within the team, the longer it takes.

The largest increase in time occurs as we shift from an individual to a two-person team. One person can respond nearly immediately, while two people have to discuss issues and perhaps resolve disagreements. Adding a third or fourth member slows the process still further.

More deadlocks

Teams are much less likely to reach agreement than individuals. First, they may take too long to agree or may even be unable to agree among themselves. They therefore cannot move toward a deal.

Second, the social power balance changes. In one-on-one negotiations both parties usually have psychological and social power over the other. They probably want the other person to think that they are fair, reasonable, and bargaining in good faith. In order to preserve their relationship and the other party's good opinion of them, they are likely to be flexible. The psychological and social rewards usually come from being reasonable and accommodating.

As members of a team, people have much less power over the other side. People focus, not on the other side, but on their own teammates. They want the team's approval, and the other side's opinion becomes much less important.

Unfortunately, the teammates' approval often comes from being tough and competitive. One is rewarded for taking a hard line, stonewalling, and attacking the other side's position. "Now, John, I've told them we are not moving one inch. Make sure that you support me. Don't sell out to them."

Blake and Mouton, authors of *The Management Grid*,[11] call this the "hero-traitor dynamic." The hero upholds the team's position, even when it is wrong. The traitor sells out by accepting the other side's position, making concessions, or being friendly.

For example, let's say that you are a member of a union involved in a long and bitter strike. You have not worked in 16 weeks, management has hired scabs, and there has been violence on the picket lines. You are sitting in the union hall, drinking coffee with your friends. The conversation naturally turns to the strike, and you decide to speak up: "I've been trying to look at this situation objectively. I've read the papers pretty carefully, and I think that management really is right about this competitive costs issue."

What is likely to happen to you? Your friends will probably get angry and tell you off. Some of your union "brothers" may not be very brotherly for a while. You might even get beaten up!

The greater the conflict of interests or personalities, the more important this hero-traitor dynamic becomes. The hard-liners may take over one or both teams. Therefore, if there has been a history of unpleasantness, or if there is a high degree of conflict between both parties' interests, teams are much less likely to reach an agreement than individuals.

Which Way Should You Go?

Should you negotiate as an individual or as a team? It depends upon the situation, and you frequently cannot be sure which is better. You should therefore step back, analyze the costs and benefits of each approach, and then make your decision.

Sometimes, this decision is irrevocable, but it can usually be changed. If you decide to negotiate individually and later decide that you need other people, you can usually bring them in. You may not even have to ask the other side, or you can say something like this: "I can see that a lot of these issues will require our purchasing department's approval. Do you mind my bringing our purchasing manager to our next meeting?" Most people would agree (but they might bring someone to balance your psychological edge).

Conversely, you may decide to negotiate as a team only to find that you need the greater speed and flexibility of 1:1 discussions. Just pick up the telephone and say: "Harriet, I'm wondering whether these meetings with four or five people on each side are the best way to go. We seem to be moving pretty slowly. We might make more progress if just the two of us got together next time. What do you think?" She might agree, or propose that both teams consist of only two people.

ORGANIZING YOUR TEAM

If you or your organization decide to negotiate as a team, you must organize the team and agree on each member's role. A good negotiating team is like a good business organization: each member has a specific job to do, and different kinds of people should be assigned to each position. Quantitative people keep the books. Relationship-oriented people fill most sales jobs. Natural leaders tend toward management.

Individual Roles

There are seven distinct roles on a negotiating team: chief, spokesperson, tough person, friendly person, behavioral analyst, data analyst, and specialist. We will describe each set of responsibilities and the kinds of people to assign to each role. If the team is too small, certain roles can be combined.

Chief

The first person to select is the chief, the team's leader. This is the most important role, and the person taking it should always be carefully selected. Alas, this selection is often extremely haphazard, even whimsical. "Sue Ann, you are the last one to get here; so you're the chief."

Perhaps she should be the chief, but base that decision on more rational criteria. Pick the person who has the qualities needed to lead *this* team. Those qualities may be different from the ones needed to lead another team, but for most teams some general principles do apply.

Responsibilities

The chief is the boss, the *only* boss. Negotiating teams are not, and should not be democracies. Decisions can be made in a semidemocratic manner, but the chief should retain the final authority. Somebody has to say, "Do it" or "No," and the chief is the logical candidate.

Many people feel uncomfortable with this autocratic principle. They want to have co-leaders or even complete equality for all members. That approach can work if you are willing to spend an immense amount of time resolving your internal conflicts (and if these conflicts can be resolved, which is not always the case).

Since reasonably prompt decisions are usually desirable and you must present a united front, a strong leader is probably better. Let's give an absurd example of the limitations of democratic decision making. You are in an airliner at 35,000 feet. Suddenly the plane starts to dive and the captain announces, "Our engines have just broken down. What would you like me to do?" You do not want to participate in the decision; you just want a fast, effective decision. The same principle often applies to negotiations.

The chief has several specific responsibilities.

1. *To select the team.* The first task is obviously to select the negotiating team. If, as is customary in most negotiations, the chief has to report to a higher-level person, that person may select some of the people, but the chief should certainly be consulted. The chief probably cannot maintain control and perform effectively without the authority to select the team (and to remove people who do not accept the chief's authority).

Unfortunately, this principle is violated almost constantly. Again and again, people are given the chief negotiator's responsibilities, but have little or no authority to select the team. Senior people insist that Harry or Gertrude be part of the team, and the chief knows that they are loyal, not to him, but to their sponsor. They are, in fact, spies.

If you put your spies on a team, do not be surprised if it does not accomplish very much. A chief cannot function effectively while looking over his shoulder, wondering how you and the other people will second guess any decision.

2. *To plan the overall strategy.* The members should certainly be consulted, but the ultimate responsibility and authority for strategy must be the chief's. Otherwise, a fragmented strategy and extremely slow responses are quite probable. Each member may insist upon a specific position; the overall strategy could lack coherence, and the team will probably spend excessive time on its internal conflicts.

3. *To maintain control.* The chief must be a leader and manager, assigning tasks to people, ensuring that the tasks are performed satisfactorily, and coordinating all the members' activities. The chief cannot possibly perform these difficult tasks without authority, and it is often withheld or undermined.

The Vietnamese War illustrates the danger of not giving a chief sufficient authority. For literally thousands of years experts have insisted that the local commander must have decision-making authority. Higher levels are too isolated to make intelligent decisions.

President Johnson and Secretary of Defense McNamara repeatedly violated that principle. They selected targets for air raids, shifted their favorite officers from one unit to another, even became involved in plans for small infantry engagements. Neither was knowledgeable about military tactics or local conditions, but they got involved in almost everything, ignoring or even firing field commanders who disagreed with them. Their interference was just one of the reasons we lost that war, but it was certainly a factor.

If you appoint a negotiating team, select a chief, discuss strategy in whatever level of detail you think is appropriate, then shut up and let him or her do the job. If you are dissatisfied, replace the chief, but do not try to do the job yourself. As the British say, "Don't buy a dog, then bark yourself."

If you are selected as the chief, request full authority. If you cannot get it, agree on the exact limits of that authority and insist that higher levels respect those limits. Under no circumstances should you allow the higher-ups to get involved in the details. If they do, it is a no win game for you and your organization.

Personal characteristics

Since relatively few people can perform the chief's functions, you must select someone with the right skills and personality.

1. *Able to think strategically.* As the primary strategist, the chief must be able to think in strategic terms—set clear objectives, anticipate the other side's actions, and plan an overall strategy.

The chief must also plan contingent strategies. What will they do if the other side acts in unanticipated ways or the original strategy does not work?

2. *Able to lead consultatively.* The chief must be a leader, but not an autocrat. There must be natural leadership; without it, a chief is useless. If, for example, the team does not accept the chief's directives, the team may drift aimlessly. However, the chief must also listen to the group and use their ideas. Otherwise, the members are unnecessary, and they will resent wasting their time and being ignored.

Leadership and listening ability are a relatively rare combination. Because of their egotism and arrogance far too many leaders ignore information that conflicts with their ideas. For example President Nixon's top aides, Haldeman and Erlichmen, went to great lengths to protect their boss from unpleasant facts. Other leaders pretend to listen, but pay no real attention to anything they do not want to hear. Try to select a chief who sincerely wants to understand and use the team's ideas.

3. *Able to keep quiet.* The chief should be a thinker, not a talker. Someone who needs to talk a lot should not be made chief. First, talking and thinking naturally conflict. If the chief is concerned about what to say next, the strategic decisions will be neglected.

Second, the chief can say something carelessly that binds the team to an undesirable position. If a spokesperson makes a careless remark, the chief can clarify or correct it. The White House and State Department have repeatedly done so when they disliked the reaction to a position taken by a press secretary or UN ambassador (even when they approved that position in advance). But, if the President says something, it is said. It cannot be withdrawn; the government has to live with it.

Unfortunately, many talkers end up as the chief. In fact, *the most common error that chiefs make is to talk too much.* They thereby undermine the spokesperson's authority, confuse the other side, put their side into undesirable positions, and neglect their strategic and managerial responsibilities.

Ronald Reagan offers many examples. "We will bomb the Soviet Union in five minutes." The Russians are in charge of "an evil empire." "When you have seen one tree, you've seen them all." The record of his misstatements would fill a far larger book than this one; he is just too impulsive to realize how damaging his remarks can be.

Many high-level people have made stupid, destructive statements: "What's good for General Motors is good for the USA." (Charles Wilson, then Secretary of Defense, former Chairman at GM). "I was brainwashed" (George Romney, then a leading candidate for the presidency; a few days later, a has-been). "Flight attendants don't need to make much money because they are not bread-winners" (Carl Icahn, primary owner of TWA; his remark made a nasty strike even nastier.) "Poland is not controlled by any foreign power" (Gerry Ford, then president of the US, shortly after, ex-president).

4. *Able to keep completely out of some sessions.* The chief should avoid sessions if there is a clear danger of questions or requests for concessions that you do not want to answer. For example, if you need additional information before taking a position on an issue, it is safer to have the chief avoid the negotiating session. The spokesperson can then honestly say, "I do not have instructions or authority to respond to your question."

Sometimes the chief should avoid sessions that focus on preliminaries or minor details. Let lower-level people solve the little problems; they can usually do so more quickly and efficiently without both chiefs' inhibiting presence.

The chief should concentrate on larger issues, utilize information from the various team members and focus on strategy. As the negotiations progress, the chief should attend more sessions and take a more active role. In fact, doing so signals that the negotiations are entering their final phase.

For example, summit meetings normally occur only after extensive preparation. President Reagan and Chairman Gorbachev normally met only after the stage had been properly set, the issues had been defined, and both sides' positions had been stated and clarified. When this preliminary work has been completed, the chiefs meet to resolve the final issues.

Again, Ronald Reagan offers a splendid negative example. At the Reykjavik summit meeting the Russians raised several disarmament issues for which he was totally unprepared.[12] In complete violation of all the rules of diplomacy, they asked a head of state to make decisions without any warning or preparation, and they let the media know of their proposals. Since they had not allowed him to prepare, their proposals were not at all serious, but the gullible media applauded them as a major breakthrough: "The Russians want total disarmament!"

Nonsense! If they had wanted it, they would have given the American government time to prepare an intelligent response to their proposals. But the media cannot deal with such subtleties; they do not fit their need for simplistic headlines.

President Reagan should have insisted on deferring discussion of those issues to a later meeting. Nobody can negotiate complex issues without preparation. Instead he tried to negotiate, naturally with the media's rapt attention.

When the inevitable occurred, when President Reagan found that he could not solve a forty-year-old problem in a few hours, the media jumped all over him. Once again, Reagan was the warmonger; Gorbachev, the man of peace. The summit had failed because "nasty old Ron" had not accepted a proposal that was not even on the agenda!

All of these problems could have been avoided if President Reagan had simply said: "I have not had time to prepare for that issue, but I will be glad to discuss it later."

If you find yourself in a similar situation—if the other side raises an issue and you do not know how to respond—just remember the three R's (Ronald Reagan Reykjavik) and keep your mouth shut.

Spokesperson

The spokeperson presents the team's positions, a visible and apparently glamorous role. However, many spokespeople find it frustrating, even humiliating. Ambassadors, the quintessence of this role, have said: "Once we were decision makers. Now, because of modern telecommunications, we are messengers at the end of the telephone."

Responsibilities

1. *To communicate the team's positions.* The spokesperson must understand and communicate the team's position. Sometimes that position should be communicated very clearly. At other times the team or chief may want some "waffle." The spokesperson must understand exactly what the team wants to communicate, then follow directions.

2. *To communicate the team's attitudes.* The spokesperson must also let the other side know that the team is pleased with progress, dissatisfied by the other side's refusal to make concessions, or outraged by their actions.

Personal characteristics

1. *Flexible ethics.* We have started our list of personal qualities with the most controversial one, but it may also be the most important. The simple, inescapable fact is that nearly every spokesperson will occasionally be forced to take objectionable, even repugnant positions. The spokesperson's job is to state what the chief and higher levels want, *even if that position is morally repugnant to the spokesperson.* This sometimes creates a dilemma. For instance, an ambassador has been described as an honest man who goes abroad to lie for his country.

If you cannot accept that rule, if you cannot say things you do not believe, we applaud your ethics, but we must also insist that you avoid the spokesperson role.

If you are the chief, you must make sure that the spokesperson will follow your directions. Grill all the candidates, and be quite skeptical. Can they sincerely and credibly express your position, even when they disagree with it? If they cannot do so, if their personal ethics force them to act in a less than whole-hearted manner, select someone else.

2. *The ability to comunicate clearly.* Obviously, the spokesperson must be a good communicator. The other side must know exactly what has been said, and this clarity is often missing. The spokesperson may send messages which he or she thinks are clear, but the other side misunderstands them.

3. *Acting ability.* A spokesperson must also be a good actor. The other side must believe that one is angry, confused, pleased with progress, or any other attitude the team wants.

Many spokespeople fail here. They are simply unable to act effectively. For example, their side's strategy might be to appear outraged, but they just cannot do it. Their entire manner says, "I'm faking it."

For example, they might look down, speak slowly in a soft, subdued voice, and say: "We are very angry about your offer." The other side quite properly concludes that they are not at all angry.

4. *The ability to follow directions exactly.* The spokesperson must be controllable. The job is to communicate not what he or she wants to say, but what the chief wants said. At times the spokesperson must take positions that are personally uncomfortable or even offensive. In extreme cases the chief may even deceive a spokesperson to make sure that directions are followed. For example, many Presidents have deceived their press secretaries to make sure that they were credible when they unwittingly deceived the media.

The spokesperson must also communicate the team's attitudes, even when disagreeing with them personally. For example, if one is angry, but the team wants to be conciliatory, personal anger must not show, and one's words and manner must be pleasant.

Lawyers are professional spokespeople ("mouthpieces"), and most of them learn that they are paid, not to say and do what they want, but to protect their clients' interests and follow their directions. One of their standard aphorisms is: "A good lawyer can get angry any time that it is in the client's interests."

Having to follow directions can be so frustrating that diplomats and other spokespeople have bitterly complained that they are little more than a ventriloquist's dummy. That frustration can become so intense that they violate their instructions and say what they really feel. The results are often disastrous.

Purely by chance, the public information officer of a major oil company attended one of our workshops while that company was trying to buy another oil company. We asked him: "What is the most important personal qualification for your job?"

He answered: "A complete lack of creativity. My job is to say what they... (pointing upward) want me to say, not to express my own feelings."

We agree, and we hope that you accept that simple, but rather unpleasant principle. Of all the qualities a spokesperson must have, the ability to follow directions is the most important. Make sure you assign this role to someone who can do so.

The powerless or unofficial spokesperson

Sometimes an organization, especially a government, will use a powerless or unofficial spokesperson to protect itself if things go wrong. They can then deny any responsibility for a position or action.

For example, toward the end of World War I, Palestine and other parts of the Ottoman Empire were divided into French and English spheres of influence by two relatively junior French and English officials.

When Jimmy Carter, Pierre Trudeau, or Helmut Schmidt travel, they may carry messages to or from foreign leaders, perhaps even make public suggestions for resolving conflicts. If the press or another government learns of these messages, or if the public reaction is negative, the government can deny all responsibility.

> "President Reagan, do you support Jimmy Carter's proposals for the Middle East?"
> "Jimmy Carter? He is not part of my administration or even my political party. He was just talking as a private citizen."

Tough person

In some negotiations you need someone who can take a tough, hard line, who can let the other side know that there is a stick as well as a carrot. On the other hand, most negotiating teams do not and should not include a tough person.

Responsibilities

1. To threaten the other side. In power-oriented negotiations the other side often has to believe that you have both the power and the will to use it against them. They must believe that their refusal to compromise will lead to some form of punishment such as a strike, lost contract, or lawsuit.

Frequently, the tough people communicate that message. They may or may not be the official spokesperson, but they must communicate that at least some members of the team intend to take a hard line.

In extreme cases the tough person may deliberately try to intimidate the other side by acting irrationally or viciously. At other times the message may be that the facts simply require a hard line. But, one way or another, the opposition must believe that refusing to compromise will have painful consequences.

2. *To respond to other tough people.* If the other side threatens you, your tough person must respond to show that you cannot be intimidated. Most teams in professional sports contain an enforcer, someone who will punish the other side for hurting one of their players. For years, whenever Wayne Gretzky, the world's greatest hockey player, was on the ice, Simenko was also there. He was big, mean, and aggressive. Just putting him on the ice was the Oiler's way of saying, "You touch Gretzky, and you go home in two pieces."

Personal characteristics

1. *A genuinely tough image.* The tough person must be credible; the other side must believe that they will be punished. Without that credibility, the tough person is useless, perhaps even a minor annoyance. So select someone that the other side believes is tough (a Simenko).

2. *Self-restraint.* Toughness must be balanced by self-restraint. Aggression is a weapon, and all weapons should be used judiciously. Threats and outbursts should be made only when the chief wants them to support the team's overall strategy.

Many tough people lack that self-restraint. They become so involved with their roles, so genuinely angry, that their feelings take over. They may then become so aggressive that the negotiations get stalled or even break down. If that happens, the chief must take over and stop the aggression immediately, even if the tough person resents it. Sometimes the chief must even expel the tough person from the team to recover control. Allowing uncontrolled aggression can easily lead to a disaster.

Friendly Person

The friendly person's job is to relieve tensions, protect people's face, and act as an alternative communications channel if the negotiations break down. If your team contains a tough person, or if the overall strategy is aggressive, you *must* balance the team by including a friendly person. A team does not have to include both a tough person and a friendly one. It is often better to have neither so the negotiations remain unemotional. It is also acceptable for every member of the team to be friendly. But *do not have a tough person without also having a friendly one.* Otherwise, the negotiations can easily break down.

Responsibilities

This role is difficult and demanding because its responsibilities often conflict with personal feelings.

1. *To maintain contact if the negotiations break down.* This is the ultimate responsibility. The friendly person must be able to approach the other side after the official negotiations break down.

This responsibility is crucial because no one else may be able to fulfill it. The chiefs and spokespeople may be so committed to conflicting positions and strategies that they cannot reopen the negotiations without losing a great deal of face. The friendly people must then quietly talk to each other.

"Virginia, you've got problems with Tom, and I've got the same kind of problems with Charlotte. They are both so angry that we can't get anywhere. Perhaps you and I should talk to see if we can make any progress."

2. *To ease tensions.* The friendly people can also prevent breakdowns and make the negotiations progress more smoothly by relieving tensions. Just listening and showing appreciation to the other side's position can prevent or reduce some problems. They can also make jokes or change the subject when tensions get too high.

These two responsibilities interact with each other. By easing tensions, the friendly people establish their character and create positive relationships with the other side. Then, when things get nasty, they can build on the foundation of personal relationships.

3. *To provide a face-saving way to compromise.* Even if the negotiations are continuing, the principal members of both teams may be reluctant to offer certain compromises. A quiet conversation between the friendly people can lead to compromises on issues that could not be resolved during the formal meetings.

Personal characteristics

In some respects the friendly person is the most difficult role on a team. It certainly requires a great deal of self-control because one must remain friendly even when personally irritated or even furious.

1. *A genuinely friendly image.* The friendly person's image is even more important than the tough person's. If the other side does not believe the tough person, they may take liberties, but at least the negotiations will continue. If they do not trust the friendly person—and distrust is common during negotiations, particularly heated ones—the negotiations may break down permanently.

The friendly person's image is therefore critically important, and it must be created in advance. Mr. Dobrinyen, the former Soviet ambassador to the United States, illustrates this principle. In the fall of 1962 during the Cuban missile crisis, the Politburo suddenly realized that it had no representatives in Washington that the Americans trusted, and they desperately needed someone there.

A few months later Ambassador Dobrinyen arrived, and he stayed in Washington for more than 20 years. He worked very hard to develop positive relationships with the White House, State Department, and Congress; he even sent his grandchild to Washington public schools. His job was to be ready, when things got nasty, to talk quietly to the president, secretary of state, speaker of the house, and so on. He did that job so well that he became a member of the Politburo and a top advisor on foreign policy.

2. *Perceptiveness and tact.* The right image is not enough; there should be substance too. The friendly person's tasks require genuine tact and perceptiveness. He or she must be able to see when tensions are getting dangerous, and then smooth things over with a word, gesture, or bit of private advice to the chief.

Of course, smoothing things, defusing crises, and showing understanding of the other side's position also help to build that friendly image.

3. *Self-restraint.* Friendly people need this restraint even more than the tough person does. They must remain friendly even when they feel angry. That is an extremely difficult task, and one that many people fail to perform. Again and again we have seen friendly people step out of their role and attack the other side.

They usually do so when the negotiations have become heated. In other words, at precisely the time that they must remain in their role to smooth tensions and provide a face-saving communications channel, they express their anger and destroy their effectiveness.

They also need another type of self-restraint. They must walk a very fine line between friendliness and making substantive concessions. They must communicate understanding of the other's position and feelings without making concessions or binding their team in any way. Their task is emotional and procedural—to ease tensions and facilitate communications—not substantive. They should not make concessions (unless, of course, the chief has instructed them to do so).

4. *Tolerance for pressure from one's own team.* Friendly people frequently encounter great pressure or even abuse from their own team. Even though they are doing their jobs, they may be seen as "traitors" who have sold out.

For example, Armand Hammer, the chairman of Occidental Petroleum Co., performed this role for the United States from the 1920s to the 1980s. His personal relationships with Soviet leaders were extremely valuable to this country, but he was repeatedly attacked as a Communist or fellow traveler. When groups are in conflict, people who show friendliness toward the other side are often perceived as traitors.

Behavioral Analyst

This person must study the other team's actions to try to understand its objectives, priorities, concerns, and so on. Since understanding the other side is so critically important, it is a pity that this role is often omitted or minimized.

Responsibilities

1. *To analyze the other team's actions.* Behavioral analysts focus on the verbal and nonverbal cues of the other side's MSP, priorities, and strategy. They should always focus their attention on the other side of the table, even when their spokesperson is speaking. Their task is to understand how the other side reacts to a point.

The foreign ministries of many major powers may contain literally dozens of these analysts, and some of them spend years studying one or a few key people. Their primary job is to understand, for example, Gorbachev. What does he want? How will he probably react to a particular demand? What does his latest proposal really mean?

Major diplomatic delegations often have one or more behavioral analysts. For example, during a United Nations' debate the United States' analysts focus their attention on the Russians, Chinese, or other delegations. They are not concerned about the speech that their ambassador is making. All of their attention is focused on the indifference, anger, boredom, enthusiasm, and other reactions of these delegations.

When the other side communicates, they intensely study every word and gesture, looking for subtle nuances. They might even compare a long series of diplomatic notes to detect any signs of changes over time. To you or me the cues might be meaningless, a slight change in wording in otherwise nasty prose.

> On April 18 they called us fascist, imperialist, warmongers and accused us of trying to destroy their economy. Yesterday they made the same accusation, but left out the term "warmongers." Maybe their position is softening a little.

These examples may seem farfetched, even unbelievable, but they are true. Governments understand the critical importance of understanding each other, and they have learned through painful experience that the signals are often extremely subtle and ambiguous.

Your team obviously cannot afford to spend so much time and effort, but if the negotiation is important, someone should clearly be assigned to this task. The analyst should prepare in advance, learning how the key people on the other side think, act, and negotiate.

2. *To report their analyses to the chief.* Obviously, these analyses are worthless unless they influence the chief's decisions. The analyst must therefore report them promptly and clearly to the chief.

Personal characteristics

1. *Perceptiveness.* Behavioral analysts must obviously be perceptive. They must see and understand subtle signals.

2. *Comfortable with the observer's role.* They must be able to take a passive role. They should almost never speak during the negotiating sessions. Someone with a high need to get involved in the negotiations will be uncomfortable and ineffective.

3. *Ability to influence the chief and the team.* The behavioral analyst is useless if nobody takes the analyses seriously or acts on the recommendations. Unfortunately, many perceptive people are not persuasive or forceful. It is therefore quite common for the behavioral analyst to understand the other side better than the rest of the team, but no one listens. During breaks the active, forceful members of the team often dominate the discussion and ignore the behavioral analyst's insights.

To reduce this problem, select someone who is both perceptive and influential, the sort of person who seldom speaks, but gets a respectful hearing. In addition, the chief should make a point of listening carefully and encouraging other people to do so.

Data Analyst

This analyst records and makes sense out of both sides' numbers and other information. It can be a dirty, unpleasant, and unglamorous job, but it is absolutely essential. If it is not done well, the team can get confused or make unnecessary concessions, and the entire negotiation can get bogged down in the details.

Responsibilities

1. *To record and analyze all the numbers and other data.* The data analyst should keep careful records of both sides' proposals, compare them, determine the size of the gaps between the position, compute ratios of movement, and generally make sense out of both sides' numbers and other facts.

Many teams have a "number cruncher," but they may unduly restrict the role and its influence. They have the analyst compute the percentages or do other book-keeping tasks, but do not ask or perhaps even allow the analyst to make inferences or recommendations about strategy.

Since analysts will usually have and understand more information than anyone else, they should be directly involved in strategic discussions. What do you think are their key priorities? What is their MSP on this issue? If we continue the current pattern of offers, where will we end up? Should we change our strategy? In what ways?

If these discussions also involve the behavioral analyst, the team's analysis and plans will really improve. Conflicts and inconsistencies between the numbers and the other side's words and actions will reveal more than you can learn from either in isolation. You may see, for example, that the pattern of concessions supports the behavioral analyst's suspicion that their real priorities are considerably different from the ones they have directly stated.

Then the chief can pull together all this information, plus the suggestions of the rest of the team to revise the strategy and plan specific moves.

2. *To work with the other side's data analyst.* Occasionally, both sides' analysts should work together to reduce confusion about the offers. This confusion is extremely common. Each side may use a different system to organize its information, or they may present their offers in different formats. Neither side can evaluate or respond to the other's offer until they have translated it into their own format.

Trying to do so during an interteam meeting is extremely difficult and inefficient; too many people talk, extraneous issues are raised, and the central goal of understanding the offers gets lost. It is far better to have the data analysts meet privately to understand each other's offer and the supporting logic and analysis. Of course, they should not meet unless directed to do so by their chiefs, but these meetings can often save a great deal of time and prevent confusion and distrust.

During these meetings they should not make any form of concession or discuss anything other than the meaning and computation of their offers. They are there to learn what the offers mean, not to respond to them. The latter task should be left to the chief and the entire team.

Personal characteristics

1. *Skill at analyzing numbers and other information.* Data analysts must obviously be good with figures and other information, have an orderly mind, calculate very quickly, and be able to keep track of all the offers from both sides.

2. *Communication skills.* They must also be able to communicate to people who do not fully understand numbers and other information. Many excellent analysts cannot do so. They are so fast and so good at data processing that they cannot understand how other people are confused, or even frightened, by numbers or other kinds of information. They may therefore talk as if they were dealing with another expert, while the rest of the team gets confused and frustrated.

If you must choose between a genius who cannot communicate, and a merely competent analyst who can communicate with nonexperts, you should probably avoid the genius.

3. *Comfortable with the role.* Data analysts must also be comfortable with a supporting, analytic role. They must focus on the information and keep quiet during the negotiating sessions. They must accept the limitations of their role and not feel a strong need to get directly involved in the discussions.

At times, data analysts do not even have to be at the negotiating session. They should be someplace else, clarifying the other side's last offer, computing the costs of making various concessions, and so on.

Specialist

Many negotiating teams need specialists such as lawyers, purchasing agents, contract administrators, engineers, buyers, and operations personnel. These specialists must be used effectively.

Responsibilities

Specialists normally have only one responsibility: to provide their specialized expertise. They should not usually try to usurp other responsibilities.

This point is particularly important with lawyers. Many of them disrupt negotiations or cause deadlocks by taking over the chief's or spokesperson's role. Of course, some lawyers are highly skilled negotiators who should take those roles, but that is a decision that the chief and team must make. However, if they want the lawyer to act as a specialist, they must insist the lawyer remain in that role. Lawyers (or other specialists) who insist on a more active role should be asked to leave.

Personal characteristics

1. *Genuine expertise.* Since specialists are there to provide expert advice, they should obviously be experts.

2. *Credibility with both teams.* It is highly desirable to have their expertise accepted by both teams. Professional credibility, particularly with the other team, is as important as technical expertise. If their opinions are accepted by both sides, a great deal of time can be saved, and technical decisions can be based on objective analyses rather than negotiated compromises.

3. *Comfortable with the specialist's role.* Since a specialist must remain within that role, being comfortable with it is obviously essential. The specialist who wants a more active or influential role will often create severe problems.

Combinations of Roles

Since many negotiating teams contain only a few people, team members may be forced to take two or three roles. Combining roles is far from easy because some roles make such conflicting demands.

First, we will discuss the unnatural role combinations, the ones that you should avoid. Then we will discuss the natural combinations. These recommendations are just general guidelines; you must also consider the team members' personalities and skills when assigning roles. Combinations which would not work with most people might be best for your team.

Unnatural combinations

Unless you have no other choice, avoid the following combinations.

Chief and spokesperson

These two roles just do not go together. The chief is a managerial, thinking, and strategic role; the spokesperson is a talking role. This distinction is so important that virtually all lawyers retain another lawyer to represent them whenever they have legal problems. They will make the major decisions, but their lawyers will do most of the talking. In fact, the legal profession has a succinct aphorism: "People who act as their own lawyers have fools for clients."

Trying to perform both roles virtually guarantees that neither role will be performed well. The spokesperson must concentrate on what he or she will say, which prevents one from thinking of larger, more strategic issues.

In addition, combining those roles increases the risks that a careless statement will damage the team's position. If a spokesperson says something damaging, it can be denied, withdrawn, or clarified. If the chief (e.g., the President of the United States, CEO of your company, head of a union) says something, you are stuck with it.

Although it is an unnatural combination, it occurs very frequently. Far too often the most senior person is both the chief and the spokesperson. He or she says, in effect, "I will do the thinking and the talking. The rest of you carry my suitcases and make sure that I get plenty of coffee." It may be good for their ego to take both roles, but it is usually bad for the team and the organization it represents.

Since the spokesperson's role presents more immediate demands, the larger strategic decisions are probably made poorly. The boss's mind naturally focuses on what to say next, and nobody looks at the larger picture. Minimize those dangers by dividing these two roles.

Tough person and nice person

These two roles obviously conflict with each other, but occasionally someone tries to take both of them. It just does not work. Acting tough here and friendly there just undermines credibility and creates distrust. The other side will not believe you and may even feel that you are playing games.

Behavioral analyst and data analyst

If possible, these roles should be assigned to different people. They have fundamentally conflicting responsibilities and require different sorts of personalities. The behavioral analyst is an eyes-up role; one must focus on the other side of the table. The data analyst is an eyes-down role; one must look down at pages of numbers and other information.

In addition, they require different kinds of people. The behavioral analyst must be a perceptive "people person." The data analyst should often be a numbers person. Very few people are both.

Despite their conflicting demands, both roles should be taken by the same person—the chief—in a two-person team. The spokesperson is just too busy to analyze either the data or the other side's actions.

Chief or spokesperson and data analyst

The data analyst is too busy making sense of the information to focus on the chief's strategic responsibilities. The spokesperson is too busy talking or planning what to say to analyze the data effectively. These combinations should therefore be avoided (except in two-person teams which force you to combine the chief and the data analyst).

Natural combinations

If you have enough people and they are the right kinds of people, try for the following combinations.

Chief or spokesperson combined with tough person or friendly person

Either the chief or the spokesperson can take either emotional role (friendly or tough). In fact, these combinations are often used to send a signal to the other side. For example, if their chief is a notorious hard-liner, they are telling you not to expect many concessions. Conversely, if their chief is known to be reasonable, you can expect a friendlier, more problem-solving approach.

At times there may be more than one spokesperson on a team. Some issues may be discussed by one person, others by another person. This pattern can be used to send a signal. For example, if all pricing issues are discussed by the tough person, and payment terms are discussed by a friendly person, the team is saying they will be more flexible on terms than on price. However, because this signal is so indirect, they are not committimg themselves to anything at all. They are just hinting.

Chief and behavioral analyst

These two roles are fairly compatible because both require focusing on the other side's reactions and thinking of the effects of different approaches. In addition, personal characteristics required by both roles are fairly similar. Both the behavioral analyst and the chief must be able to keep quiet and understand other people.

Tough person and data analyst

This is a fairly natural combination, if the team wants to communicate that their toughness is based ultimately on rational factors. Instead of using emotional toughness and aggression, the data analyst/tough person essentially says, "Your numbers just don't make any sense."

Friendly person and behavioral analyst

Because they care about people and want to understand them, many friendly people are quite perceptive. These two roles therefore fit together very nicely. Both roles require understanding of the other side and a generally perceptive personality.

CONTROLLING YOUR TEAM

Control is absolutely essential, and maintaining it is often quite difficult. Members disagree about strategy and tactics; political conflicts spill over into the negotiations; personal animosities are openly or indirectly expressed.

Without control, the disadvantages of negotiating as a team far outweigh the advantages. Therefore, unless you can maintain control, do not negotiate as a team.

The following guidelines will reduce, but probably cannot completely solve control problems.

Have Exactly One Chief

Generally, only one person can be the boss. However, for political reasons many teams have more than one chief. They have co-chairpersons, or they try to resolve disagreements by voting, or the formally appointed chief abdicates the responsibilities, or is too busy to come to meetings. Without a chief who is clearly in control, the team may drift aimlessly, waste time on pointless arguments, even tear itself apart because of political and personal conflicts.

If the team disagrees emphatically with the chief's position, or if the chief fails to maintain sufficient control, you should change chiefs (if it is possible). But do so explicitly. Do not just let someone else take over while the original individual remains. Discuss the issues thoroughly, and then put a new person into that role. In addition, it may be necessary to ask the former chief to leave. Otherwise, you can easily have constant disagreements or unclear authority.

Agree on Everything in Advance

The spokesperson should almost never be allowed to "wing it," even if people have confidence in him or her. The complexity of team negotiations normally requires more careful planning and tight discipline.

During its private meetings the team should agree on what will be done at the next session and make sure that the spokesperson knows exactly what to do. If something unanticipated occurs during the negotiating session, the spokesperson should not respond without getting clear instructions from the chief or team. These instructions can be communicated in a note, a brief conference, or a formal team meeting, but the spokesperson must be told what to do.

Resolve Questions and Disagreements Privately

Disagreements and questions are nearly inevitable, and they must be resolved privately. If you disagree in front of the other side, or if some people reveal their lack of understanding of an issue, you will reduce your bargaining power and perhaps the other side's trust as well.

One reason that the American government has lost so many international negotiations is that our disagreements are reported on the front pages of the *New York Times*, while most disagreements of the Politburo or the Japanese Cabinet are settled quietly behind closed doors.

Forbid Unauthorized Private Conversations with the Other Side

The key word here is "unauthorized." It is perfectly appropriate, perhaps even strategically necessary, to have private conversations. However, the chief should always authorize the contact, the topics to discuss, the concessions to make, and the questions to ask. And the individual should follow these instructions exactly.

If your people just talk to members of the other side without the chief's approval or even knowledge, they can easily misunderstand your team's position. They may believe your team is willing to make concessions that are absolutely impossible, or that there are larger disagreements within the team than really exist, or that the team's priorities are considerably different from the real ones.

Demand That Everyone Support the Team's Strategy or Leave

Occasionally, someone will disagree completely with the objectives, analysis, or strategy of the rest of the team, but want to remain on the team. "I think your entire approach is wrong. You have misread the situation, and your strategy can't work. But I'll come along to help out."

Taking that person to the negotiations would usually be a serious mistake. A team must work together, and it cannot do so if some of its members do not support its position. The need for support is not absolute. Not everyone has to be a "yes man." However, there must be a fundamental agreement that once people have voiced their objections, they will support the team's positions, even if they disagree with them. If they are not able to do so, if they insist on maintaining their positions, they should be asked to leave.

That rule is, however, far from absolute. At times a "devil's advocate" can be extremely useful. The team may be so committed to a position or strategy that they overlook or misinterpret the other side's signals or information from other sources.

They may even demand uncritical acceptance of their position and regard criticisms, including justified ones, as evidence of disloyalty.

In *The Best and the Brightest*[13], David Halberstam showed that the American government repeatedly ignored very obvious signs that its Vietnamese strategy was failing, and it fired almost anyone who had the temerity to say so.

Since you need both objectivity and unified, decisive action, you might allow a critic or skeptic to *observe* the negotiations if you can be sure that he or she will not communicate with the other side or with your management in any way whatsoever. They can say what they like during private meetings, but they cannot say anything during negotiating sessions, communicate their disapproval nonverbally, nor can they go over your head to management, write memos to the file, or otherwise undermine the team's position. They are there to help you to understand and adjust to the situation, not to act as spies or rebels.

Stay in Your Role

A negotiating team is like a project team. Each member has a role to play and a specific job to do. For example, if one person is supposed to keep the accounts, but neglects them, problems are almost inevitable. Exactly the same principle applies to a negotiating team. If your job is to be the friendly person, you must be friendly, even if you are personally angry. If you are the chief, you must not take over the spokesperson's job. You would then be too busy to think strategically or to manage the team.

Unfortunately, people frequently step out of their role. They let their frustration, impatience, or desire to play a different role override the team's needs. Your team must be more disciplined. You must agree on the roles and insist that everyone stays in their own role.

If you find that people cannot stay within an assigned role, take a break and renegotiate the roles. But do not just allow people to shift from one role to another. If some people cannot accept that discipline, if they insist on taking roles that do not conform to the team's strategy, demand that they leave.

If other things, such as power, are equal, a well-disciplined team will normally get a better deal than a more talented, but less-disciplined one.

SUMMARY

It is far from easy to negotiate as a team. The negotiation process is a complex one, and many of its demands conflict with each other. If you add the complications of organizing and controlling a team, you make the problem very complex indeed. Therefore, your first decision is: Should I negotiate as a team or as an individual?

There is no easy answer to that question. It depends on the issues involved, the people on the other side, the range of talent and information available to your team, and the team members' styles, knowledge, and skills. We cannot make unequivocal recommendations about whether you should negotiate as an individual or as a team.

We can only suggest that you carefully consider the advantages and disadvantages before making that decision. Countless errors have been made by people negotiating singly when they should have worked with a team and vice versa.

Once you have decided to negotiate as a team, you must carefully select its members. In most cases you should select people who have complementary knowledge, skills, and personalities. The classic and very common error is to select people like yourself because you feel comfortable with them. Doing so can create the disadvantages of negotiating as a team without gaining its major benefits: diversity of information and ideas, effective performance of a variety of roles, and superior analysis.

After selecting the team, you must agree on each member's role and responsibilities. Doing so can be very difficult. Several people may want the same job, or nobody may be willing to take some essential role, or a powerful person may want an unsuitable role. If you cannot agree on a rational organization, you may have to change the team. Drop the people who will not accept the roles they should take, and bring in new people to ensure that all roles are performed properly.

The final, and perhaps the most difficult problem is to control the team while you prepare and negotiate. Some people may fail to prepare thoroughly. Others may refuse to stay within their roles. Others may take actions that undermine the team's strategy. If these problems occur, the chief or the entire team must get tough. Discipline is not pleasant, and enforcing it can be extremely stressful, but it *must* be enforced. An undisciplined team can cause a disaster.

We have seen that discipline is an underlying issue that affects every aspect of team negotiations. You must base your decision on whether to negotiate individually or as a team, not on your personal preference, but on the demands of the situation. You must select the people you need, not the ones who make you most comfortable. You must insist that these people take the roles that help the team, not the ones they enjoy. And you must make sure that everyone stays in their role and works within the team's strategy.

11

Cultural Factors Affecting International Negotiations*

As the world shrinks, more and more of us must negotiate with people from different cultures. As each culture has traditions and rituals that affect these negotiations, ignoring these cultural factors can cause extremely serious problems. You will usually get better results by understanding and adjusting to their culture.

This principle is, of course, just another application of our most important theme—understand and adjust to the other party. We have repeatedly urged you to understand the other side's situation, objectives, perceptions, and strategy, and cultural factors influence every one of them.

You should therefore learn what cultural factors are and how they affect the negotiating process so you can adjust to their effects. For example, when negotiating with Japanese, you need a completely different Beginning Game. They often want to spend days or even weeks creating a friendly, trusting atmosphere before discussing business. Positions are expressed indirectly to obscure conflicts, even though you are negotiating to resolve these conflicts. Direct questions are regarded as rude, and the meaning of answers may depend upon extremely subtle signals. Certain ways of saying yes actually mean no.

Cultural factors similarly affect every other part of the negotiating process. If you do not understand these effects, cultural differences can complicate and interfere with your negotiations. Cultural conflicts may even become important issues in themselves, forcing you to work on them when you should be resolving substantive conflicts.

Their impact can be enormous because cultural factors affect virtually everything about people and their ways of relating to each other, because they are often un-

*This chapter was coauthored by Stephen Rhinesmith, Ph.D., and much of its content is based upon his experience and research.

conscious, and because we all feel strongly about them. Despite its impact, most of us rarely think about our culture; it is just there, a natural part of the way we think, talk, and feel.

Only when we encounter people from different cultures do we realize how strongly we feel about cultural factors. People who think differently appear illogical; those with different values seem immoral. For example, Americans regard bribes as immoral and illegal, but in many countries gifts and commissions for services (both of which we might regard as bribes) are quite normal.

Let's apply our most basic principle and look at things from the other side of the table. You and I would not give a second thought to crossing our legs in a way that points the soles of our feet toward another person, but doing so is an inexcusable insult to a religious Buddhist. They sit in the lotus position (with the soles of the feet facing inward) to avoid insulting other people, and some very religious Buddhists will not walk under a bridge or enter a multistory building because other people's feet would be pointing at them.

Or we can look at attitudes toward time. We Americans naturally regard our attitudes toward time as correct, but the Swiss, Germans, Scandinavians and Japanese are often offended by our tardiness, while the Spanish, Africans, and Latin Americans can become extremely annoyed by our obsessive punctuality.

Until fairly recently Americans and other Westerners (such as Canadians, Europeans, and Australians) could afford to ignore cultural differences. We dominated the world economy and could insist that everyone else do business on our terms.

Americans have always been the worst offenders: most of us do not speak any foreign language, and very few Americans speak a noneuropean one. We often insist on calling everyone by their first names, even though in nearly all other cultures that right is reserved for one's family and close friends. We tend to confront issues and criticize people very directly, a quality that many people regard as boorish. Even our multinational corporations have made absurd errors such as shipping American model cars to Japan where they drive on the left side of the road. We have many times deserved that ignoble, but memorable, label, "the ugly Americans."

We cannot get away with it any more. Whether we like it or not, we have to adjust to other cultures. We no longer dominate the world's economy, nor does the rest of the world owe us money. In fact, we have the largest trade deficit in history and are rapidly becoming the world's largest debtor. One reason for that trade deficit and its resulting debt is that we have not adjusted to other cultures. Many people and organizations would rather buy from people who respect and adjust to their customs and speak their language.

Furthermore, our trade deficit and other economic factors have changed the power balance; other countries are no longer forced to do business with us. The Japanese, Europeans, Arabs, and other people naturally and legitimately expect to be treated as equals. Otherwise, they will just do business with someone else.

A few people have accepted that unpleasant fact and learned how to adjust to cultural differences, but the learning process is usually slow and inefficient. Each person must learn through trial and error, with perhaps some informal advice. This chapter will speed up the learning process.

Ideally, we would provide detailed advice on how to negotiate with people from several specific cultures. Unfortunately, since little research has been done on this subject, we can offer only general guidelines and a few specific examples.

We must also point out that there is absolutely no substitute for understanding the specific people with whom you are negotiating. All cultural differences are general tendencies, not absolutes. Hardly any cultural principle applies to all Americans, Japanese, or members of any other culture, and differences within a culture can be much greater than those among the typical members of different cultures.

You must therefore apply our principles very cautiously, while trying to understand the specific people on the other side of the table. How do *they* think? What do *they* want?

This chapter is divided into three sections:

   I. Cultural Dimensions
  II. Negotiations Issues
 III. Final Remarks

CULTURAL DIMENSIONS

The term "culture" is not at all precise; it means different things to different people. It can, for example, refer to people who share the same national boundaries (e.g., Americans), but it may also refer to subcultural groups who share a particular perception of themselves, others, and the world. In that sense, one can talk about a black culture, a southern culture, a city culture, a rural culture, a male culture, or a female culture.

We can also carry the concept of culture to functional specialties. Engineers tend to share values, beliefs, and patterns of thinking; so do economists and physicists. Each profession has a culture, which may be stronger than the native culture. For example, while working internationally, you might find that you have more in common with a local engineer than you do with some other Americans; your functional culture might be stronger than your native culture.

This is an extremely important point. You must realize that in any society there is a wide range of cultural viewpoints. In fact, there can be equal or even greater differences within a society than there are among people from different societies with similar social, economic and educational backgrounds. This complexity plays a very confusing role in international negotiations.

Therefore, there is no such thing as the Arab culture or the Japanese culture. Saudi Arabs are different from Gulf or North African Arabs. Young Japanese are much more westernized than their elders.

Because of these differences, a critical question is how generally one defines a culture. Although it will cause us to overlook important points, we are forced to simplify the issues. To illustrate the importance and impact of cultural factors, we will focus on the differences between Americans and people from cultures that are both different and important to us: Russians, Japanese, and Arabs. We will also make occasional references to Latin Americans, Africans, and even Europeans.

All of these references are made primarily to illustrate principles. We would like to be able to compare all four cultures on every dimension, but it is impossible to do so simply because there has not been enough research. In addition, since such large differences exist within every culture, all our points must be regarded cautiously.

We will generally ignore differences between Americans and Europeans. Doing so is, of course, hazardous since there are important cultural distinctions between, for example, America and Norway. Despite these differences, we are, when dealing with nonwesterners, essentially one culture.

Because the term culture has so many confusing connotations, we will use an oversimplified definition: *Culture is the way that people think about and behave toward themselves, others and the world.*

We will also ignore differences within cultures, such as those between young, westernized Japanese and older, more traditional Japanese or those distinguishing Saudi, Gulf and North African Arabs. Since we are ignoring these differences, we must repeat our earlier warning: There is no substitute for understanding the specific people on the other side of the table.

We will discuss five cultural dimensions: values, beliefs, patterns of thinking, language, and nonverbal actions. Together these dimensions constitute the ways that people express their culture.

Values

Values are the standards by which a culture evaluates actions and their consequences. A value is an *explicit, conscious* preference for one behavior or pattern of thought over another.

Values are explicit and conscious in that people are aware that they hold them. For example, they may feel that society should be governed by a representative democracy, while other people prefer a military government.

Values affect perceptions and can have a strong emotional impact upon people. The other party's actions can be seen as wrong in a moral sense. For example, Americans regard nepotism as immoral, while most African cultures regard it as a duty: One is expected to provide jobs for relatives—even if they are absolutely unqualified. People from different cultures may therefore debate values, trying to persuade the other side that they are wrong (a nearly hopeless exercise).

Beliefs

Beliefs, on the other hand, are *implicit, unconscious* preferences for one alternative behavior or pattern of thought. For example, most Americans believe that everyone wants to be treated equally. We simply cannot believe that someone would be willing to accept an inferior role in the Hindu caste system or a master-servant relationship. We not only value equal treatment, but we also assume that everyone else shares that value.

However, in many societies people willingly trade social differences for a secure life. They want the security of a clearly defined social role, even if it is an inferior one. Many researchers have found that people are more satisfied with their status in traditional societies that allow hardly any upward movement than they are in societies that allow a person to get ahead. In fact, when advancement opportunities start to occur (e.g., when industrialization begins), people become *more* dissatisfied.

Beliefs are much more disruptive than values in cross-cultural relations because *people are unaware that they see things differently from other people.* Since beliefs are implicit and unconscious, people naturally assume that everyone sees things the same way that they do. Therefore, while negotiating, we must pay particular attention to beliefs and their effects.

Patterns of Thinking

Patterns of thinking reflect an implicit preference for one rationale, logic, or method. The basic question is how information is handled. Americans tend to be pragmatic empiricists. We think inductively and focus on practical results: Principles are induced from the facts, and we are almost always concerned with concrete results. If new facts conflict with the principles, the principles are modified to take into account this new information. If the results are unsatisfactory, we reanalyze the situation.

Many cultures think deductively. They begin with a religious or ideological principle and either ignore or redefine contradictory facts or unacceptable results. For example, Russian communists interpret nearly everything in terms of their communistic ideology. The Polish workers can't strike because they would be acting against the party, which represents their true interest. The fact that the Poles are dissatisfied just shows that they do not understand their true interests. They therefore need the party to protect these interests.

Another, even more obvious example is the Communists' insistence that their system is clearly superior to capitalism. Since West Germany, South Korea, and Taiwan are unquestionably more successful than the Communist parts of their previously united nations, and America is much more successful than the Soviet Union, this success is irrelevant, and unworthy of discussion. If America were Communist, its people would be more prosperous, freer, happier, and so forth.

Different patterns of thinking are also extremely troublesome in cross-cultural relations. Since they are implicit, we usually do not realize that our preference is only a preference. We just assume that everyone thinks that way. When other people act differently, we see them as irrational. Since no one trusts or wants to do business with an irrational person, the relationship can break down.

Language

Language has three major cultural effects. First, it defines who is in or out of that culture. People who speak the same language tend to regard themselves as belonging to the same culture.

Second, languages vary widely in their semantic richness. For example, in English there are numerous words for modern technology such as data processing. Equivalent words do not exist in many other languages. On the other hand, English does not allow one to translate directly the words for the many forms of sand that exist on the Saudi Arabian peninsula. To us, sand is sand. But to the Arabs there are many types of sand. This variety can easily be described in Arabic, but would be completely lost in an English translation. This sort of linguistic problem must be overcome, even among bilingual people.

Third, language influences the way that people think and relate to each other—their cognitive and relationship style. An obvious example is the pronoun and verb for "you." English is extremely informal with only one way to say "you." Most European languages have a familiar and formal "you." They must therefore decide whether to have a formal or informal relationship. The net result is that many Americans regard Europeans as stuffy, while they regard us as ill-mannered.

This point was made quite forcefully to me during a workshop in Europe for an American multinational. One of the participants was Charles (not Charley), the Graf (Count) von X, and he let us all know that he had attended the same school as Prince Philip, Queen Elizabeth's husband. One day at lunch I asked him, "Charles, how do you feel about my calling you by your first name?" "Alan, since this is an American company, and we are speaking English, it does not bother me at all. But, if the situation were different, and you called me 'du' [the German familiar form of 'you'], I would be so upset that I would not sleep tonight."

This problem is multiplied many times when relating to Asians such as Japanese, Vietnamese, or Thais, who may have as many as thirteen ways to say "you." In these societies, one must know the age, status, and background of a person before selecting the appropriate form of address. Language reinforces the status differences. Americans are informal, while many Asians stress formality and status.

Nonverbal Actions

Our facial expressions, eye contact, postures, gestures, and so forth, have a very powerful, but often unacknowledged, impact upon the negotiations process. For example, Americans believe that looking directly at another person is a sign of honesty, and we distrust people who do not look us right in the eye. But doing so is extremely rude to a Japanese. We may therefore believe that they are dishonest, while they regard us as rude.

Another example, if an American nods his head and smiles as he makes a point, we naturally assume that he understands and agrees with our point, but exactly the same actions by Japanese people just mean that they are trying to understand us; they may completely disagree with everything we have said.

The effects of nonverbal behavior are obvious at any mixed social gathering. Americans are most comfortable talking to people about an arm's length away. Southern Europeans stand much closer. Japanese stand slightly further away and will avert their eyes if people come too close. People from the Middle East often touch or hold people as they talk. Since each pattern makes someone uncomfortable, everyone is constantly moving closer or further away, almost as if a choreographer had told the cast to keep moving.

If you doubt our point about the emotional impact of cultural differences, just imagine talking about serious business issues with someone who holds your hand. Would you be your usual, calm, analytical self?

NEGOTIATIONS ISSUES

Many issues affect negotiations in all cultures, but we will discuss only five of them. We briefly describe each one, analyze the way cultural factors affect it, and recommend ways you can adjust your negotiating approach.

A. Context
B. Authority
C. Self-concept
D. General approach
E. The Agreement

Context

Context is the parties' conception of how a negotiation should be conducted. Five issues have exceptionally large cultural implications.

1. Working session versus formality
2. Problem solving versus debate
3. Direct versus indirect
4. Formal versus informal
5. Work versus play

Working session versus formality

Americans regard negotiations as working sessions; we expect a give-and-take process that leads toward an agreement. We come prepared to make concessions and to get them in return. Anything less is unsatisfactory.

At the other extreme are meetings that are essentially a formality. The parties come together primarily for a symbolic ritual. For example, when the heads of two countries such as the United States and the USSR meet to sign agreements, the real work has already been done. The heads of state usually just sign agreements that have already been negotiated by subordinates.

For the Japanese, negotiations sessions are usually formalities. People present and listen to preestablished positions. Then both sides retire to the real working sessions that occur within each team. They do not expect to give and take during the negotiating sessions.

Problem solving versus debate

Because we value problem solving and want to end with a firm conclusion, Americans regard a negotiation session as an attempt to solve problems. We may debate, but we do so as a means to an end, not an end in itself.

People from other cultures may regard these sessions as debates, as an opportunity to attempt to persuade the other party, to convince them of the logic of one's own position and to get them to admit that they are wrong. For reasons discussed earlier, such debates can be endless; one never reaches a firm conclusion. Nobody will admit: I was wrong; you are right.

The Russians tend to regard negotiations as debates. They are so ideologically oriented that giving and taking are seen as immoral, a compromise of their principles. Instead of trading concessions, they restate their original position, with all of the arguments supporting it. This process can continue indefinitely; they keep repeating themselves until the other side sees the errors of its position and accepts the Russian position.

People may also debate rather than trade concessions because they are trying to demonstrate to their management or constituents that they have faithfully expressed the group's position or philosophy and have not sold out by compromising. Union leaders and negotiators for many undercapitalized organizations and countries often debate.

For example, many Third World countries such as Brazil and the Philippines have essentially said, "We do not care what previous governments have said, nor will we accept our obligations. It is immoral for you to expect us to pay our debts, and we insist on debating this morality, not negotiating a method to pay our debts."

Similar philosophical debates occur in Arab countries and many other Third World countries. They love to discuss issues such as the nature of man or the proper relationship between corporations, individuals, and the government. Westerners generally regard these debates as irrelevant, but they are quite important to many people. To them pragmatism is much less meaningful than abstract moral principles.

Because they dislike confrontations, debates are less frequent in Japan, but philosophical issues are extremely important. The Japanese often want to know what philosophy is behind a position. In fact, they generally regard Americans as narrow pragmatists who do not even think about these philosophical issues. They feel that Americans are so overconcerned with efficiency that we ignore larger issues.

Unfortunately, they are right. We often assume that everyone agrees on philosophical issues or that they are irrelevant. We therefore ignore these debates and try to focus on what we feel is the central purpose of the meeting: solving the problem by reaching some sort of compromise. Doing so just increases many people's confusion and discomfort.

Direct versus indirect

There are two meanings of "direct." The first refers to who meets with whom. Direct negotiations are between the principals or their clearly defined representatives. Indirect negotiations use third parties such as brokers or mediators.

The second meaning refers to the way conflicts are expressed. They can be expressed directly: "I disagree." Or they can be expressed quite subtly: "I think that everything you have said is absolutely right. However, I must check this matter carefully with my management."

Both types of directness can speed up the negotiations. Issues that take weeks for third parties can often be settled quickly by the principals. Conflicts that are not clearly understood can be clarified and resolved if they are expressed directly.

Indirectness can, however, be quite valuable. It can save people's face. We have repeatedly pointed out how important saving face is, and it is much more important in most other cultures than it is in America. In fact, preserving face is so important in Japan and the Arab countries that many people would rather lose a profitable deal than lose face, and they will say or accept transparent lies to preserve their own or other people's face.

This near obsession with face causes both types of indirectness. If conflicts are not directly stated, neither party can appear to lose. If third parties are used, they serve as a buffer; they also allow people to deny that they ever took certain positions.

Because diplomats are absolutely obsessed with face, many important diplomatic negotiations are indirect. For example, Algeria mediated between the United States and Iran during the hostage crisis. Russia mediated between India and Pakistan to end one of their wars. The UN has mediated dozens of disputes. In fact, summit conferences (direct meetings between the heads of two countries) are a relatively recent invention, and, in the opinion of many people, a dangerous one. There is too great a danger of public embarrassment (as Khrushchev humiliated Eisenhower at the 1958 summit).

Because Americans are impatient and value frankness, we greatly prefer direct negotiations. We want to meet face-to-face and lay all the issues out on the table. Our directness is particularly important during negotiations because they do not occur unless there is a conflict.

Most other cultures are less direct. They are more patient and are much more concerned with saving everyone's face. In fact, our directly confronting style makes many people, particularly the Arabs and Japanese, quite uncomfortable. They regard open disagreements as rude and contemptuous.

The Arabs want direct, face-to-face discussions, but do not want direct confrontations. Face-to-face meetings help them to establish a trust relationship, but they do not want to bring open disagreements into a formal session.

In fact, rather than say that they disagree, many Arabs will say they agree, but then take actions that gently hint they do not agree at all. They hope that the other party will get the message. In Algeria an American consultant said: "My clients never disagree with my recommendations. They just do not try to implement the ones they dislike."

The Japanese are willing to meet face-to-face, but they also use third parties much more frequently than we do. They like to have that buffer. They are also so uncomfortable with open conflict that they hardly ever express it directly. They talk around it, or do not react at all, or give indirect hints that they disagree. In fact, they hardly ever say no directly; one must infer it from the way they say yes. In Tokyo we even saw a book for foreigners titled *Fifty* [or one hundred or some such number] *Ways to Say "No" in Japanese.*

Unfortunately, we Americans lack the subtlety to understand such messages. We are so direct and insensitive that we often focus on the words and miss the real message. If, for example, a Japanese says, "Your proposals are very interesting and will be studied very, very carefully," we do not realize that he may have said no.

Formal versus informal

Formal negotiations occur in a prearranged, clearly defined negotiating context. Informal ones can occur anywhere; in fact, at times some of the people involved may not even realize that they are negotiating.

Varying degrees of formality and directness give us four approaches to negotiations: direct formal; direct informal; indirect formal; indirect informal.

Direct formal

This is the classical negotiating approach. In fact, when some people say "negotiations," this is what they mean. Both sides sit at opposite sides of a table. Agendas and procedures may be clearly established. Positions are often expressed in formal language. There may even be written proposals.

Direct informal

This approach involves direct negotiations in an informal setting. For example, the principals meet in the corridor or the bar. This sort of negotiation is the major reason for the UN to exist. The formal meetings are usually worthless because everyone makes speeches to their own constituents. The real work is done in the delegates' lounge where people can talk off the record.

Direct, informal negotiations can also be conducted by telephone. During a phone conversation about another subject, one principal might casually mention a negotiating point.

The direct informal approach can be the primary one used throughout an entire negotiation or an adjunct to the formal negotiations. If the formal negotiations are not progressing satisfactorily, one side may suggest an informal meeting where they can talk in a more relaxed manner. "Let's have breakfast tomorrow."

Indirect formal

Indirect informal negotiations involve clearly designated third parties such as mediators or brokers. For example, many real estate transactions use brokers, and most realtors have a simple rule: Keep the principals apart. They know that people often say things that offend the other party (e.g., "If we buy this house, the first thing we will do is paint it to get rid of that terrible color.")

Some mediation sessions are extremely formal, with procedures that have been derived partly from courtroom practices. The most famous recent example of indirect formal negotiations concerned the Iranian hostages. The American and Iranian governments passed their proposals through Algeria, and both sides repeatedly denied positions that they allegedly had taken earlier.

Indirect informal

Indirect informal negotiations involve third parties who are not clearly designated and may not even be acknowledged. If things go wrong, the principals can claim that meetings never, ever happened or that the mediator was never authorized to do anything.

Governments often use prominent private citizens to sound out the other side on sensitive issues. Corporations may use informal go-betweens for the same purpose. If someone gets upset, they can deny any responsibility. "Jim Johnson? I may have met him once or twice, but he certainly does not have any authority to negotiate for us."

Americans generally prefer direct, formal negotiations. We do not like the extreme formality of certain rituals, but we do regard negotiations as clearly defined, essentially formal events. Two or more people sit down at a table and attempt to reach an agreement. We may also negotiate at the dinner table or over cocktails, but we still regard negotiations as relatively formal sessions.

The Japanese, Arabs, and most other people regard negotiations as much less formal events. Social rituals such as dinners and parties are an essential part of the negotiation process—even though it may be bad manners to discuss business during these social rituals.

Work versus play

Americans are much more work-oriented than most other people. A few people (e.g., the Japanese and Germans) work harder than we do, but they seldom talk as much about business as Americans. We discuss it at times that other people regard as rude and uncultured.

In fact, we tend to ignore the fact that in most countries there are two distinct processes: the formal negotiations, and an informal, essentially social process. We are so work-oriented that we regard the informal process as irrelevant or even an obstacle to the really important activities.

In Japan and the Arab countries the direct negotiations are combined with social activities. One purpose of these activities is to demonstrate hospitality. Another, more serious purpose is to determine whether you are the sort of person with whom they want to do business. An easy way to create a bad impression is to discuss business at the wrong time. That is, *the social process can be as important as the negotiations process.*

We must make an amusing digression. Good manners are so important to the Japanese, and they are so subtle that they have a novel way of punishing boors. A high-level person negotiating an important contract could be invited to a geisha party. Contrary to popular opinion, geishas are highly skilled entertainers, not prostitutes. While one geisha is singing or playing an instrument, another tops off everyone's glass; it is therefore impossible to keep track of how much one has had to drink.

If the foreigner has acted courteously, at an appropriate time the host will stand, bow, and say: "The party is over." If the foreigner has been impolite, the host just lets the party continue until the guest has gotten so drunk that he makes a complete fool of himself.

RECOMMENDATIONS

1. *Study the culture before you negotiate.* You cannot understand the negotiating context or anything else without studying the overall culture. So take the time to read about the history, traditions, and customs. So few Americans do so that you will have an immediate advantage.

2. *Analyze the context of your negotiations.* We have given you some general principles, but you must apply them to your own negotiations. During your planning ask the questions that are implicit in this analysis.

Is this a working session or a formality? Are we going to debate or try to solve a problem? Are the formal sessions only a small part of the process? Should disagreements be expressed directly? Should I use a third party? Am I working when I should be playing?

3. *Adjust your approach to fit the situation.* Your analysis is useless unless you use it to adjust your approach. Ignore or minimize your own comfort and act in the ways that will get you the best results.

4. *Slow down.* People from virtually all cultures prefer to move more slowly than Americans. Spend as much time as necessary on social rituals and relationship building; wait until they tell you that they are ready to talk business. Move slowly during the actual negotiations. Curb your natural impatience when they make apparently pointless speeches about philosophy; those speeches are not pointless to them. Accept digressions as a necessary and inescapable part of the negotiating process.

This recommendation must be related to our general positioning principles. You cannot afford to slow down if you are under extreme time pressures. You should therefore make sure that schedules are not so tight that you must negotiate at an unacceptable speed. Time pressures can weaken your position, cause you to make unnecessary concessions, and offend the other party. Most countries take a lot of time for negotiations—be sure to allow for it or you may lose.

5. *Avoid confrontations.* Do not express disagreements openly or directly. The frankness and openness that you admire may seem rude or even frightening.

6. *Pay particular attention to the informal, social process.* Unless you are unusually perceptive, you will have to work hard to understand and adjust to the demands of this process. Learn how social activities relate to the negotiations and how you are expected to act. Then do what they expect, even if it bores or irritates you.

7. *Use a local person as cultural advisor.* This person can help you to interpret the other party's actions, understand the situation, and plan a more effective strategy and tactics. Select someone who understands both cultures, yours and theirs; a local person who has also worked or studied in your country would probably be best. He or she can tell you how the cultures differ, the effects of these differences, and how you can be most effective.

8. *Do not assume that our way is the only way.* This is a general recommendation that applies to virtually every issue. All cultures tend to think that theirs is the only way, but Americans and westerners in general are particularly arrogant. That attitude was always questionable, and it is certainly unacceptable today. We must therefore be careful not to regard other cultures as inferior, their values as wrong, their thinking as illogical.

We Americans have always been arrogant about our culture; we were cultural imperialists long before we had anything resembling an empire. We believed that God had smiled on us, that we should bring "light to the heathen," and show them the ignorance of their ways.

It was a lot of fun while it lasted, but the party is over. The Japanese are now richer than we are; so are certain Arabs, the Swiss, and many Germans. The Russians, despite their economy, are about equal to us militarily. Since we can no longer insist upon our superiority, we must learn to negotiate as equals, and an important part of that shift is to show respect for other cultures.

Authority

The negotiators' authority is an important factor, and it is clearly affected by cultural differences. We will consider four issues affecting authority:

1. Achievement versus social factors
2. Institution versus individual
3. Technician versus politician
4. Racism and sexism

Achievement versus social factors

The question is whether the negotiator's authority is based on achievement or on social factors, such as family, age, or seniority.

Americans, and to a somewhat slighter degree Europeans, emphasize achievement. Theoretically at least, people are promoted according to achievement. Family, social position, and connections help, of course, but achievement is usually a major determinant of one's position and authority.

Most other cultures place more emphasis on social factors. Therefore, the American negotiator will often be much more technically competent than his counterpart, and will think and talk in achievement terms that may be almost meaningless to the other party.

In most Arab countries one's family is the primary determinant of one's position. People get their jobs, status, and social position because of their family connections, almost without regard for their abilities. The same is true in most of Latin America and the Third World in general.

Despite their egalitarian rhetoric, the Russians follow the same basic pattern, with one important exception. The children of high ranking party officals go to the best schools and get the best jobs almost regardless of their ability, but their privileges are much less secure than those of the wealthy people in other countries. If the father is purged or demoted, the entire family suffers.

In Japan the picture is more complex. The Japanese measure individual achievement much less frequently and closely than we do, and promotions are based upon seniority except at the highest levels. For example, some companies do not formally evaluate an employee's performance for the first ten years of service, and every person hired at a certain time might get similar raises and promotions. However, Japanese companies do have an enormous commitment to the group's achievement.

Therefore, a Japanese negotiating team would normally be chosen on the basis of both seniority and achievements; it would contain the best members of a group of people with sufficient seniority. It would not normally include any truly incompetent fools (as it could in Africa, Latin America, or the Arab countries), nor would it include any young "hot shots" (as it could in America).

The official spokesman would often be chosen on the basis of seniority and eloquence. He might not be the most competent person technically, but he would be the one whom the team felt could present their case most effectively. Incidentally, he would normally be the only person to speak, and it would be considered quite rude to direct comments or questions to any other member of the team.

Institution versus individual

Americans, Europeans, and Japanese tend to relate to each other as representatives of their organizations. Everyone's personality is much less important than the organization's power, reputation, and ability to do what is needed. In addition, people are much more interested in each other's organizational position than in their personality or family. The critical questions are: What can your organization do? Where do you fit in that organization?

For example, an American negotiating team would probably want to determine the negotiator's formal authority and the organization's abilities before agreeing to anything, and they would probably sign a contract with the vending organization that offered the best price and performance, even if they did not like that organization's representative. Refusing to do so on personal grounds would be regarded as irrational or even disloyal to their own organization.

In most other countries one's personality and family are much more significant. This pattern is particularly true in Arab countries. If they do not respect, trust, and like you personally, they will not do business with you, regardless of your formal authority or your organization's size, reputation, and abilities.

In addition, one's family and personal relationships would have a much greater impact upon one's ability to influence his organization. A young, well-connected middle manager might have much more influence on an organization than a high level executive.

This difference is particularly great for expatriates. Because of a shortage of trained people and several other factors, many Arab countries rely heavily on expatriates. They may have impressive titles, but much less influence than people who are nominally their subordinates. In fact, there are countless cases of senior executives being overruled by people several levels below them. You must therefore learn how much influence a negotiator really has; it may be much more or less than would appear from an organization chart.

Technician versus politician

This issue is closely related to the last two. Americans respect technical competence and expect people to gain positions and power because of it. In many other cultures, particularly Third World and Communist cultures, technical competence is often less important than political connections. It is not all unusual to find totally incompetent fools with good connections in very high-level jobs.

For example, Marcos' chauffeur became head of the Philippine Armed Forces. Lysenko, a total fraud who faked his data, was once the most influential biologist in the USSR; his theory and data were nonsense, but he told his bosses what they wanted to hear.

When dealing with such people, Americans make many mistakes. For example, we often assume that other people are technically competent because they hold certain positions. We may also assume that they want to reach the best technical solution when, in fact, they may be more concerned with maintaining or expanding their political power. For example, we assumed that Marcos' army wanted to defeat the communist insurgents, while they were much more interested in preserving the corruption that was making them rich.

We may also make the opposite mistake. We may dismiss people with limited technical competence as "just politicians" and try to deal directly with the technical experts. Doing so is extremely dangerous; in many societies technical expertise is the servant of political, social, or bureaucratic authority.

Racism and sexism

These extremely sensitive subjects are rarely discussed, but they are obviously important. The simple fact of the matter is that nearly all nonwestern societies are very racist and sexist. In fact, when we wrote the first version of this chapter in 1981, our Japanese cultural advisor told us: "You can't say this, of course, but the Japanese are very racist and sexist. You should never send a black or a woman to negotiate in Japan."

Japanese sexism is simply inconceivable to most westerners. For example, we have all heard about Japan's lifelong job security. Did you know that one way they provide that security to men is to provide almost no security to women? Nearly all female employees are on short-term contracts.

In addition, women, blacks, Koreans (who may have lived in Japan for three generations), and even some groups of low-status Japanese have virtually no chance of ever becoming even middle managers. They clean the toilets and do clerical work.

The Arabs are much less racist, but even more sexist. In fact, in some Arab countries women are not even allowed to drive cars, and any woman walking alone, even one going from her own house to her sister's next door, is in danger of being arrested as a prostitute!

In the Soviet Union the pattern is confusing. Their rhetoric is extremely egalitarian, but ethnic Russians dominate the party and the government, and hardly any women have important positions.

RECOMMENDATIONS

1. *Learn why negotiators have gotten their positions; then talk in the terms that are meaningful to them.* With technocrats, be yourself. With politicians, talk in terms of maintaining or expanding their political base. With older people, communicate deference for their age. With members of a powerful family, emphasize the value of the agreement for the family as a whole.

2. *Communicate respect for other people, even if they are much less techni-cally competent than you are.* Because we are so achievement-oriented, we often com-municate contempt for people who have gotten their positions for any other reason. They naturally resent our attitude, which can easily kill a deal.

3. *Take the time to develop mutually respectful and trusting relationships.* Even in America these relationships are valuable, but in most other countries they are indispensable. If people do not like and trust you, they just will not do business with you, no matter how good your organization is.

Do not schedule quick trips on tight schedules; they give people the impression that they are just one of your many appointments. Instead, allow enough time to respond to local hospitality.

4. *Be aware of racism and sexism.* You do not have to accept them, but you must be aware of them and their effects. Ignoring them will not make them go away; it will just make their effects less controllable.

Self-concept

The way that people see themselves greatly influences every aspect of the negotiations process. Cultural factors have a particularly strong effect upon four elements of people's self-concept.

1. Strength versus weakness
2. Superiority versus inferiority
3. High status versus low status
4. Control versus subjugation

Strength versus weakness

Since many negotiations are ultimately based upon power, one's strength or weak-ness is obviously extremely important. Our concern here is not the objective power balance; it is the way that cultural factors affect people's perceptions and attitudes toward power.

Americans are ambivalent about power. On the one hand, we respect it and the people who use it well. On the other hand, we want people to like us and are often reluctant to use our enormous economic and military power. Our discomfort, desire to make a deal, and tendency to focus on ourselves often cause us to underestimate or to misuse our power. For example, we spend a much greater percentage of our nation-al income on defense than our allies do, and much of that expenditure is to defend those allies. We have spent a fortune and suffered casualties to protect oil shipments from the Persian Gulf, even though we do not need that oil, while Japan, which would collapse without it, does virtually nothing. The money they and other countries save on their defense helps them to compete with us, buy our corporations, and so forth.

Israel is an even better example. It cannot possibly survive without our billions in aid, yet we wring our hands and beg them to act rationally instead of telling them what they must do to continue to receive this aid. The overall pattern of our relationships with our allies is an absolute reversal of the usual one between great powers and weaker countries; in the past the weaker ones normally paid tribute and did what they were told.

The Russians have much less power than we do, but they have generally used it more effectively. They understand power, and they are not at all afraid to use it. For example, right after World War II we were much stronger; our economy was intact, while theirs was ruined; we had the atom bomb; they did not. Yet they won nearly every major diplomatic negotiation.

One reason for their numerous victories has been our naiveté. We have repeatedly made unilateral concessions because we believed that doing so shows flexibility and encourages them to compromise. But, since the Russians regard unilateral concessions as a sign of weakness, these concessions actually made them more demanding.

The oil exporting Arabs know that they are in an extremely powerful position, despite the relatively low current price for oil. The world simply cannot live without oil, and they have a substantial percentage of the world's reserves. However, they also know that they are militarily vulnerable and extremely dependent upon other countries' technology and people. In addition, they have been rich and powerful for such a short time they naturally feel somewhat insecure.

The Japanese know that they are technically and economically very strong, but they also know that they are extremely vulnerable. Their entire economy can be disrupted by actions such as an oil embargo or a trade boycott.

The Japanese also have a fundamentally different attitude toward power. They believe that it essentially creates obligations. That is, one should not abuse one's power, at least not when dealing within one's own group or organization.

Since Japan dismantled their military forces at our insistence, they feel we have an obligation to defend them. Because of our failure to consult with them on many important issues such as recognition of China, they believe we have not lived up to our obligation. They are also extremely frightened by our threats to become as protectionist as they are; since they have almost no natural resources, they must export or die, and we are their most important market.

They therefore tend to fear and distrust our government and, to a lesser degree, all Americans. These feelings affect nearly every aspect of every relationship between us.

RECOMMENDATIONS

1. *Analyze both the objective and the perceived power balance.* How strong are both parties? What is the basis of their power? Regardless of cultural factors, the key question is always, what are each party's alternatives? Then consider cultural factors. How strong do they think they are?

2. *Analyze the other party's attitudes toward power.* Do they feel that it should be used ruthlessly? Or that it creates obligations? Are concessions seen as a sign of good faith or as a sign of weakness? Do they trust you or are they afraid that you will exploit your powerful position?

3. *Use your power in ways that they feel are legitimate.* If you ever deal with the Russians, make sure that you do so from strength and use it directly. With the

Japanese, do not appear to be abusing your power. With the Arabs, allow for concessions that can be seen as part of the process of building good will. In addition, communicate that you enjoy the bargaining process as much as you look forward to obtaining an agreement.

Superiority versus inferiority

Virtually everyone feels that their culture is superior. Our way is naturally the best way. But people from different cultures vary in the amount of confidence they have in the feelings and the way they express them.

We Americans are sometimes so arrogant that we offend nearly everybody. Many Americans sincerely believe that our culture, and our economic and political systems are immeasurably superior to all others. We therefore do not bother to learn foreign languages or try to adjust to most foreign customs. In fact, we often do the opposite: We try to teach other people the "right" way to do things. Most Europeans know at least two languages and conduct business in the other party's language, while Americans think everyone should speak English.

Many people from other cultures deeply resent this attitude. One reason for their resentment is that they grudgingly feel that our culture is superior, at least in some respects, and no one likes to feel inferior. For example, the French have forgiven the Germans for defeating them, but they have not forgiven the U.S. for defeating Germany, then rebuilding France after the war. They can forgive their former enemy, but resent their benefactor. This resentment is even stronger in Mexico and other parts of Latin America because we have been so dominant for so long. Former colonies of western countries have similar feelings toward us and Europeans.

Arabs and other Muslims feel the same way. They are particularly enraged about being portrayed as ignorant terrorists in the American media. The most visible sign of Muslims' resentment was The Ayatollah's revolution. He and his supporters said in unmistakably clear terms: "Get out! We want to return to our own traditions."

The Japanese have more mixed feelings. On the one hand, they have a long and very successful cultural history that emphasizes their uniqueness and superiority. Their recent economic success has also built their confidence, particularly among the young, technically trained people. On the other hand, they have essentially borrowed or had imposed upon them a number of western ideas such as parliamentary democracy and business suits. In addition, negotiations between us invariably take place in English, which implies that ours is the superior culture.

RECOMMENDATIONS

1. *Learn at least a few words of the other party's language.* Merely saying in their language, "Good morning. I wish that I could speak your language well enough to work in it," can greatly improve the atmosphere.

2. *Visibly demonstrate your respect for their culture.* Observe their social rituals. Eat their food. Most importantly, do not criticize anything or ask rude questions (e.g., "Do Arab women resent their inferior position?").

3. *In Japan communicate sincere respect for their organization.* Japanese identify much more closely with their organizations than we do. After all, they work for one organization for their entire life. Therefore, in the informal discussions that precede the formal negotiations, tell them how pleased you are to work with them, your successful experiences with them in the past, and so on.

These actions conflict with the Law of Indifference. You may recall that we pointed out that appearing indifferent to making a deal increases your power. However, appearing indifferent in Japan has the opposite effect because they are so concerned with creating long-term, trusting relationships.

4. *Understand and work to reduce resentment or other negative feelings.* Regardless of whether these feelings are caused by jealousy, our arrogance, foreign policy, history, or other factors, they will adversely affect the negotiations. You should therefore try to learn how people really feel about you and your society, and then work to overcome, or at least reduce, any negative feelings.

High status versus low status

Status is a particularly sensitive element of one's self-concept. In many negotiations the other side will be represented by people whose political, social, or corporate positions make them very sensitive about losing face. It is extremely important not to do anything that places them in a bad light in front of their subordinates.

RECOMMENDATIONS

1. *Never make a high status person lose face in front of lower status people, particularly subordinates.* We have repeatedly discussed the importance of preserving people's face, but it is particularly important in front of one's subordinates. The other recommendations are specific actions that may protect high status people's face.

2. *Do not force high status people to change their position publicly.* Allow them to do so in private. You might, for example, suggest a recess in which only the principals continue the negotiations. You could also suggest some other arena in which a one-to-one discussion can be used to iron out differences. The agreement could then be formally ratified when all sides reconvene with the subordinates present.

3. *Do not direct your remarks to their lower-status, but more technically competent people.* In many countries, especially in the Third World, technical advisors are important, but the higher-status people make the decisions, and they may ignore the technical advisors. The decision makers will respond much better to respect than to any technical arguments.

In Japan, causing the high-status person to lose face is unthinkable. The technical experts may have the real power within the team, but they would never publicly disagree with their spokesman. In addition, every member of the team would resent your attempts to undermine the spokesman's authority.

Control versus subjugation

People have very different beliefs about their ability to control their lives and environments. Americans are exceptionally confident about our ability to control events. We literally believe that we can and should change the world. No one but an American president would have publicly committed to put a man on the moon within a decade.

In Third World countries, people often have very little confidence in their ability to control events. For centuries their destiny has been determined by colonial powers or natural forces beyond their control. Their cultures therefore emphasize acceptance of a fixed order rather than active striving to improve things.

Arabs tend to have mixed feelings. Because of their enormous resources, they are learning that they can control events. However, their underlying culture does emphasize accepting things as they are, and almost all plans are qualified by the expression "Inshallah," if God wills it.

They are also very concerned about changing society too rapidly, especially in ways that conflict with Muslim ideals and traditions. They may therefore object to proposals that would cause more social change than they regard as desirable. That is, they are simultaneously trying to make enormous technical and economic changes, while trying to preserve their social and cultural traditions.

The Japanese generally try to balance control and acceptance. They strive essentially for harmony. They have demonstrated their ability to control economic and technical development, but they also try to work within the constraints of economic, political, and organizational forces.

They are therefore quite uncomfortable with Americans' insensitivity to order and balance. They feel that we tend to rush into things, trying to control each individual event without regard for the effects on the overall economic and social balance. For example, they are literally horrified by the way we hire and fire people, abruptly change suppliers, and focus upon extremely short-term profits.

In a negotiation they would want to consider issues that most Americans would regard as irrelevant. For example, we might want to focus almost exclusively on price, quality, and delivery, while they would also want to consider the effects of this agreement on the local economy, the environment, and their relationships with the government.

RECOMMENDATIONS

1. *Recognize that other people may not have and may even dislike our sense of control over events.* Projects that appear feasible to you may appear impossible or even frightening to them.

2. *When dealing with Japanese, pay careful attention to overall economic and social balance.* This balance may seem irrelevant to you, but it is critically important to them. If they feel that your proposal would be too disruptive, they will reject it— almost without regard to costs and profits.

3. *When dealing with Arabs, try to minimize conflicts between your proposal and their traditions.*

General Approach

Each party's general approach is obviously affected by the issues discussed earlier. We will now discuss five additional aspects of international negotiations:

1. The negotiators' flexibility
2. Past, present, or future orientation
3 Inductive, deductive, or intuitive thinking
4. Negotiating time
5. Communications styles

The negotiators' flexibility

Cultures vary enormously in the amount of flexibility they allow a negotiator. American managers tend to give negotiators fairly general limits and instructions and let them use their own judgment about what they say, concede, and demand. The amount of flexibility people are allowed generally depends upon their positions and perceived competence.

Many cultures allow considerably less flexibility. For example, Japanese negotiators may have almost none. In many negotiations all they can do is report their team's position and listen as you report yours. Their decision-making pattern requires them to develop a consensus among many people after thoroughly discussing the alternatives. Any change in a position must therefore be referred back to those who participated in the original decision.

Negotiators for ideologically committed organizations generally have little flexibility, but for different reasons. Compromise is seen, not as the normal give-and-take that helps to solve a problem, but as a violation of an important principle. For example, Russian negotiators are so constrained by their ideology that they may simply sit there repeating their original position again and again.

RECOMMENDATIONS

1. *Determine the amount of flexibility that the other party has and adjust to it.* Do not expect concessions that the other side simply cannot make without consulting with other people.

2. *Be as flexible or rigid as the other side.* The American reaction to rigidity is often excessive flexibility. We make concessions, hoping the other side will reciprocate, but they often get even tougher. Remember, if yours is the only side making concessions, you are certain to lose.

Past, present or future orientation

Americans are present- and future-oriented. We live in a young country and have little knowledge, respect, or interest in history. We tend to regard traditions as undesirable constraints upon rational actions. We often do not care how we did something yesterday because we have a better way to do it today.

Nearly all other cultures have much more respect and interest in history and traditions. In fact, many Americans have met foreigners who know much more American history than they do. Hardly any foreigner can understand why we demolish perfectly usable buildings to put up larger, and often much uglier, ones. People from many countries can tell you their families' history for several generations, while most Americans do not even know their grandmothers' maiden names.

Although Americans are future-oriented, we do not look that far forward. We are naturally impatient and have an almost insatiable need for feedback. Our evaluation systems almost force us to focus on short-term results. How does this quarter compare to the previous one?

The Japanese have a much longer time horizon, partly because they are more patient, partly because they have been taught to expect a more ordered advancement in status based upon seniority. Their system encourages lifetime employment, less frequent performance appraisals, slow promotion and long-term pay-outs.

They also have a much broader conception of their interests and strategy than we do. We tend to focus on a particular project. In fact, our accounting systems almost force us to do so. Each project must pay its own way. The Japanese look at the larger and long-term picture. They are concerned with how a project fits into an overall strategy for their company or even the entire Japanese economy and society. Therefore, the ROI (return on investment) of a particular project might be evaluated very differently.

We might feel that the ROI was too low, while they might regard it as adequate because the project is also keeping people employed or providing control over a resource needed by other parts of the company or economy. In fact, they have often been guilty of dumping (selling things for less than they cost to produce) to protect their market share and keep people employed.

The Arabs want to preserve their cultural traditions, but they also want certain changes to occur immediately. For example, during the oil boom, harbors were often full of ships that could not be unloaded because they were buying things and building so fast. Hospitals and hotels are often extremely underutilized because they were built without analyzing the need for them. They often replaced western technicians and managers with Arabs so quickly that people were assigned responsibilities for which they were not at all prepared. Sometimes a multimillion dollar project was directed by a person with no significant field experience.

Many Third World societies have the same general mixture of past and immediate future orientation. For example, many countries created national airlines and steel plants that they did not need and could not afford. They preferred the instant status of these symbols to the slow, arduous process of building up their infrastructures.

Inductive, deductive, or intuitive thinking

As we noted earlier, Americans tend to be inductive. From a base of facts, experience, or even formal studies we abstract principles. Then, if later facts conflict with principles, we modify the principles.

The Russians and people from theocracies or socialistic countries tend to be more deductive. They begin with certain assumptions or principles about the nature of man or social justice. Because they cannot violate these principles, they may take negotiating positions that Americans perceive as essentially irrelevant and irrational.

Stalemates often occur because both sides are operating on different bases. The Americans reject the philosophical arguments as irrelevant and insist that a cost-benefit analysis indicates that certain steps should be taken. The other side rejects the entire system of cost-benefit analyses and reiterates its philosophical position.

Philosophical issues are also important to the Japanese. They want to know the philosophy upon which positions are based. Since Americans ignore philosophical issues, the Japanese tend to regard us as shallow pragmatists.

Many Arabs also enjoy philosophical discussions, but they often mix them with intuitive thinking because they are most concerned about trust and personal relationships. The critical issue is often not efficiency or philosophy; it is their personal trust in you. Arabs from the wealthy countries say, in effect, "Don't bother me with technical details because I am not a technical person. Besides we have enough resources to do almost anything. If you and I trust each other and work together, we can do it."

RECOMMENDATIONS

1. *Analyze the other party's time orientation and thinking pattern.* Are they looking to the past, present, or future? How far forward are they looking?

Are they thinking inductively, deductively, or intuitively? What premises are different from yours? How do these premises affect their goals and strategy?

2. *Accept their attitudes and approach as legitimate.* The mere fact that they are different from yours does not mean they are wrong. In fact, from their perspective their actions almost certainly make sense. For example, since some Arab countries have enormous resources, they can afford inexperienced executives' mistakes. Giving young people these jobs now means they can control their own economy tomorrow.

3. *Adjust to these differences.* Do not propose actions that could cause offensive social changes. Try to deliver results in their time frame (more immediate for Arabs, longer term for Japanese). Most important of all, *make sure you are appealing to the motives that they really have, not the ones you would have in their situation.*

Negotiating Time

Because we are extremely impatient, Americans want to settle things quickly. We want to have only a few brief sessions, with relatively little time between them. People from virtually all other cultures are willing to spend more time negotiating.

The Japanese prefer relatively brief sessions, but they need many sessions with a great deal of time between them. The group must thoroughly discuss all issues and reach consensus on their next position before they meet again with the other side. Therefore, a negotiation that might require a few days for two American companies can take months in Japan.

Arabs tend to have long negotiating sessions with extensive and perhaps repetitious philosophical discussions, but there are relatively few sessions. Therefore, the total negotiating time may not be particularly long.

Russian negotiators tend to be stonewallers. They will spend an extraordinary amount of time, and repeat positions again and again, slowly wearing you down.

RECOMMENDATIONS

1. *When negotiating with Japanese, plan to have many sessions with a great deal of time between them.* Do not fly to Tokyo and expect to settle an important agree-

ment in a few days. Allow yourself weeks or even months. Failing to do so can create severe communications and trust problems; you just will not have enough time for the social rituals and numerous meetings that the Japanese require.

You will also make deadline pressure work against you. You will feel that pressure much more than they will. You may therefore make unnecessary, perhaps even excessive, concessions.

2. *When negotiating with Arabs, plan to have longer and less formal sessions.* Listen attentively to Arabs' philosophical statements and express your own philosophy. Remember, there are two fundamentally different sets of issues: the economic and technical issues that you regard as so important, and the philosophical and personal issues that they care about.

Communications styles and patterns

Cultures vary significantly in the degree to which they allow or encourage open communications. During negotiations three different communication styles can be used.

Americans generally favor a direct and open approach; we say whatever is on our minds, a tendency which appears ill-mannered to people from many other cultures.

Russians tend toward the opposite style. They often play their cards close to their chest. They may give only the information that is absolutely necessary or clearly requested by the other party; nothing is volunteered.

The Japanese often use a vague and indirect style. This style may result from a conscious strategy or from a difference in values or patterns of thinking. For example, rather than embarrass someone by turning down a direct request, that may change the subject each time the request is made. The guest is essentially being told that the request cannot be honored, without losing face from a direct answer. Alas, because we Americans lack subtlety, we might not understand that the request has been denied, while people from cultures that are more attuned to saving face would easily get the message.

Another aspect of communications during international negotiations is the degree to which members of a negotiating team are allowed to talk during a negotiation. Again, there are two extreme patterns and many intermediate ones.

One extreme is to allow anyone to speak whenever they feel that they can contribute. Americans and some Arabs often prefer this pattern. As we noted in chapter 10, this lack of team discipline can create serious problems, especially if team members openly disagree with each other.

The other extreme is to allow no one but the spokesman to speak during the formal negotiations. Subordinates may or may not be allowed to speak to the other team outside the formal sessions. Russians often favor this pattern, and the Japanese place special emphasis upon this sort of discipline. The young, competent aggressive person who tries to "sharp shoot" or show off in front of his boss is regarded as very rude.

An intermediate pattern would be to have a prearranged sequence of speakers. The sequence might be based upon a formal agenda or upon the distribution of expertise within the team. For example, engineers or purchasing specialists might speak only when their areas are being discussed.

RECOMMENDATIONS

1. *Analyze the other party's communications style.* Learn what it is, then try to determine its causes. Is it a consciously chosen style? Or is it based upon some important cultural factors?

Look also for hidden meanings in their responses to your questions and requests. Try to understand what they mean, not just what they say.

2. *Carefully select the communications style that fits your objectives.* If you want to create a comfortable, trusting relationship, you should probably use their style. If you want to put them off-balance or signal dissatisfaction, you might select an unfamiliar style. For example, you might shift from being open and direct to being closed and unresponsive.

3. *Establish a communications game plan.* Decide in advance on the order in which issues will be discussed and who will speak about each one. Do not let it just happen.

The Agreement

As we pointed out in chapter 8, an agreement is not always the end of the negotiating process. Even when dealing with people from your own culture, you may need extensive discussions to clarify and implement the agreement.

Cultural differences add to the confusion. They obviously affect both parties' perception of everything that has been said, and various cultures may have fundamentally different conceptions of agreements. Four subjects are particularly important:

1. Oral versus written
2. Tight versus loose interpretation
3. Final versus directional interpretation
4. The effects of corruption

Oral versus written

American business people live by the written word and pay very little attention to oral contracts. As a movie mogul once said, "Oral contracts aren't worth the paper they are printed on." Look at the standard conditions of almost any contract and you will see a disclaimer about any oral statements. The written contract is it, period.

Arabs and many other people still live by the oral tradition. People talk and listen rather than read. In fact, they distrust our lawyers and our contracts' archaic and abstruse language.

In addition, if there is a disagreement between the written contract and their understanding of the oral contract, they expect you, as a person they trust, to honor the oral agreement.

Tight versus loose interpretation

Americans tend to interpret contracts rather tightly. We have a well-developed law of contracts, and over the centuries certain phrases have been interpreted to have specific meanings.

The Russians interpret contracts even more strictly, at least when it is in their interest to do so. Their agreements with America, about wheat purchases are an excellent example. When the world price rises, they insist that we deliver at the original price. When the price falls, they cancel the contract or demand renegotiation.

Many other cultures interpret contracts in loose or even whimsical ways. For example, for many business issues there is no clearly defined contractual law in the People's Republic of China; a contract means whatever the authorities think it means, and they have often contradicted or ignored precedents. The entire meaning of an agreement can be completely changed if the people in power are replaced.

Wealthy Chinese are emigrating from Hong Kong because they know that the People's Republic of China's guarantee not to change the system for fifty years is absolutely meaningless. American corporations will probably lose billions of dollars before learning that their contracts are also meaningless. A new government, or even new officials will simply ignore the contracts.

Final versus directional interpretation

Americans normally regard contracts as final. If conditions change to one party's disadvantage, that's tough. You made the deal, and you will have to live with it. We generally regard attempts to renegotiate contracts as illegitimate, even dishonest.

The Japanese have a fundamentally different concept of contracts. They regard them as directional rather than final. They are a statement of the agreement now, and it is assumed that they will be reinterpreted or renegotiated if conditions change.

Therefore, if conditions change in ways that make the contract unfavorable, they expect to renegotiate it. For example, they have repeatedly canceled or insisted on renegotiating contracts for the purchase of commodities when world prices have fallen below the level in the contracts.

We regard their actions as illegitimate, but we do not recognize that they would renegotiate contracts if conditions changed in the opposite direction. In other words, we have the worse of both possible worlds. If conditions change in one direction, they cancel or renegotiate the contract. If conditions change the other way, we foolishly live by the original contract, even though they would renegotiate it.

The Arabs and the rest of the Third World have a somewhat similar conception. For example, numerous countries have either nationalized their oil industry after it became profitable, or insisted that the oil companies renegotiate their contracts. Dozens of countries have essentially torn up their loan agreements and insisted upon lower interest, longer repayment terms, *and* new loans.

Unfortunately, not just Third World countries have taken such actions. The British government, under both Labour and Conservative administrations, has repeatedly changed the financial terms for North Sea oil. The American government has also changed the game after investments were made based upon the old rules.

The simple, inescapable fact is that very few people and hardly any governments regard a contract as absolutely final under all conditions. If conditions change, most foreign corporations and nearly all governments will insist that the agreement change also.

RECOMMENDATIONS

1. *Be absolutely certain that you really agree on everything before you write the contracts.* Check everything—the words, the meaning these words have for both parties, and the way that the agreement will be implemented.

2. *Make sure that the contracts say exactly what you have agreed.* In chapter 8 we made this point for all agreements, but it is particularly important when negotiating across cultural lines.

3. *Recognize that the local courts may interpret the agreement in ways that your lawyers never even considered.*

4. *Never let lawyers without detailed knowledge of the applicable law write a contract.* Those archaic phrases that they love so much may mean absolutely nothing to a foreign court. Some American corporations have ignored this obvious fact and even insisted on terminology that violates the law in the country where the contract will be implemented!

5. *Whenever possible, consult a local attorney.* You need to know how the other parties and their courts will interpret the agreement. If that interpretation conflicts with your objectives and understanding, change the contract language.

In other words, make sure that the written contract says what you want it to say in a language that will have the same meaning to both parties. Misunderstandings can create problems as diverse as poor implementation, cancellations and lawsuits.

6. *If conditions change so that the contract becomes unfavorable, demand renegotiation.* Of course, you should not do so when dealing with cultures that regard contracts as final, but, if renegotiation is part of a culture's traditions, demand it.

If they demand renegotiation when it favors them, but you accept an unfavorable contract that you can legitimately renegotiate, you are obviously going to get less than you deserve.

The effects of corruption

Americans and other westerners are extremely naive about corruption. We know that it occurs occasionally, but we see it as an aberration, not a central fact of business life. However, in many countries it is nearly impossible to do business without paying bribes, and people do not even take corruption seriously. It is just an inescapable part of the system.

For example, former prime minister Tanaka remained the most powerful politician in Japan long after he had been convicted of accepting millions in bribes.

Contrast that with America's vice-president Spiro Agnew who was forced out of office and political life, but never convicted.

Mr. Laurel, the vice-president of the Philippines, resigned his office in August 1988 to protest the government's "institutionalized corruption," and former President Marcos is still a hero to many people despite stealing billions of dollars and impoverishing the country.

The Philippine economy has shrunk; the standard of living has declined; millions of people are homeless; and it has over 25 billion dollars in foreign debts that it cannot repay. Despite its desperate need for capital, The Philippine government allows or even colludes in frauds against foreign investors.

For example, registered letters are routinely opened, and the cash and checks are stolen. Essential documents cannot be obtained without bribing officials. The courts ignore the law and allow powerful people and organizations to do whatever they like. How do I know? Because I have been robbed in an extraordinary blatant way.

I invested $69,000 in a small business in Manila. My Filipino attorney wrote a promissory note that explicitly prohibited the borrower from selling that business without my written approval. A few months later he sold it to a much larger organization, and he had been on the board of trustees when he signed the promissory note.

In any western nation, the courts would void that sale or force the borrower to share the proceeds with me. In Manila, the legal system is so corrupt that I did not get a penny. My attorney told me that the promissory note *he* drafted was essentially meaningless because my rights were inferior to those of the "innocent buyer." The obvious fact that an organization which buys a property owned by a trustee is certainly not innocent was irrelevant, nor did the restrictions of the promissory note *he* had written mean anything at all. Since the buyer was a rich powerful organization, while I was a foreigner, it could do whatever it liked.

I must also add that my attorney charged me a fee equal to about a year's salary for a beginning physician and was not the slightest bit embarrassed by his failure to protect my interests. In fact, he became quite abusive when I criticized him; it was all my fault for not understanding the system. In the U.S. I could appeal to the Bar Association's ethics committee, but in Manila I was helpless. If I was stupid enough to trust my lawyer, I deserved whatever happened to me.

One last point: while I was trying to collect my money, various people suggested that I bribe the officials. Despite my belief in adapting to other cultures, I had to draw the line somewhere. I am simply not willing to commit a felony, even one which the local people regard as just a normal part of doing business.

RECOMMENDATIONS

1.   *Carefully investigate the pattern of corruption before you invest.* I hope that my expensive lesson helps you to avoid my mistake. I should have realized that The Philipines is hopelessly corrupt.

2.   *Flatly avoid investing in countries with endemic corruption* (such as The Philipines, Nigeria, Columbia, and many others.)

3. *Do not trust local lawyers unless someone you know very well will vouch for them.* Many of them are as corrupt as their governments, and they will cheat you as quickly and completely as possible.

FINAL REMARKS

Both negotiations and cross-cultural analysis are complex subjects, but we cannot allow this complexity to prevent us from trying to understand the subject. The more that you understand about cultural differences, the more effectively you can negotiate and implement agreements.

The dominant theme of this chapter has been the same as the theme of the entire book: Understand the other party. In earlier chapters we saw how hard it is to apply that principle even when negotiating with people like ourselves; we naturally focus on our own concerns, objectives, and positions. Cultural differences and our natural tendency to think that our own way is best make understanding much more difficult.

This chapter's principles and recommendations will help, but you have to go much further. We would like to close with four general recommendations.

1. *Study a culture before negotiating with its members.* This chapter just gave you some general principles and examples. You need to understand a culture in much greater depth to negotiate effectively.

2. *Remember that there is no substitute for knowing the individuals on the other side of the table.* No amount of study of a culture can replace personal knowledge of the other people.

3. *Do not change your values or objectives just because they conflict with the local culture.* You should be sensitive to and respectful of the local culture, but not reject your own.

4. *Do not be too eager to do business as the Romans do.* Consider cultural factors; adjust to them when necessary, but remember who you are and why you are there. Changes in your philosophies and management practices should be deliberate and based upon a collective management decision.

Appendix 1:

Preparation Questionnaire

This questionnaire will help you to organize your preparation, a formidable task that most people perform poorly.

Copy it as often as you like. You should obviously work with copies to preserve the master.

It follows the steps described in chapter 2, "Getting Ready to Negotiate." These steps should be taken, in order, for most significant negotiations.

   I. Define the issues
  II. Set your objectives
 III. Analyze the situation (from their perspective)
 IV. Plan your strategy

As this form is too detailed for most negotiations, you should not try to answer all these questions unless a negotiation is really important. It simply takes too much time to do so. You should therefore skim through it, decide which questions are important for each negotiation, and answer only those pertinent questions.

DEFINE THE ISSUES

Your first task is to define the issues: What are you negotiating about?

List the Issues

Just list all the issues, including ones that may be irrelevant. If you are unsure if you should include an issue, include it. It is far better to list an irrelevant issue than to ignore a potentially important one.

_____	_____
_____	_____
_____	_____
_____	_____
_____	_____
_____	_____
_____	_____
_____	_____
_____	_____

Group the Issues

Sometimes you can ignore this step because the issues are simple, or all of them can be combined into one overriding issue such as price.

If you cannot ignore this step, you must decide how to group the issues. Group them on any basis that you feel is meaningful. For example, you might group them by priority, by the amount of conflict on each issue, by whether they are monetary or nonmonetary issues, or by some other basis.

This form allows you to group them in whatever way you think is most valuable. First, identify the basis for grouping (e.g., conflict). Then label each group (e.g., for conflict it could be high, medium and low). Just identify the group (such as "Low conflict") and list the issues that fit into this group.

In addition, you may find it useful to group the issues in two or more different ways, such as by the amount of conflict and monetary versus nonmonetary.

<u>Basis For Grouping_____</u>

Group_____	Group_____	Group_____
_____	_____	_____
_____	_____	_____
_____	_____	_____
_____	_____	_____
_____	_____	_____

<u>Basis For Grouping</u>_____

Group_____   Group_____   Group_____

_____   _____   _____

_____   _____   _____

_____   _____   _____

_____   _____   _____

_____   _____   _____

<u>Basis For Grouping</u>_____

Group_____   Group _____   Group_____

_____   _____   _____

_____   _____   _____

_____   _____   _____

_____   _____   _____

_____   _____   _____

Relate the Issues to the Overall Relationship

Now that the issues are defined, relate them to the overall relationship. If they are much more important than the relationship, you might be willing to damage or sacrifice the relationship to get a good deal in this negotiation. The converse is equally true. If the relationship is supremely important, you might settle moderately or even generously. It is foolish to damage an important relationship for a minor issue.

<u>Importance of the issues</u>   <u>Importance of the relationship</u>

_____   _____

IMPLICATIONS FOR ACTION

How should you negotiate?_____

_____

_____

_____

SET YOUR OBJECTIVES

What are you trying to accomplish? You must know what you are trying to achieve; otherwise, you have no direction.

For important issues you should set an MSP, but you cannot do so for every issue. An MSP has no flexibility; if there are too many of them, you can create a null set, meaning that no deal is satisfactory.

You should therefore set an MSP for every important issue, and a target for less important ones. You *must* achieve every MSP, and you would like to achieve those targets.

Set Your MSP's

Base each MSP entirely on your economics. At what point are your alternatives more attractive than a deal with these people?

Remember, you should set an MSP only for the most important issues. Otherwise, you may try for a deal that is simply impossible.

Issue	MSP
_____	_____
_____	_____
_____	_____
_____	_____
_____	_____
_____	_____

Set Your Priorities

There are two reasons for explicitly setting your priorities. First, you need to know what is most important to you so that you try for a deal that satisfies your most important objectives. Second, any differences between your priorities and those of the other party create opportunities for value-adding trades. These trades are ones in which both parties gain because they receive something that is more valuable than whatever they have conceded.

To simplify your analysis, divide the issues into three categories: high, medium, and low priority.

Issue	High	Medium	Low
_____	____	____	____
_____	____	____	____
_____	____	____	____

Issue	High	Medium	Low
_____	____	____	____
_____	____	____	____
_____	____	____	____
_____	____	____	____
_____	____	____	____
_____	____	____	____
_____	____	____	____
_____	____	____	____

Set Targets For Less Important Issues

Indicate what you would like to achieve on the less important issues.

Issue	Target
_____	_____
_____	_____
_____	_____
_____	_____
_____	_____
_____	_____

ANALYZE THE SITUATION FROM THEIR PERSPECTIVE

This step is an extremely important one, and it is usually performed poorly. People naturally focus their attention on their own perceptions, objectives, and concerns, thereby missing the critically important information.

Their Objectives

In nearly all negotiations, the most important information for you to seek is the other side's objectives. If you can accurately estimate their goals, priorities, and MSP's, you have an enormous advantage.

Of course, you hardly ever get complete information on their objectives, but you should be constantly trying to read them. Make a preliminary estimate of their objectives before the negotiations begin, and then revise that estimate as you acquire more information.

Their MSP'S

Since this information is so critically important, people guard it carefully. Make a very preliminary assessment now and then keep trying to improve it as the negotiations progress. Take the following steps:

a. Make a preliminary estimate of their MSP on each major issue now
b. Base your initial strategy on that estimate
c. Keep probing to improve that estimate
d. Revise it as you get new information
e. Base your final strategy on your best estimate

Major Issue	Initial estimate of their MSP	Final estimate of their MSP

Their Priorities

Learning their priorities is only slightly less important than learning their limits. Every difference in priorities creates an opportunity for a value-adding trade. Estimate their priorities the same way that you estimated your own.

Issue	High	Medium	Low

Issue	High	Medium	Low
_____	_____	_____	_____
_____	_____	_____	_____
_____	_____	_____	_____
_____	_____	_____	_____
_____	_____	_____	_____
_____	_____	_____	_____
_____	_____	_____	_____
_____	_____	_____	_____

Now compare their priorities to yours. Every significant difference in priorities creates a potential trading opportunity. Record every significant priority difference and plan your trades.

TRADING OPPORTUNITIES

Issue	Your priority	Their priority
_____	_____	_____
_____	_____	_____
_____	_____	_____
_____	_____	_____
_____	_____	_____

Their Perceptions of Your Situation

People react, not to reality, but to their perceptions of it. In fact, to a considerable extent, negotiating concerns influencing the other party's perceptions.

Try to understand how they see you; then plan ways to change those perceptions toward ones that support your objectives and strategy.

Their perceptions of your objectives

These perceptions are, of course, the critical ones. They will respond, not to your real objectives, but to their perceptions of them. Write down your beliefs about how they perceive your objectives on the major issues and then plan ways to influence those perceptions toward ones that are more favorable to you.

Major issue	Their perception of your objective	What should you do?

Their other perceptions of your situation

Chapter 2, "Getting Ready to Negotiate," listed a number of perceptions that can influence the negotiations. Since the influential perceptions vary so much from one negotiation to the next, we will not list all those dimensions here.

We encourage you to look through that chapter and record the potentially significant perceptions and your plans for coping with their effects or trying to change them.

Potentially significant
perception_____   What should you do about it?

_____   _____

_____   _____

_____   _____

_____   _____

_____   _____

_____   _____

_____   _____

_____   _____

_____   _____

The Power Balance

When all is said and done, it is power that makes the difference. You may be charming, friendly, and reasonable, and your position may be absolutely correct. But power will usually determine who gets what.

Power is partly objective, partly psychological. Objective negotiating power comes primarily from having attractive alternatives. Psychological power comes from the other side's beliefs. If they think you have power, you have it. Conversely, no matter how good your alternatives, if they believe you are weak, they will probably react to your "weakness."

You should therefore analyze the power balance and its sources, consider its implications, and, if necessary, plan to change it.

A simple, but reliable, way to assess this balance is to divide 100 percentage points of power between both parties.

Your power _____%   Their power _____%

Power does not exist in a vacuum, nor is it created in one. You should therefore understand the sources of both sides' power.

SOURCES OF POWER

<u>Your power</u>	<u>Their power</u>
_____	_____
_____	_____
_____	_____
_____	_____
_____	_____
_____	_____

Their Strategy

After reviewing your analysis of the situation, consider their personalities and negotiating style. What strategy are they likely to use?_____

_____

_____

What other strategies might they use? _____

_____

_____

PLAN YOUR STRATEGY

Pure Bargaining versus Joint Problem Solving

Which will you emphasize? _____

_____

Offers

List your offers in the order you intend to make them.

1. _____
2. _____
3. _____
4. _____
5. _____

Questions

What questions will you ask?

1. _____
2. _____
3. _____
4. _____
5. _____

Attitudes

What attitudes will you communicate?_____
_____
_____
_____

Team Issues (if you will negotiate as a team)

1. Should you negotiate as an individual or a team?_____
2. Why?_____
3. Who should be on the team?_____

   _____
4. Why?_____
5. Who should take each role?
   Chief_____
   Spokesperson _____
   Tough person _____
   Friendly person _____
   Behavioral analyst _____
   Data analyst _____
   Specialist _____

Appendix 2:

Feedback Loop Questionnaire

This questionnaire will help you to organize your thoughts while you are working on the Feedback Loop. It can be used at any time you take a break during a negotiation.

Copy it as many times as you like. You should obviously work with copies to preserve the master.

It is too detailed for most negotiations. In addition, since it covers every negotiating step, some questions may be irrelevant. For example, if you refer to it before starting the Middle Game, questions on the Middle Game are obviously irrelevant.

Unless a negotiation is very important and nearly completed, do not try to answer all the questions. It would take too much time to do so. Just skim through it, decide which questions are important for this negotiation, and answer them.

However, *you should answer all the questions in the final two sections, "Interpreting the Information" and "Revising your Strategy."* They pull things together and help you to make the overall decisions.

Your analysis will be improved if you have taken detailed notes and refer regularly to them.

The Feedback Loop contains four steps:

1. Acquire information
2. Interpret that information
3. Use that information to revise your strategy
4. Implement your revised strategy

This form will focus on steps 2 and 3. There will be a few questions on step 1, but you obviously cannot acquire information during a break; you can only interpret and use it. Step 4 will occur after the break.

REVIEW OF YOUR PREPARATION

Refer to your notes and to the Preparation Questionnaire.

Inconsistencies between Their Actions and Your Expectations

Any inconsistency suggests that your analysis and perhaps your strategy are based on incorrect assumptions. For example, if the buyers' opening offer is higher than your preliminary estimate of their MSP, that estimate is obviously incorrect, and their entire situation may be considerably different from your expectations.

You should therefore take three steps.

1. Carefully review your preparation questionnaire, your notes, and your recollections of the negotiations.

2. Write down any apparent inconsistencies between your expectations and their actions.

3. Write down the possible meaning and implications of each inconsistency. Please note that there may be more than one meaning or implication to an inconsistency.

Their inconsistent action

Meaning and implications

Their inconsistent action

Meaning and implications

Their inconsistent action

Meaning and implications

Their inconsistent action

Meaning and implications

Inconsistencies between Your Plans and Your Actions

These inconsistencies suggest that you have not executed your plans properly. For example, you may have intended to create an indifferent atmosphere and then sold hard.

The obvious questions are: "Why?" and "What does it mean?"

You might just have planned a strategy that you cannot execute well because it is unnatural for you. If so, what should you do now? Continue the new strategy? Move to one that is midway between your planned and actual strategy? Do something else? The important thing is to make explicit plans; do not just do what comes naturally.

Another possibility is that you have adapted to the other side's actions, perhaps without even consciously thinking about it. For example, you might have planned to act indifferently because you expected them to be eager for the deal. When they seemed uninterested, you started selling hard. Again, the important thing is to make an explicit analysis. Decide whether you have adjusted to something they did and analyze why they did it.

Follow the same procedure as in the last section: Identify the inconsistency and discuss it.

Your inconsistent action.

Why did you do it?

What should you do now?

Your inconsistent action.

Why did you do it?

What should you do now?

Your inconsistent action.

Why did you do it?

What should you do now?

Your inconsistent action.

Why did you do it?

What should you do now?

REVIEW OF THE BEGINNING GAME

Most of the remaining sections use the same general approach as the previous one, but the questions are more specific. We are breaking down the negotiation process into smaller steps. There are obvious overlaps between sections. If a question has already been answered, or if it seems unimportant, ignore it.

Creating the Right Atmosphere

1. What atmosphere was created?

2. Was it appropriate?

3. What should you do now?

Communicating Your Position

1. Did you communicate the position you intended to communicate?

2. Did you communicate it in an effective way?

3. What should you do now?

Learning Their Position

1. Do you believe that you understand their position?

2. What is it?

3. If you have not learned it, what specific information did you need, but not get?

4. What prevented you from getting the necessary information?

5. What should you do now?

REVIEW OF THE MIDDLE GAME

Creating Momentum

1. Was it unexpectedly easy or difficult to create momentum?

2. Why? What does it mean?

3.   What should you do now?

Maintaining Momentum

1.   Did the momentum ever stop?

2.   Why? What does it mean?

3.   Has it been unexpectedly easy to maintain the momentum?

4.   Why? What does it mean?

5.   What should you do now?

Controlling the Momentum

1.   Are you satisfied with your control of the momentum?

2.   If not, why not?

3.   Are you moving in the right direction? That is, if current trends continue, will you end up where you want to end up?

4.   What should you do now?

REVIEW OF POSITIONING YOURSELF

Creating Credible Alternatives

1.   Do they believe that you have attractive alternatives?

2.   What can you do to make those alternatives more credible?

Selecting Appropriate Attitudes

1.   Have you selected and communicated the right attitudes?

2.   What should you do now?

Setting Up Trades

1. Do you have enough bargaining room?

    Compute the future ratio of movement (ROM) on the major quantitative issues; if it is greater than 1 (meaning that they have to move faster than you to get a deal within your range), you could be heading for trouble.

ISSUE	ROM	Implications
_____	_____	_____
		_____
		_____
_____	_____	_____
		_____
		_____
		_____
_____	_____	_____
		_____
		_____
_____	_____	_____
		_____
		_____

2. What should you do now?

3. Have you explicitly set up the trades you want to make?

4. If not, why not?

    For example, if you have offered trades, but the other side has rejected them, you may have misread their position or priorities.

5. What should you do now?

6. Have you created bargaining chips with real trading value? Which ones?

7. What should you do now?

Managing Time Pressures

1. Do you have enough time to complete the negotiations in a controlled orderly way?

2. If not, what should you do now?

3. Which side handles time pressures better?

4. What are the implications of this answer?

5. What should you do now?

REVIEW OF THE END GAME

1. Have you tested their limits on every important issue? That is, are you satisfied that you know those limits?

2. What should you do now?

3. Have you laid a foundation for communicating finality? That is, have your offers and other actions made it likely that they will believe you when you say, "That's it"?

4. What should you do now?

5. If there is a deadline, will it create more pressure on you or on them?

6. If there is not a deadline, does its absence favor you or them?

7. What should you do now?

8. Should you plan final concessions or other actions to let them save face? What concessions or actions?

ADDITIONAL INFORMATION NEEDED

What information do you need? How should you get it? Perhaps you should use external sources. If you should get it directly from the other side, you might ask a direct question, probe gently, make an outrageous or unexpectedly generous offer, or propose a trade to see how they react.

Information needed	How should you get it?
_____	_____
	_____
_____	_____
	_____
	_____
_____	_____
	_____
_____	_____
	_____

INTERPRETING THE INFORMATION

Rapidly review your answers to the preceding question, then try to answer the critical questions.

What Are Their MSP's and Priorities?

Issue	MSP	Priority
_____	_____	_____
_____	_____	_____
_____	_____	_____
_____	_____	_____
_____	_____	_____
_____	_____	_____
_____	_____	_____
_____	_____	_____

What specific actions should you take?

m Issues

Should you continue to negotiate as an individual or as a team, or should you change?

Why?

Should anyone be added to or dropped from the team? Why?

ple to add   Reason for adding them

_____   _____

_____   _____

_____   _____

ple to drop   Reason for dropping them

_____   _____

_____   _____

_____   _____

Should any role assignments be changed? Why?

le changes   Reasons for the change

_____   _____

_____   _____

_____   _____

her Strategic Changes

ould you make any other strategic changes? Why?

rategic change   Reasons for the change

_____   _____

_____   _____

_____   _____

What Is the Power Balance

Your power_____%   Their power _____%

On what evidence did you base this estimate?

What Is Their Strategy?

REVISING YOUR STRATEGY

Review your answers to the questions in the last section, plus your answ
"What should you do now?" questions; then revise your overall strategy,

Pure Bargaining versus Joint Problem Solving

1.   Should you change your emphasis?

2.   Why?

3.   What specific actions should you take?

Offers

1.   Should you change your plans regarding offers?

2.   Why?

3.   What specific actions should you take?

Attitudes

1.   Should you change the attitudes you communicate?

2.   Why?

Appendix 3:

Record of Offers

The simple form on page 287 will help you toward two objectives: (1) to keep track of both sides' offers and (2) to understand the significance of the pattern of these offers. What does it *mean*?

The first objective is simple, but essential. If you do not know who offered what, when, you cannot discern the meaning of any pattern.

The second objective is quite demanding. Interpreting meaning from a pattern of offers is often quite difficult. It is exceptionally difficult if you cannot easily and quickly see exactly where and when both sides have moved.

While we discuss our procedure, please look at both the directions and the form for recording offers.

To grasp the pattern of offers, we urge you to follow our directions *exactly*. Doing so is rather tedious, but it is often worth the effort. Understanding the pattern of movement can help you to understand the other side's priorities more clearly than any other activity.

The first step is easy. Just make as many copies of this form as you think you will need. Do not worry about copyright violations. Purchasing this book gave you the right to copy the appendices (but not the rest of the book).

Second, list all the issues in the left hand column. If you need more space, use more than one form.

Third, record the opening offer, regardless of who makes it, in the second or third column, depending on who made it.

The boxes for recording an offer on any issue are quite small because this form's primary purpose is to help you to see and understand the overall pattern of offers. Since there is so little space, you will often be forced to make a quick summary of the opening or subsequent offers. In fact, an offer on a particular issue may be so long that you do not have enough space to summarize it. Then, just make an identifying title, such as "Our opening offer," and record it in your notes. That method helps you to keep track of who is doing what.

Use the same principle whenever any part of an offer is too complex to fit into the box. You might, for example, indicate that you will make a specific concession on issue X, that you flatly refuse to make any concession on that issue, or that you will trade concession Y for concession Z on a different issue. You obviously cannot write so much information in the small box on this form, nor should you try to do so. The important point is that you should be able to see exactly who is moving, and where and when they are moving.

Note the label of each column, "Theirs," "Yours," and so on. Simply recording both sides' offers will help you to see the overall picture.

If they make two concessions in a row, just leave the column for your offer blank. Doing so will help you to see that they have moved twice, while you have not moved at all.

Most important of all, do not record offers on any issues that are essentially the same as one that either side has made earlier. For example, if their offer on price has not changed, but they have moved on down payment and the total payment period, leave the "price" box absolutely empty, but insert the new offers for down payment and repayment period.

Recording data this way will help you to see exactly how, where, and when both sides are moving. "Aha, they have moved twice on down payment and three times on the total repayment period, but they have never moved on the price." Then you can easily conclude that price is their critical priority.

We have provided this sort of form to our workshop participants for nearly twenty years, and most of them misuse it. They record every bit of data, including the details of offers that vary on only one of several issues. They therefore essentially obscure the forest with the trees. They prevent themselves from seeing exactly where and when movement has occurred.

Please be more selective. Record enough information so that you know what is happening, but be sufficiently selective so that you can see the overall pattern.

RECORD OF OFFERS

ISSUE	Yours	Theirs	Yours	Theirs	Yours	Theirs	Yours	Theirs

Appendix 4:

Self-Analysis Questionnaire

OBJECTIVES

A. To help you apply the negotiating principles directly to yourself
B. To help you understand your negotiating style, strengths, and weaknesses
C. To help you develop your negotiating skills

PROCEDURE

A. Review all the information you have received from any source at any time about your negotiating style, strengths, or weaknesses.
B. Skim the text and relate its principles directly to your own negotiations. How well do you perform each task? How can you improve?
C. Look for patterns in all that information.
D. Complete the questionnaire as carefully as possible.
E. Discuss it with your boss, co-workers, friends, or spouse. Take careful notes of their comments.
F. Implement your plans for developing your skills.
G. From time to time review the questionnaire and people's comments. Compare your progress to your plans. Take whatever actions seem necessary.

THE QUESTIONNAIRE

The Negotiating Process

1. Describe your style in your own words.

2. Describe your strengths and weaknesses.
   Strengths   Weaknesses

3. Vulnerability
   Which negotiating styles get the best results from you? That is, to which styles are you most vulnerable? How can you become less vulnerable?

   Style

   Ways to reduce your vulnerability

   Style

   Ways to reduce your vulnerability

4. Pure bargaining versus joint problem solving
   Which one is more natural to you?

   What are the implications of your preference?

   What should you do to become more effective?

Getting Ready To Negotiate

Rate yourself on each of the following tasks, then write down ways to improve:

$$E = \text{excellent, } VG = \text{very good, } G = \text{good,}$$

$$F = \text{fair, } P = \text{poor}$$

1. Defining the issues   Rating_____

   Ways to improve

2. Setting ojectives   Rating_____

   Ways to improve

3. Analyzing the situation (from their perspective)   Rating_____

   Ways to improve

4. Planning your strategy   Rating_____

   Ways to improve

The Beginning Game

1. Creating the right atmosphere   Rating_____

   Ways to improve

2. Communicating your position   Rating_____

   Ways to improve

3. Learning their position   Rating_____

   Ways to improve

The Middle Game

1. Creating momentum   Rating_____

   Ways to improve

2. Maintaining momentum   Rating_____

    Ways to improve

3. Controlling momentum   Rating_____

    Ways to improve

The Feedback Loop

1. Acquiring information
    Each of the major techniques should be analyzed separately.
    a. Listening   Rating_____

        Ways to improve

    b. Observing   Rating_____

        Ways to improve

    c. Probing   Rating_____

        Ways to improve

2. Interpreting information   Rating_____

    Ways to improve

3. Using information to revise your strategy   Rating_____

    Ways to improve

Positioning Yourself

1. Creating credible alternatives   Rating_____

Ways to improve

2. Selecting appropriate attitudes   Rating_____

   Ways to improve

3. Creating trading power
   a. Bargaining room   Rating_____

      Ways to improve

   b. Bargaining chips   Rating_____

      Ways to improve

The End Game

1. Testing the limits   Rating_____

   Ways to improve

2. Communicating finality   Rating_____

   Ways to improve

3. Using deadline pressure   Rating_____

   Ways to improve

4. Letting them save face   Rating_____

   Ways to improve

Reviewing Your Negotiations

1. Implementing the agreement   Rating_____

Ways to improve

2. Planning your future negotiations with these people   Rating_____

Ways to improve

3. Developing your skills   Rating_____

Ways to improve

Overall Development

Review your answers to all of the preceding questions, and then write down three general actions that will improve your overall negotiating skills.

1.

2.

3.

Appendix 5:

Recommended Readings

We encourage you to read some of the following books.

COHEN, HERB. *You Can Negotiate Anything*. Secaucus, N.J.: Lyle Stuart, 1980. A big best seller, with both the virtues and faults of most best sellers; it is well-written and entertaining, but quite superficial.

FISHER, ROGER, AND WILLIAM URY. *Getting to Yes*. New York: Viking Penguin, Inc., 1981. A well-written and useful guide to joint problem solving, but one that essentially ignores conflict. It is also oversimplified; they claim there are only four basic principles.

KARRASS, CHESTER L. *Give and Take*. New York: Thomas Y. Crowell Co., 1974. Too many anecdotes and very poorly organized. It has no organizing principle other than the alphabet. However, it has excellent tips for pure bargaining negotiations. A useful balance for the books that overemphasize joint problem solving.

KARRASS, CHESTER L. *The Negotiating Game*. New York: Thomas Y. Crowell Co., 1970. A solid, well-written book; much better than *Give and Take*.

NIERENBERG, GERARD I. *The Art of Negotiating*. St. Louis: Cornersone Press, 1981. A best-selling book. Useful and easy to read, but it overemphasizes joint problem solving.

WALTON, RICHARD E., AND ROBERT B. MCKERSIE, EDS. *A Behavioral Theory of Labor Negotiations*. New York: McGraw-Hill, 1965. The best and most comprehensive book, and the only one we know with the proper balance between problem solving and bargaining. Their principles apply to all types of negotiations, not just ones between labor and management. Academic and hard to read, but worth the effort. This book had so much influence on me that I did not feel free to write my own book for several years. Now I have sufficient original material to justify my own book, but I am still very indebted to them.

Appendix 6:

Notes

[1]Robert J. Ringer, *Winning Through Intimidation* (Los Angeles Book Publishers, 1973, 1974).

[2]Henry Kissinger, *White House Years* (Boston, Mass.: Little Brown & Co., 1979).

[3]William J. Dickson and F.J.Roethlisberger, *Counseling in an Organization: A Sequel to the Hawthorne Researches* (Boston, Mass.: Division of Research, Graduate School of Business Administration, Harvard University, 1966).

[4]New York Times 2/24/88. L, A 3 col. 2.

[5]New York Times 10/20/86. L, A 8 col. 2.

[6]Time Magazine, 10/20/86, p. 16.

[7]Walton, Richard E., and Robert B. McKersie, eds. *A Behavioral Theory of Labor Negotiations* (New York: McGraw-Hill, 1965).

[8]Cyrus Vance, Hard Choices: Critical Years in America's Foreign Policy (New York: Simon and Schuster, 1983).

[9]James A. Michener, *Texas*: (New York: Random House, 1985).

[10]Ian Fleming, Goldfinger (Great Britain: Glidrose Productions, 1959). Also (New York: Macmillan, 1959).

[11]Robert R. Blake, Ph. D. and Jane Srygley Mouton, Ph. D., *The Managerial Grid* (Houston, Texas: Gulf Publishing Co. 1964).

[12]Time Magazine, 10/20/86, p. 19.

[13]David Halberstam, *The Best and the Brightest* (New York: Random House, 1969, 1971, 1972).

Index